Modern Office Technology and Administration

Modern Office Technology and Administration

Third Edition

Joan Gallagher and Siobhán Coghlan

Gill & Macmillan

Gill & Macmillan Ltd
Hume Avenue
Park West
Dublin 12
with associated companies throughout the world
www.gillmacmillan.ie

© Joan Gallagher and Siobhán Coghlan 2006
ISBN-13: 978 0 7171 4029 9

Print origination in Ireland by Carole Lynch

The paper used in this book is made from the wood pulp of managed forests.
For every tree felled, at least one tree is planted, thereby renewing natural resources.

Contents

Preface

The objective of *Modern Office Technology and Administration* is to explain in detail the business environment, the workings of an office, the impact of technology on the office and the services available to a business from the Banks, the Post Office and the Telecommunication sector.

A third edition of this book was necessary to take account of the changes in the working environment such as: legislative changes and advances in electronic and mobile communication.

The book is divided into five Units to facilitate the presentation of related topics. Each unit deals with a particular aspect of the Office Environment and consists of between two and four chapters, as outlined in the Table of Contents.

All units have a common structure designed to facilitate comprehension, self-study and retention. Each unit begins with an Introduction — a brief summary of the major topics covered. The introduction acts as a preview to the chapters and illustrates how the chapters are related to each other.

Each unit concludes with a Summary — a concise review of each chapter. Short Questions at the end of each chapter are in line with FETAC examination requirements. Assignments are given at the end of each unit. Some assignments are based on individual chapters and others require an integrated approach. These assignments are designed to guide the student toward further research of the topic and can be used as either individual or group projects, at home or during class time.

The text is written from both a practical and an educational point of view. It explains the activities of an office and how technology has helped to improve efficiency levels within the office. Essential administration and reception skills are comprehensively covered in a step-by-step approach such as: planning and organising work, operating the switchboard, dealing with correspondence, filing, wages and business transactions. The impact of technology on the office and its capabilities are presented in a style suitable for the beginner and yet comprehensive enough to enable the student to make informed decisions about technology.

Modern Office Technology and Administration was written to meet the requirements of the FETAC Level II Information and Administration syllabus. It is also a suitable text for the HETAC syllabus – National Certificate in Office Administration Systems, and the City and Guilds Information Technology and Business syllabus. Furthermore, it can be used as a supplementary text for any office practice or office technology examination and is an ideal book for any 'back-to-work' course.

We wish to thank our families and colleagues for their support in this third update, particularly our partners John Hegarty and John Creedon, both of whom took on the role of childminding and entertaining to make this edition possible. Since the last update, technology has moved on and so have our lives.

For Joan, little Niamh and baby Siobhan are now 6 years and 4 years, respectively. A big thank you goes to Niamh for her contribution to the book, namely: minding her sister, entertaining herself and allowing me to do it. They were both very good and deserve a big reward!

For Siobhan, her quiet house and freedom is now replaced by two lovely children: Eve, 4 years, and Eoin, 2 years — neither of whom has yet grasped the difficulties of updating a book!

We also extend a special thanks to our colleagues at Senior College, Dún Laoghaire, and the Institute of Technology, Tralee, for their continued support.

Acknowledgments

For permission to reproduce material, grateful acknowledgment is made to the following:

- Apple Computers
- Cable & Wireless
- Canon (UK) Ltd
- M.J. Flood (Ireland) Ltd
- O'Sullivan Graphics
- An Post
- Sygma Wireless Communications Ltd (Motorola Distributors)
- Eircom
- Zefa Pictures
- Dell
- Viking Direct

Unit 1 —
The Business Environment

Introduction

Unit 1 provides an overview of the business environment, concentrating on how businesses are legally formed and organised, the functions of the office, banking services available to businesses and legislation in the workplace.

Unit 1 is divided into four chapters:

Chapter 1 — Business Organisations and Functions

Deals with the business as an organisation, how a business can be set up, and examines the main functions of a business, ie, marketing, finance, production and human resources:
- ◆ Types of Organisation
- ◆ Legal Forms of Business
- ◆ Organising the Business
- ◆ Business Functions

Chapter 2 — Office Functions, Design and Equipment

Examines the primary functions of the office in relation to receiving, storing, processing and distributing information. Office design and typical office equipment are discussed.
- ◆ The Office and its Functions
- ◆ General Sources of Reference
- ◆ Office Design
- ◆ Office Equipment

Chapter 3 — Banking

Reviews banking for business and the major technological advances made in routine banking activities such as telephone banking and Internet banking are reviewed.
- ◆ The Euro
- ◆ The Irish Banks
- ◆ The Current Account
- ◆ Bank Cards

- ◆ Lodgements
- ◆ Withdrawals
- ◆ Electronic Funds Transfer (EFT)
- ◆ Foreign Exchange
- ◆ Electronic Banking

Chapter 4 — Legislation in the Workplace

Provides a review of legislation that affects the workplace, such as laws governing: terms and conditions of employment, health, safety and welfare at work and the protection of personal information stored manually or electronically:

- ◆ Conditions of Employment
- ◆ Employee Welfare Legislation
- ◆ Data Protection Legislation

Chapter 1 — Business Organisations and Functions

To understand the role of the office within the context of an organisation, it is necessary to examine the types of organisation that exist. An organisation exists where people and resources combine to achieve some objective. Objectives will differ according to the type of organisation. For example, the objective of a voluntary organisation may be to provide a social service to the community, while the main objective of a private enterprise, ie, a **business,** is to make a profit.

Types of Organisation

Three main types of organisation exist in Ireland.

Voluntary Organisations

Voluntary organisations are non-profit-making organisations that depend on State funding and/or voluntary contributions to survive. This type of organisation is run largely by volunteers and the main objective is to provide aid, support or some social service to the community. Examples of voluntary organisations are charities, (eg, Goal and Concern) and non-profit-making sporting societies (eg, local GAA and rugby clubs). Registered charities are exempt from paying tax on donations received.

Public-Sector Organisations

The main objective of public-sector organisations such as the Health Boards is to provide cost-effective services to the community, rather than to make a profit. While the general public is charged for the use of the services, these organisations are heavily subsidised by the Government. They are managed by civil servants and are accountable to the Government.

Private-Sector Organisations

Private-sector organisations are privately owned business enterprises. A business is an organisation that is set up to produce or distribute a product or service. The primary objective of a business must be to make a profit. Without profits or some spending power, the business will not survive in a competitive market. Business objectives will vary depending on circumstances. For example, in the first year of trading the main objective may be to *break even*, (ie, to cover expenses, not make a profit or a loss). If the business is successful, increasing market share or developing new products may become important objectives.

Legal Forms of Business

When setting up a business in Ireland, it is important that all the relevant documentation is complied with, so that the business can legally commence trading. For example, a company must have a Certificate of Trading before trading can begin.

All businesses must register with the Register of Business Names, and register with the Revenue Commissioners to pay tax on profits and to collect taxes from employees, eg, PAYE and PRSI. Sole traders and partnerships pay income tax on profits, while companies and co-operatives pay corporation tax on profits.

A business must also register for VAT with the Revenue Commissioners if the turnover of the business exceeds €51,000 on goods and €25,500 on services.

The most common forms of private business enterprise in Ireland are:
1. Sole trader
2. Partnerships
3. Limited companies
   a) Public limited company (PLC)
   b) Private limited company (Ltd)
4. Co-operatives.

Sole Trader

Sole trader is a term used to describe a business wholly owned by one person. The owner takes responsibility for all the activities of the business, such as selling, purchasing, marketing, hiring staff and preparing the accounts. Typical examples are: small retail outlets and local grocery shops.

Features of a sole trader
◆ Sole owner of the business, with control over all business functions.
◆ Generally small in nature, with a small number of staff employed.
◆ Has *unlimited liability*. This means that while the owner controls all aspects of the business and reaps all the profits, s/he is also personally liable for any debts that the business may incur. Therefore if the business goes bankrupt, the sole trader may sacrifice personal assets to pay creditors.

- The sole trader is charged income tax on profits and can offset business losses against personal income.
- The business ceases to exist on the death of the sole trader.

Partnerships

A *general partnership* exists where two or more people (usually to a maximum of 20) come together and contribute finance and/or expertise to a business. Accountants, solicitors and doctors commonly practise under the partnership structure.

Features of general partnerships

- When forming a partnership, it is usual to draw up a Deed of Partnership. This is an agreement between the partners that specifies the duties and responsibilities of each partner. As the partners may contribute to the business in varying ratios, the Deed of Partnership also specifies the extent of liability of each partner and how profits and losses are to be distributed.
- If a partnership agreement is **not** drawn up, then each partner is jointly liable for the debts of the partnership, ie, each partner has unlimited liability.
- It may be easier to access credit facilities where more than one person is responsible for repayments.
- Partners, like sole traders, are charged income tax on profits and can offset business losses against personal income.
- A new partnership must be formed on the death or resignation of a partner.

A *limited partnership* may be set up in which the partners' liability is limited to the debts of the partnership. However, a limited partnership must have at least one partner with unlimited liability and must register with the Companies Registration Office (CRO).

Limited Companies

Most Irish companies are formed as limited companies. The owners of the company are the **shareholders** who purchase shares in the company. A limited company has a legal status (separate entity) distinct from the owners. The liability of the shareholders is limited to the amount invested, ie, if the company is declared bankrupt, the shareholders are liable for any amount remaining unpaid on their shares. The shareholders elect a Board of Directors and/or a Managing Director to manage the company on their behalf.

When forming a limited company, the following documentation must be sent with the appropriate fee to the Companies Registration Office (CRO):

1. *Memorandum of Association*: a document detailing the nature of the business, who is involved in the company, and the amount of shares that will be issued.
2. *Articles of Association*: a document detailing the internal rules of the company, eg, how meetings are convened, the rules governing transfer of shares, election procedures, etc.
3. A declaration, signed by the company secretary or director, stating the amount of money received from shares that are paid to date. A company must have 25% of its authorised share capital paid up before trading.
4. A declarational compliance with the *Companies Act,* signed by the company secretary, director or solicitor.

When all the documents are forwarded, the CRO will issue a Certificate of Trading and the company can commence business.

A limited company can be formed as a public limited company or as a private limited company:

Public limited company (PLC)

A public limited company (PLC) is formed with a minimum of seven members, and with no upper limit. PLCs are companies that are quoted on the stock exchange. This means that the company can raise finance by selling shares to the general public. Depending on the type of shares purchased, the shareholder may be entitled to a share of profits, known as a *dividend*, and may be entitled to vote at the Annual General Meeting (AGM) of the company. Examples of Irish PLCs include the commercial banks, Kerry Group PLC and Waterford Wedgewood PLC.

Another form of PLC is a company *limited by guarantee*. With this form of PLC, the members of the company agree to contribute an amount towards the debts of the company if the company is declared bankrupt. Charities, clubs, societies and professional bodies may form this type of public company, as it allows the members to have the benefits of limited liability without raising funds from the members.

Private limited company (Ltd)

A private limited company (Ltd) is formed with a minimum of one member and with an upper limit of fifty members. A private limited company is similar in legal standing to a PLC; however, private companies are not quoted on the stock exchange and there are strict regulations regarding the buying and selling of the company's shares.

A *single-member company* (ie, where one member owns all the shares) must have at least two directors and a secretary (who can be one of the directors).

Both public and private companies must file audited accounts with the CRO; however, the accounts of a private company are not as detailed as the accounts for a public limited company.

Features of a limited company

- A limited company can be formed as a public or private limited company.
- The limited company is legally recognised as a separate entity.
- Liability of the shareholders is limited to the amount unpaid, if any, on shares purchased.
- The company is managed by a Managing Director and/or a Board of Directors.
- Detailed documentation is required to register as a limited company.
- A limited company is charged corporation tax on profits, unlike partnerships and sole traders.
- Financial accounts (such as Profit & Loss Accounts, Balance Sheets, Auditors' Reports and Directors' Reports) are filed annually with the CRO and must be available for shareholders, auditors, creditors and potential investors.

Co-operatives (Co-ops)

A co-operative is formed with seven or more members and the ethos is based on values of fairness, democracy and mutual support. The purpose of a co-op is to gain better trading terms and to reduce the business risks that the members would be exposed to if they were trading as individuals.

Most Irish co-ops are members of ICOS (Irish Co-operative Organisation Society — www.icos.ie), a coordinating body that provides advice and expertise to its members. Co-ops in Ireland play a major part in the Irish economy, contributing almost 50 per cent of total food exports.

Features of a co-operative (Co-op)

- A co-op consists of seven or more members.
- A co-op must register with the Registrar of Friendly Societies, and can also register with the CRO to avail of a separate legal identity and limited liability for the members.
- Members invest in the co-op by purchasing shares and appoint managers to run the business on their behalf.
- There is a maximum limit on the amount invested by each member.

◆ Members have an equal vote regardless of the amount of shares held.
◆ Shares are not directly transferable between members.
◆ Co-ops are charged corporation tax on profits.

Comparisons of Business Forms					
Business Form	No. of Owners	Owned By	Managed by	Liability	Tax
Sole trader	1	Owner	Owner	Unlimited	Income
Partnership	2–20	Partners	Senior Partners	Unlimited	Income
Private (Ltd)	1–50	Shareholders	Directors	Limited	Corporation
Public (PLC)	7+	Shareholders	Directors	Limited	Corporation
Co-operative	7+	Members	Manager	Limited	Corporation

The decision to form a business as a sole trader, partnership, company or co-operative depends on:
a) the number of people involved
b) the nature of the business and level of risk attached
c) the resources necessary for the business.

Sources of funds available to a business include private funds, loans from financial institutions and Government grants.

Grants are available from a variety of government agencies to help start up a business, train staff, purchase equipment, etc. Enterprise Ireland and Shannon Development offer assistance to businesses, from the initial feasibility stage, research and development to the actual production and marketing of a product or service. Some agencies (eg, Leader programmes) offer a mentor system, where experienced consultants offer assistance to a start-up situation.

Organising the Business

When the business is formed, the resources must be organised so that the objectives can be achieved. Organising means how the business is structured so that work can take place effectively. Once the structure is in place, rules and procedures for carrying out tasks can be developed and responsibility for the performance of these tasks can be allocated to individuals or teams within the business. The formal structure of a business can be depicted by an **organisation chart**.

Organisation Chart

An organisation chart is a diagram outlining the work relationships between people and tasks. It shows:

a) formal lines of communication, ie, who reports to whom

b) the framework of the business, ie, departments

c) levels of management (or the 'chain of command').

The organisation chart does not show:

a) the duties associated with the positions shown on the chart

b) informal relationships between staff.

The diagram below depicts a simple organisation chart for a company, showing 6 levels of management in a hierarchical structure, ie, the general workers report to the supervisor, the supervisor reports to the department manager, etc.

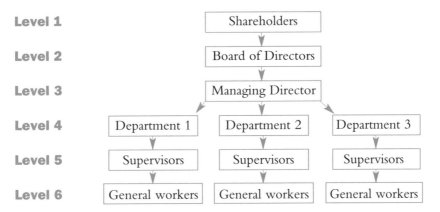

Business Functions

In a small business, all the business activities may be carried out by one person or a small number of people. For example, a sole trader will order supplies, market and sell the goods or services, negotiate finance with the banks, keep accounts, recruit and train staff.

As a business grows, both in physical size and complexity, it may be necessary to divide business activities into departments according to their function, such as:

- Production
- Marketing & Sales
- Finance
- Human Resources
- Administration.

These functions may be further divided as shown in the organisation chart below:

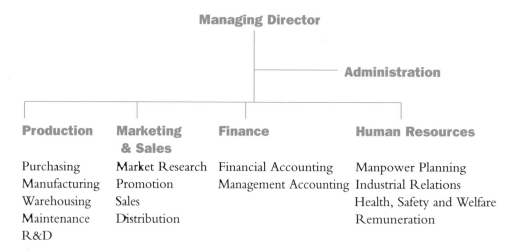

Production	Marketing & Sales	Finance	Human Resources
Purchasing	Market Research	Financial Accounting	Manpower Planning
Manufacturing	Promotion	Management Accounting	Industrial Relations
Warehousing	Sales		Health, Safety and Welfare
Maintenance	Distribution		Remuneration
R&D			

Production Activities

The Production Department is concerned with the complete manufacturing process, which includes: purchasing raw materials; scheduling work orders; quality control; maintaining premises, machinery and equipment, warehousing and developing new products; and improved procedures for carrying out the production process.

Purchasing

A Purchasing Officer may be appointed within the Production Department to negotiate with suppliers to obtain the best available terms, such as: prices, discounts, credit terms, and delivery. S/he ensures the quality of the materials purchased, establishes a system for ordering and is responsible for stock control.

Manufacturing

The Production Manager must ensure that the production process is operating at an optimum level. This involves devising a schedule to minimise disruptions to the production process and liaising with the Purchasing Manager to ensure raw materials are available.

The planning and scheduling process can be aided by computer software such as MRP (Materials Requirements Planning), which facilitates materials planning and machinery scheduling, and CAM (Computer-Aided Manufacture), which controls the production process.

At all times, the quality of inputs (eg, raw materials) to the production process and the resulting outputs (eg, finished goods) must be monitored.

Warehousing

The stock-control manager must ensure that correct procedures are in place for the storage of raw materials and the finished goods waiting for distribution. The costs of warehousing can be quite significant; among the costs involved are: security, insurance (on premises and contents), lighting, heating, rent of premises, fit-out for orderly rotation of goods, and costs of replacing obsolete products if storage is not organised properly.

Many businesses try to reduce the amount of stock in storage by using computerised ordering systems which ensure that raw materials are ordered on a 'just-in-time' basis as required by the production process.

Maintenance

The maintenance team ensures that machinery and equipment are regularly maintained to avoid breakdowns in the production process. Breakdowns are a serious cost to the business in terms of production time lost in fulfilling orders and paying employees for non-productive work. Equipment should be checked regularly and a reporting procedure should be implemented to report faulty equipment, in accordance with recent safety-at-work legislation.

Research and development (R&D)

The R&D team is responsible for researching, designing, testing prototypes (models) of new products and devising new procedures to carry out production more efficiently. Computer software such as Computer-Aided Design (CAD) can aid the R&D team in designing new products.

Marketing Activities

The function of the Marketing Department is to satisfy consumer needs by selling a quality product at an appropriate price. This is achieved by identifying:

1. what the *product* is
2. what *price* to sell the product at
3. what *marketplace* to sell the product in
4. how to *promote* the product.

The above activities are often expressed in marketing terms as obtaining the correct *marketing mix*. The marketing mix refers to all aspects of the *four Ps*

(Product, Price, Place and Promotion). To obtain the correct marketing mix, the Marketing Department must engage in market research to identify what the consumer requires.

Market research

Market research is a process of gathering and analysing information to identify who the customer is, what products or services are required by the customer and how best the Marketing Department can meet the requirements of the market.

Promotion

Promotion involves bringing the products/services to the attention of the customer. The promotion campaign can consist of:

(i)   *advertising:* aimed at a wide audience through the media (ie, television, radio, papers, journals, magazines and the Internet);

(ii) *sales promotions:* such as samples, in-store demonstrations, price cuts and competition offers. This form of promotion is best suited to retail products such as food items, cosmetics and general household items;

(iii) *publicity:* is concerned with obtaining 'good press' reports from the media. A business may gain publicity by supporting local or national events, eg, donating money to charity or sponsoring sporting events;

(iv) *personal selling:* suitable for selling products/services on a one-to-one basis that require demonstration or explanation (eg, software or financial products).

Sales

The marketing team must sell products. Apart from the product itself, the level and quality of service offered to a customer can often be a distinct selling advantage.

The sales team regularly supplies invaluable information to the marketing research team directly from the customer to maximise competitive advantage.

Distribution

Large businesses will have a separate distribution department responsible for getting the product to the final destination. However, in a small business the Marketing Department is responsible for deciding what *channel of distribution* is most suitable to get the product to the market. Once the channel of distribution is decided upon, the marketing team can organise warehousing and coordinate transport for effective delivery to the market.

The three main channels of distribution are:

Manufacturer ⟶ Consumer

Typical businesses that use this channel produce customised products, eg, specially commissioned furniture, paintings, etc.

Manufacturer ⟶ Retailer ⟶ Consumer

Typical businesses that use this channel are producers of perishable items, or where the manufacturer needs an agent or broker to distribute goods in wide geographical locations on their behalf. For example, car manufacturers will sell to an agent (garages) for sale to the customer.

Manufacturer ⟶ Wholesaler ⟶ Retailer ⟶ Consumer

Typical businesses that use this channel are manufacturers of large volume, non-perishable consumer goods such as detergents, and household items.

Financial Activities

The Finance Department is responsible for controlling the finances of the business and prepares final accounts, eg, Trading, Profit and Loss and Balance Sheet at the end of each trading period — usually yearly. Financial systems (eg, accounts receivable and accounts payable, etc) are implemented so that an accurate statement of the trading position of the business can be established.

Financial Accountant

The Financial Accountant is responsible for recording accounting activities. S/he prepares the yearly final accounts, and throughout the trading year will produce monthly or quarterly reports (interim reports) stating the current trading situation. This information is used by management for decision-making purposes. For example, if the first quarterly report shows that sales are falling in a particular foreign market, management may decide to invest more in advertising, employ a local agent to distribute the product or discontinue the product.

Management Accountant

The Management Accountant is responsible for analysing and controlling business costs and preparing overall budgets for the business. Budgets are plans of how money should be allocated in the future. Usually budgets are based on historical information, such as what the costs of production were last year, and what is the likely cost this year, given inflation, wage increases, material increases, etc. The individual departments are then required to operate within the allocated budget.

Human Resources Activities

The Human Resource Department (HR) is not directly linked to the manufacturing of products. It provides a service to all the departments within the business by developing overall employment policies such as: manpower planning; industrial relations; employee health, safety and welfare; and remuneration policies.

Manpower planning

Manpower planning is an ongoing process to ensure that the business has employees who are skilled to perform the tasks necessary for the survival of the business. The planning process involves:

(i) *job evaluations:* An evaluation of the job is carried out to assess the level of skill and ability necessary for the job. Job evaluations are necessary to devise job descriptions and pay structures.

(ii) *recruitment, selection and training:* A combination of selection processes such as psychometric tests, aptitude tests and interviews may be used when *recruiting* staff. When staff are *selected,* an *induction course* should be arranged so that new employees can become familiar with the business policies, their duties and responsibilities. Initial and ongoing *training* should be provided for staff to develop and maintain skill levels.

(iii) *performance appraisal:* Performance appraisal interviews should be carried out with all employees on a regular basis. The information received is used to provide extra training, support, reward staff, etc where appropriate.

(iv) *management development:* It is important that the business has a management development policy to ensure the management structure is not weakened. Training for potential managers should include courses on: Time Management, Leadership Communication and Stress Management.

(v) *terminations (redundancies and retirement):* The HR Department negotiates with management and unions in the event of redundancies. The business may devise its own redundancy package, but it must adhere to the legal requirements. Conditions of retirement are detailed in the employee's contract of employment.

Industrial relations

The HR Department will facilitate at consultations between management, unions, employees and the various adjudication bodies such as Employment Appeals Tribunal and the Labour Court.

Grievance and disciplinary procedures are usually drawn up by the HR Department in consultation with other interested parties (eg, trade union representatives and senior management) to establish guidelines for acceptable standards of behaviour at work and to provide formal channels for making a complaint.

Health, safety and welfare

Every business is legally obliged to provide a safe place of work. The HR Department is instrumental in devising health and safety policies and ensuring that health and safety procedures are in place and monitored.

Remuneration

This involves devising reward systems so that employees are paid/rewarded in line with duties and responsibilities. Pay structures should be clearly defined and regularly reviewed. Reward systems can include: share option schemes, medical insurance, assistance with child care or further education, etc.

Restructuring the Organisation

As a business grows in size and complexity it may relocate geographically and some functions may be centralised, ie, operated from head office. For example, in the organisation chart below, the Marketing Department will coordinate the marketing functions for all branches; the Transport/Distribution department will be responsible for ensuring stock is delivered to all the branches; the HR department will carry out all the personnel activities for all branches; and the Finance department will control the major financial functions such as preparing overall accounts, setting budgets and monitoring costs. The Information Technology (IT) department will be responsible for monitoring networks and information systems between the branches.

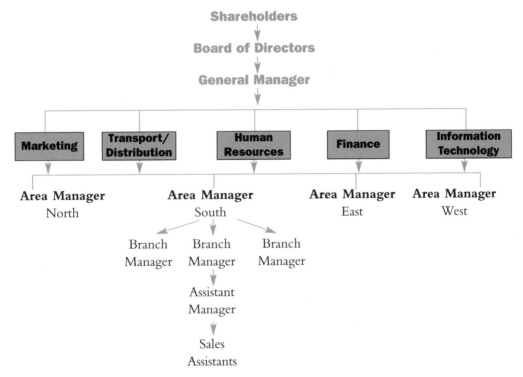

Organisation Chart by Geographic Location — Retail Chain.
Note the shaded functions are centralised and service all the branches.

Short Questions

1. Distinguish between public-sector organisations and private-sector organisations.
2. List four legal forms of business.
3. Describe two main differences between a sole trader and a partnership.
4. Briefly describe four features of a private limited company.
5. Draw up a table to contrast a private company with a partnership and a sole trader. List four points.
6. State two main differences between a private limited company and a public limited company.
7. List features of an organisation chart.
8. Briefly describe four activities carried out by the Production department.
9. Outline the costs involved in maintaining stock in a warehouse.
10. Briefly describe four activities carried out by the Marketing department.
11. What do the 'four Ps', as used in marketing terminology, refer to?
12. List three main channels of distribution.
13. List four promotional activities a Marketing department may utilise when marketing a new product.
14. Briefly describe four activities carried out by the Human Resources department.
15. What is manpower planning? List four activities that generally form part of the planning process.
16. What is the function of the Finance department in a business?
17. Distinguish between the Financial Accountant and the Management Accountant.

Chapter 2 — Office Functions, Design and Equipment

The Office and its Functions

The **office** is responsible for handling information that flows to and from the business. The location and size of the office is determined by the nature and size of the business.

A large business will have offices attached to each department. Administration will carry out work specific to that department: for example, in the Marketing department they may be responsible for preparing sales presentations, processing sales orders and calculating travel expenses for sales representatives. However, it is common practice for a large business to have a **centralised office** to deal with the activities that are common to all departments.

Some of the support services that may be centralised are shown below:

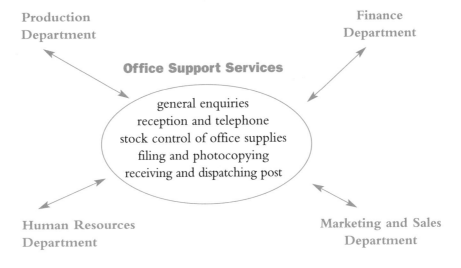

Production Department

Finance Department

Office Support Services

general enquiries
reception and telephone
stock control of office supplies
filing and photocopying
receiving and dispatching post

Human Resources Department

Marketing and Sales Department

The functions of the office can be classified as follows:

Receiving and Sorting Information

Typically the office deals with information received from:
— *Customers*, ie, enquiries, quotations, orders, payments, complaints
— *Suppliers*, ie, invoices, statements, catalogues, promotional literature
— *Government bodies*, ie, Revenue Commissioners, Department of Enterprise, Trade and Employment, Central Statistics Office, Employment Welfare Agencies
— *Financial institutions*, ie, bank statements, interest rates, currency rates, stock valuations
— *The business itself*, ie, company reports, internal mail, minutes of meetings, final accounts and other internal business documents.

The information received is sorted for further processing or immediate distribution.

Processing and Communicating Information

Generally information received requires some further processing before it can be used effectively or distributed. The office must impart the processed information to the recipient in the most effective way for clear understanding. There are four ways to communicate:
— *Orally:* eg, face-to-face meetings, telephone, videoconferencing
— *Written:* eg, letters, reports, minutes
— *Electronically:* eg, e-mail, fax
— *Visually:* eg, bar charts, pie charts, histograms.

Storing and Protecting Information

When information is processed, it is stored for future reference using a manual filing system or an electronic document management system (EDM — see Chapter 16). Information regarding individuals that is held on computers must be maintained according to the Data Protection Acts 1988–2003. Confidential information should be safely stored to prevent unauthorised access.

General Sources of Reference

Most offices deal with a variety of general business enquiries during the working day. The office personnel should have a series of references (books and websites) to access for accurate and up-to-date information. The following section lists typical reference sources that should be available in the office. The list is not exhaustive, as the references required will depend on the nature of the business.

Dictionary and Thesaurus

A dictionary is used to check the meaning and spelling of words and a thesaurus is used to find different words with the same meaning (synonyms), eg, 'busy' can be interchanged with 'occupied', 'engaged' or 'employed'. In addition, computer-application software, ie, word processors, have a spell checker and a thesaurus facility.

Accommodation References

Office personnel who prepare travel arrangements should have information on accommodation available and places of interest in the surrounding area. Up-to-date information is available from the Tourist Offices and relevant websites such as www.failteireland.com.

Timetables

Timetables are necessary to check transportation times for employees travelling on behalf of the business. Timetables of buses and trains can be obtained from the local Bus Éireann and Iarnrod Éireann stations respectively. Iarnrod Éireann operates a 'talking timetable' facility and the telephone numbers for specific routes are listed in the telephone directory. When the number is dialled, a recorded message gives the times of departures and arrivals for that route. Travel timetables can also be viewed on 'Aertel', RTE's Teletext service, or relevant transportation websites such as www.buseireann.ie and www.irishrail.ie.

Road Maps

Road maps are necessary in any office where employees travel as part of the business. Maps of local areas, national and international routes may be obtained from the AA (Automobile Association) or any bookshop.

Some maps have a mileage chart which gives details of distance in kilometres and miles. The mileage chart can be used to calculate travel expenses and the duration of the journey.

Internal Telephone Directory

The receptionist will maintain a list of all employees' telephone extension numbers, and an internal telephone directory for commonly used telephone numbers.

Telephone Directory and Golden Pages

The Telephone Directory lists telephone numbers and addresses in alphabetical order according to the name of the telephone account holder. National and international dialling codes are also listed.

The Golden Pages is a business directory, organised alphabetically under products and services, with a fast-finding index at the back of the directory.

Businesses that want more than a single-line listing can purchase advertising space to highlight their products or services.

Both the Telephone Directory and the Golden Pages are available in each of the six telephone zones and can also be referenced on-line at www.eircom.ie and at www.goldenpages.ie

Kompass

Kompass is a national directory of businesses in Ireland. This directory gives a brief description of the organisation, types of product/service supplied and a list of executives involved in the business. Kompass can also be referenced on-line at www.kompass.ie.

Stubb's Gazette

This journal is invaluable for checking the performance and solvency of trade partners such as customers and suppliers. It publishes information on businesses that have had judgments made against them, have been struck off the companies register or have been declared bankrupt. Competitors' solvency can also be analysed for business opportunities.

Postal Guides

Postal guides, available from the Post Office, list national and international costs of postage for letters and parcels.

Industry Magazines

Industry magazines, journals, newsletters and reports may be left with the administrator for circulation among employees. The variety of magazines available in the office will depend on the nature and budget of the business.

Office Design

Office design refers to how the office is organised in terms of the number of workstations and the equipment used in the office.

Motivation theories suggest that the physical environment of the workplace has a significant effect on employee morale and productivity. An unpleasant physical environment, such as cramped space, inadequate natural light, or extremes of temperature, can cause unnecessary stress, fatigue and strain on employees and can result in poor productivity – so-called 'sick-building syndrome'.

In many cases the Office Manager will be constrained by the amount of physical space allocated to the office and by financial constraints, which will affect the eventual design selected.

There are three common types of office design.

Open-plan Office

In open-plan offices there are no obvious divisions or partitions between working areas. The workstations are normally organised so that the work **flows** from station to station in a logical manner.

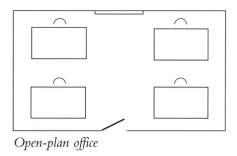

Open-plan office

With an open-plan office, space is optimised and economies of scale are obtained with the shared use of electricity, heating and resources such as printers and photocopiers. However, there may be a lack of privacy and background noise may be distracting. An important consideration when designing an open-plan office is to ensure that pedestrian traffic routes are kept clutter-free and are clearly defined.

The open-plan office is suited to a business that handles a large volume of general (non-sensitive) information, for example, a travel agent.

Landscaped Office

This is generally the preferred style. The landscaped office can consist of semi-permanent partitions or else a modular approach can be used. A modular approach uses furniture to create work areas and can be easily rearranged. Within the landscaped office, a section of the office space can be portioned off as a

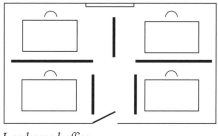

Landscaped office

'cellular office' to facilitate meetings or briefings of a sensitive nature.

Landscaped offices are suited to a business that deals with a large volume of work, but also requires some privacy for group work.

The Corridor/Closed Door Style

Some offices operate a corridor style, where a small number of staff are segregated into separate private offices. Usually the manager will have a private office.

This style of office design is suited to a business that handles

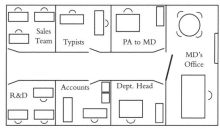

Corridor-style office

highly sensitive information. For example, banks will have private offices for advising customers on loans, solicitors will have private offices where confidential issues can be discussed with the client.

Planning Office Layout

A change in office layout or a move to a new office needs to be carefully planned to avoid or reduce any resistance from office staff. A work-study analysis may be carried out to determine the optimum layout. In planning the office layout, the number of staff working in the office and the office equipment must be considered before space can be allocated to each individual work area. The Office Manager should consider:

1. *Space:* What space is available for the office? How should it be utilised, ie, open-plan, closed door style, etc? Present and future staff requirements?
2. *Work flow:* Volume of work? Frequency and confidentiality of the work?
3. *Equipment:* Location of shared equipment such as a printer, fax, photocopier, etc, for easy access and minimum disruption?
4. *Safety legislation:* Are procedures in place for implementing and maintaining a safe and secure office?

Depending on the volume of work in the office, it may be necessary to plan for centralised equipment areas, for example for dispatching post, filing, printing and photocopying, etc, to minimise disruptions in the main office.

Office Equipment

General office equipment typically includes a photocopier, binder, guillotine, laminator and desktop sundries as described below.

Photocopier

A photocopier is a reproduction machine used to make copies of written or printed material. Modern photocopiers range in size from desktop multifunctional device (ie, a photocopier that incorporates other functions such as fax, scanner and printer) to dedicated, freestanding machines. Typical features of a dedicated photocopier are:

◆ *Number selector:* Used to set the number of copies required.

◆ *Page size and type:* A variety of page sizes ranging from A6 to A3 may be catered for and the type of photocopiable material may include bond paper (high quality), card, photocopiable overhead transparencies. etc.

◆ *ARDF (automatic reverse document feeder):* A loading facility located generally on the lid of the photocopier, which automatically 'feeds' pages to be copied, thus eliminating the need to lift the cover of the photocopier each time a page is to be copied.

◆ *Duplex feature:*Enables copies to be made on both sides of one page from two single pages, or vice versa.

◆ *Sorting and stapling:* A facility to produce sorted copies of a multi-page document. The sorted copies can be automatically stapled.

◆ *Automatic grouping:* A facility that copies a series of **separate** pages multiple times. For example, if the operator required 20 copies each of 3 pages, the grouping facility would produce 20 copies of the first page as a group, 20 copies of the next page as a group, etc.

◆ *Zoom facility:* Documents can be increased or decreased in one-per-cent increments. For example, a small diagram on an A4 page can be increased to fill the page or the content of an A4 page can be increased to an A3 page. Likewise, a magazine article which is slightly wider than A4 can be reduced to A4.

◆ *Two-single-copy feature:* For example, a magazine when opened is often approximately A3 in size. This feature will automatically photocopy an A3 page onto *two separate* A4 pages. This saves the time involved in moving the magazine by hand.

◆ *Auto exposure:* This facility analyses the page to be photocopied and selects the proper image density, ie, how dark or bright the copy should be.

◆ *Interrupt mode:* An interrupt temporarily stops a job in progress to allow somebody else to use the photocopier. The interrupted job resumes from where it was stopped.

◆ *Code facility:* Codes can be allocated to individuals or departments to monitor and control copying costs. A code is entered before using the photocopier and the number of copies made is recorded against that code.

◆ *Diagnostic display:* A control panel that indicates problems with the machine, ie, paper jam, no paper, etc.

Using the photocopier

1. Remove any staples to prevent damage to the glass surface.
2. Align the page according to the correct paper size displayed on the glass surface screen and close the lid of the photocopier. Alternatively, use the ADRF facility.

3. Select the correct settings for the machine before starting, ie:
   — the size of paper required, such as A4
   — the density of the copy, which is generally set halfway between bright and dark. However, if photocopying from dark-coloured paper, select a brighter setting
   — required functions, ie, sort, group, duplex, etc.
4. For complicated tasks, a test copy should be photocopied and checked.
5. Set the number of copies required and press the 'start' button.

When photocopying onto overhead transparencies, check that they are the photocopiable type. Write-on transparencies will melt in the machine, causing damage.

Purchasing a photocopier

Consider the following factors:
1. *Budget allocated:* This will limit the purchaser's choice of models.
2. *Costs:* The purchase price must be analysed. Is servicing and delivery included? What are the typical running costs? Is training required for operators?
3. *Requirements:* What functions are required? How frequently is the machine used? What is the volume of work? How often are special features used?
4. *Size:* Will the machine take up too much space in the office?
5. *Noise:* Will the machine be noisy and interrupt work?
6. *Durability:* Will the machine need to be maintained regularly?

Binding Equipment

Binders are used to secure individual pages together in booklet form. Typical binders on the market are: spiral, velobinder and thermal binder.

Spiral binder

1. A spiral binder punches holes along one side of the pages by means of a lever which is operated manually or electrically.
2. When all the pages are punched, a 'plastic comb' is inserted on the spikes of the machine and opened with the lever.
3. The punched paper is then placed into the opened 'plastic comb', working from the back of the document to the front.

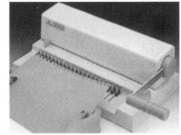

Spiral binder and combs

4. When all the pages are inserted, the 'plastic comb' is closed with the lever and the bound booklet is removed.

Velobinder

1. A velobinder punches holes along one side of the pages, similarly to the spiral binder.

2. When all the pages are punched, they are inserted into the velobinder strips, which consist of two parts: one part has prongs to hold the punched paper and the other part is a clamp that holds the pages together. A document bound with a velobinder can be easily reopened and reclosed to insert or remove pages. The booklet, however, does not open out flat as it does with spiral binding.

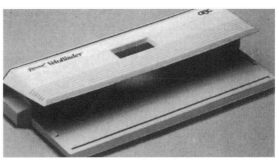

Velobinder

Thermal binder

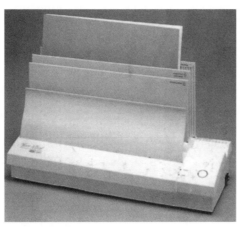

Thermal binders

Velobound product

Thermal-bound products

A thermal binder operates by melting the glue on the inside spine of special 'thermal covers'.

1. The pages to be bound are placed in a thermal cover.

2. The spine of the thermal cover is placed upright into the heated thermal binder.

3. The glue on the spine of the thermal cover melts, causing the pages to stick to the spine.
4. The booklet should be allowed to cool before opening.

Guillotine

A guillotine is used to cut paper, cards, etc to the correct size evenly. It consists of a flat table area pre-printed with paper sizes, a safety guard to the right, with a blade behind to cut the paper.

Guillotine

To cut paper:
1. The blade is moved upright by a handle.
2. The pages to be cut are positioned on the paper size required, the excess going under the blade.
3. The pages are held firmly by a movable clamp which is locked into position.
4. The blade is pushed down by its handle, cutting the paper.

Laminators

A laminator machine places a transparent plastic, durable cover over paper and cards. It is used to protect documents such as ID cards, certificates, charts, photographs, etc. There are two types of laminating machine: a pouch laminator and a roll laminator.

Pouch laminator

Laminator with an assortment of pouches

A pouch laminator machine is suitable where usage is not constant, owing to the cost of the pouches. The document is placed in the correct-sized pouch and inserted into the machine. The machine uses heat to bind the plastic pouch to both sides of the document. The item to be laminated should be at least 3mm smaller than the pouch to give a protective border.

Roll laminator

Roll laminator machines are more expensive but are very economical for frequent long runs. The document is inserted into the machine and a roll of transparent film is used to laminate the document. The finished product may have to be trimmed at the edges.

Label Maker

A machine used to make self-adhesive labels for shelves, folders, letter trays, etc. The label maker has a small keypad and screen, with up to four lines of text and a variety of print fonts available for each label. The user can check the label on screen before printing.

Label maker

Sundry Desktop Equipment

The following items of equipment may be placed on desks:

Letter trays: Also known as 'in' and 'out' trays for holding incoming and outgoing correspondence.

Tape dispenser: To hold and cut Sellotape.

Desk organisers: To hold sundries such as pens, pencils, rubbers, pencil parer, paper clips, Post-its (note paper), highlighters, treasury tags (string with metal at both end to hold punched documents together), etc.

Copyholder: To hold pages at eye level while entering data.

Puncher: To punch holes in paper to place into ring-binder folders.

Stapler: To hold pages together with a metal fastener (staple): more secure than paper clips.

Calculators: To perform arithmetic calculations.

Short Questions

1. Outline three activities carried out by the office in relation to the management of information.
2. List four office activities that can be centralised.
3. List four methods of communicating information, stating when it is more suitable to use each method.
4. Where would you find the following:
   a) a synonym for the word 'assist'
   b) times of trains leaving Dublin for Cork after 2 pm on a Tuesday
   c) the distance by road from Athlone to Galway
   d) a list of businesses in South Dublin that offer secretarial services?

5. What information is found in the following sources of references:
   a) Kompass
   b) Stubb's Gazette
   c) Postal Guide
   d) Golden Pages?

6. Distinguish between the following office designs: open-plan, landscaped and the corridor-style office.

7. Outline four factors to consider when planning a change in office layout.

8. Describe a typical workstation.

9. Describe four features of a photocopier that would make the task of producing 20 copies of an eight-page document easier.

10. List four factors to be considered when deciding on purchasing a photocopier for a business.

11. Distinguish between the following types of binder: spiral binder, velobinder and thermal binder.

12. Which binder is most suitable for inserting more pages into a bound document at a later stage? Why?

13. Distinguish between a pouch laminator and a roll laminator.

14. What office equipment is used to:
    a) cut paper to the correct size
    b) place a transparent plastic cover over certificates, charts, etc
    c) make self-adhesive labels for shelves, in/out trays, etc
    d) hold pages at eye-level while entering data?

Chapter 3 — Banking

The Euro

When the euro came into being on 1 January 2002, there were 15 countries in the European Union (EU): Austria, Belgium, Finland, France, Germany, Ireland, Italy, Luxembourg, the Netherlands, Portugal, Spain, Greece, the United Kingdom, Denmark and Sweden.

Of these 15 countries, the United Kingdom, Denmark and Sweden did not join the 'Euro Zone' and have not done so to date.

On 1 May 2004, ten new member states joined the EU: the Czech Republic, Estonia, Cyprus, Latvia, Lithuania, Hungary, Malta, Poland, Slovenia and Slovakia. These countries will introduce the euro as soon as they have fulfilled the necessary conditions laid down in the Maastricht convergence criteria, which include: price stability, public finances (ie, absence of excessive government deficit), exchange-rate stability and long-term interest rates. The target date for euro adoption for these countries varies from mid-2006 for Estonia to 2010 for Hungary and the Czech Republic, with the other countries mostly aiming for 2007 or 2008.

Euro Notes and Coins

The symbol for the euro, '€', was inspired by the Greek letter epsilon, in reference to the cradle of European civilisation and to the first letter of the word 'Europe'. The parallel lines represent the stability of the euro.

The design of the euro notes is symbolic; windows and gateways dominate the front side of each banknote as symbols of openness and cooperation in the EU. The reverse side of the banknotes features a bridge, a metaphor for communication among the people of Europe and between Europe and the rest of the world.

Euro coins carry a common European face, which represents a map of the European Union against a background of transverse lines to which are attached the stars of the European flag. The reverse side of each coin is different for each country. In Ireland, the reverse of the coin features the harp symbol, the word Éire, surrounded by the stars of the EU flag.

Benefits of the Euro Zone

The euro as a common currency has brought many benefits, such as:

◆ eliminating the need to change currencies when travelling within the euro zone. Travelling outside the euro zone is also easier, as the euro is an international currency and widely accepted in many places outside the euro zone, particularly in tourist destinations

◆ price transparency, ie, easier price comparison within the euro zone, leading to improved competition and lower prices for the customer

◆ a more stable trade environment within the euro zone, due to the elimination of exchange-rate fluctuations of currencies for both importers and exporters

◆ the benefit of lower interest rates in line with the European Monetary Union (EMU) recommendations, which include low inflation and improved control of government debt.

The Irish Banks

The Central Bank of Ireland was renamed as the 'The Central Bank and Financial Services Authority of Ireland' (CBFSAI) on 1 May 2003. This new authority has two divisions: the Central Bank and the Irish Financial Regulatory Authority.

The Central Bank has been part of the EMU since 1999, along with 11 other national central banks. Together with the European Central Bank these banks form the '*Eurosystem*', the primary function of which is to maintain price stability in the euro zone. Domestic responsibilities of the Central Bank in Ireland include:

◆ provision of banknotes and coins

◆ managing investment assets on behalf of the State

◆ acting as agent for and banker for the government

◆ maintaining a stable financial system

◆ ensuring safe and reliable payment systems

◆ provision of advice and guidance on Irish economic policy.

The majority of the banking requirements of business and personal customers will be catered for by a **commercial bank**. Well-known commercial banks are: Allied Irish Bank (AIB), Bank of Ireland (BOI), Ulster Bank (UB), National Irish Bank (NIB), Permanent Trustee Savings Bank (PTSB), etc.

General services offered by the commercial banks include: current and deposit accounts, mortgages, loan facilities, foreign exchange, electronic funds transfer, telephone banking and on-line banking.

The Current Account

Current accounts are used to cater for day-to-day financial transactions, ie, lodgements and withdrawals. An overdraft facility can be obtained on a current account for an extra fee, ie, the bank will make extra funds available for a short period of time, usually up to one year. The bank requires: identification, (ie, passport or driving licence), two references, proof of address (ie, recent utility bill), specimen signature(s) and a sum of money to be deposited before a current account can be opened.

When a current account is opened, a cheque book and a bank card are issued to facilitate the payment of bills.

The Cheque

A cheque is a written instruction to the bank to pay the sum of money that is written both in words and figures to the person named on the cheque.

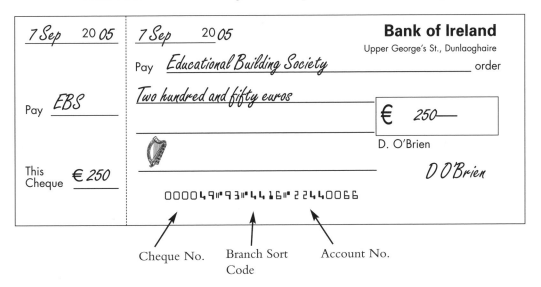

Cheque and stub

A cheque contains the following pre-printed information:
◆ the government stamp
◆ name and address of the bank, plus the bank logo, generally at the top
◆ the cheque number, branch sort code and the current account number, generally at the bottom
◆ a space for writing the value of the cheque in words and figures
◆ a space for dating and signing the cheque.

There are three parties to a cheque:

a) the *drawer*: the account holder or persons authorised to sign the cheque

b) the *drawee*: the bank on which the cheque is drawn

c) the *payee*: the person named on the cheque to receive the payment.

Completing a cheque

The cheque is completed by filling in the following details:

1. • date
   • name of payee
   • amount of the cheque in words and amount in figures, which should be written close together to prevent alterations.
2. The cheque is signed by the drawer.
3. The drawer may cross the cheque to make it more secure.
4. The cheque counterfoil (stub) is completed and retained by the drawer to check against his/her **bank statement**.

In practice, office personnel may fill in the cheque and obtain the signature(s) from management or whoever is authorised to sign the cheque for the business.

If the cheque is incorrectly completed, the bank will return it to the payee marked *refer to drawer*. This is sometimes referred to as a *bounced cheque* as the cheque was not honoured by the bank. The payee must return the cheque to the drawer, who may write a new cheque or initial any alterations made on the existing cheque.

Crossing a cheque

The purpose of crossing a cheque is to prevent an unauthorised person from cashing it, as a crossed cheque must be lodged to a bank account. Cheques that are not crossed are referred to as *open cheques*.

A cheque is crossed by drawing two parallel lines across the face of the cheque. Between the parallel lines, any of the following words are generally written:

a) the words '& Co' (or no words at all).
   This cheque can be lodged to the payee's account or the payee can transfer the cheque to another person by *endorsing* it. The payee endorses the cheque by signing his/her name on the reverse of the cheque. An endorsed cheque must be lodged.

b) the words 'not negotiable' or 'a/c payee only'.
   This cheque must be lodged to the payee's account.

c) the bank and branch specified.
   This cheque must be lodged to the payee's account in the bank and branch specified.

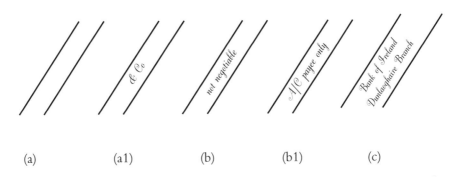

Examples of crossing a cheque

Receiving a cheque for payment

When a cheque is tendered for payment:

a) Request the customer's bank card and check expiry date.

b) Check that the drawer's name and signature on the cheque correspond with the card.

c) Check the payee's name and date on the cheque. *Post-dated cheques* (cheques written for a future date) and *stale* cheques (cheques more than 6 months old) should not be accepted.

d) Check that the amount in words and the amount in figures on the cheque correspond.

e) Write the bank card number and expiry date on the back of the cheque. This guarantees that the cheque will be honoured by the bank, if the amount does not exceed €130.

Bank statement

A bank statement is sent to the account holder on a monthly basis or is available on request. The statement shows all transactions that have occurred on the account within that period, eg, lodgements made, cheques presented to the bank for payment, standing orders and direct debits processed, bank charges and any other withdrawals made from the account.

		Account Statement		

Account Holder
PAT KELLY
Current Account

Bank of Ireland
DUN LAOGHAIRE, CO. DUBLIN
Tel: (01) 2800273
Fax: (01) 2800810

Post to
Mr Pat Kelly
"Woodview"
Leixlip
Co. Kildare

Page   1   of   1

90–11–16
Branch Code

103
Statement Number

30 Dec 2005
Date of Statement

862700256
Account Number

DATE	DETAILS		PAYMENTS OUT €	PAYMENTS IN €	BALANCE €
2005					
29 Nov	Balance Forward				1120.20
2 Dec	New Ireland – Life	DD	31.90		1088.30
	Pass 29 Nov		60.00		1028.30
	Pat Kelly	SO	100.00		928.30
4 Dec	AMV00102281	DD	14.41		913.89
6 Dec	PASS 06 Dec		10.00		903.89
	Banking 365 Access		296.60		607.29
9 Dec	Cheque	493	50.00		557.29
	Current Account Fees		10.80		546.49
11 Dec	Giro Credit			1500.00	2046.49
16 Dec	Pass 16 Dec		150.00		1896.49
17 Dec	Cheque	495	120.00		1776.49
20 Dec	In Branch Cr			250.00	2026.49
23 Dec	Banking 365 Access		420.00		1606.49

Bank statement

The final figure on the statement is the *bank balance*, ie, the amount of money in the account on a particular date. However, this may not be the true balance at the time the business receives the statement. For example, there may be cheques that the business has lodged to the bank, but that have not yet been processed.

When the business receives the bank statement, the account clerk should check the entries on the statement with the business records (ie, cheque stubs, lodgement and withdrawal counterfoils, credit-card receipts, etc) to establish the current balance. A *bank reconciliation* statement is prepared, which shows what the final balance on the account should be after adjusting for lodgements or withdrawals not shown on the bank statement.

The Journey of a cheque

The following example simplifies what happens to a cheque when it is presented for payment.

Example

Mr Hegarty has a current account in the Bank of Ireland, Limerick. He writes a cheque for €350 to Ms O'Sullivan, whose bank account is in the Allied Irish Bank, Tralee.

1   Ms O'Sullivan lodges the cheque to her bank account in the Allied Irish Bank, Tralee. (It may take up to 3 working days to clear a cheque drawn on another bank.)

2   AIB sends the cheque on to its clearing centre. The clearing centre sends the cheque details (ie, bank sort code, drawer's account name and number, cheque number, value of the cheque and date) electronically to the Bank of Ireland, Limerick.

3   The Bank of Ireland then debits (decreases) Mr Hegarty's account with the value of the cheque, and the AIB bank credits (increases) Ms O'Sullivan's account with the value of the cheque.

Bank drafts

A bank draft is purchased at a bank and, like a cheque, it is an instruction to a bank to pay the amount of the draft to the payee. The bank guarantees payment on the draft. Bank drafts can be purchased in foreign currencies. Bank drafts are commonly used where:

1.   A customer does not have a current account upon which to draw a cheque.

2.   Once-off or non-routine payments are required (eg, examination fees).

3.   A business is dealing with a new customer for the first time and requests a draft rather than risking a cheque as payment.

4.   The customer wishes to send money abroad.

Bank draft application form

Bank Cards

Two main bank cards are available from all banks: a debit card (eg, Laser) and a credit card (eg, Mastercard). Both cards enable payments for goods and services to be made electronically and for money to be withdrawn from an ATM. However, their main difference is in the timing of the payment.

All new bank cards are based on the *chip-and-pin* technology. A microchip containing the account details is embedded in the card, making it more difficult to duplicate the card. A PIN (Personal Identification Number) is issued for each card and the customer is required to enter their PIN to complete a transaction. Chip-and-pin technology ensures that the customer is the genuine cardholder. (With the previous technology of the magnetic strip, the customer just had to sign a receipt.) The cardholder should never:

◆ carry the PIN with the card
◆ reveal the PIN to another person
◆ disclose the PIN when carrying out telephone, Internet or mail-order transactions.

Debit Cards

A debit card is used to pay for goods and services electronically, directly from a current account. With debit-card purchases the customer's account is reduced (debited) almost immediately; therefore the customer must have the necessary funds in the account or an overdraft facility must be available. Some retailers will also facilitate a cash withdrawal of up to €100 at the time of purchase. This service reduces the transaction cost involved in making cash withdrawals at ATMs.

A debit card can also be used as:

◆ *a cheque guarantee card*: a guarantee that the bank will honour cheques drawn on the customer's account to the value of €130, provided that the bank card number and expiry date are written on the back of the cheque;

◆ *an ATM card*: to allow the withdrawal of cash, 24 hours a day, from an Automatic Teller Machine (ATM). The customer enters the PIN to access the account and can also order a statement or cheque book, change the PIN and top up mobile phone credit on prepaid phones. Customers can also withdraw foreign cash from ATMs abroad that display either the 'Cirrus' or the 'Maestro' symbol.

Credit Cards

A credit card is used to purchase goods and services on credit, ie, the customer is allowed a period of time (usually 30 days) before payment is required, and can also be used to withdraw cash from ATMs at home and abroad.

A customer who wishes to obtain a credit card must complete an application form and, based on the information received, the bank's credit-card centre will determine a credit limit for the customer. The bank's credit-card centre will issue the PIN number and credit card separately. The card should be signed at the back immediately it is received.

A statement is sent to the customer on a monthly basis, showing transaction details, balance due, any interest charged and the minimum payment required. Credit cards should be managed with care, as the interest rates charged on unpaid bills is very high.

Retailers who operate a credit-card payment system pay a one-off set-up fee and a percentage commission on sales to the credit-card company. In return, the retailer is guaranteed payment by the credit-card company, which collects the payment from the customer.

When accepting a payment by debit or credit card, the retailer should:
1 Request the customer to insert the card in the 'PIN reader' to authorise the card.
2 Request the customer to enter their PIN to authorise the payment.
3 Issue the customer with a printed receipt and return the card to the customer.

Lodgements

Lodgements to the bank can be made by:
♦ completing a lodgment slip at the bank
♦ using the automatic teller machine (ATM)
♦ using the night-safe facility
♦ using the express lodgement facility in the bank.

Lodging Money Using a Lodgement Slip

Businesses that lodge money regularly will be issued with a lodgement book containing a series of lodgement slips, with the business account number and business name pre-printed on the slip. Alternatively, individual lodgement slips are obtainable at the bank. When preparing money (notes, coins and cheques) for lodgement to a bank account:
1. Count all coins and place in appropriate money bags, available from the bank.

2. Sort the notes into similar denominations, facing upwards to facilitate counting. Place into bundles that are easy to count, eg, bundles of €100, and secure with an elastic band.

3. Count the number of cheques and total the value of all cheques. Note the drawer and value of each cheque for your own records.

4. Complete the lodgement slip before you go to the bank by filling in:
   - the date of the lodgement
   - the account name, bank account number and bank sort code where the money is being lodged, if you are not using a pre-printed slip
   - the amount of the lodgement in notes, coins and cheques
   - the signature of the person lodging the money
   - the lodgement counterfoil (stub).

5. Ensure that the lodgement counterfoil is date-stamped by a bank official as your record of the lodgement.

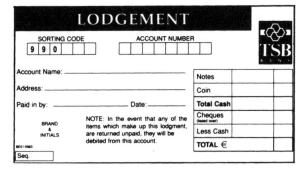

Lodgement stub   *Lodgement slip*

For security reasons:
- Count cash in a private area, eg, a back room with the door locked.
- Request an escort when going to the bank with large sums of money.
- Vary the times and days of carrying out the lodgement.
- Reduce the amount of cash held on the premises by making frequent lodgements.

Lodging Money Using the Night Safe

The night-safe service enables a business to lodge money after banking hours. The business is issued with a lodgement book, money pouch, security seal (which contains the customer's identity details) and a key to the night safe.

The completed lodgement slip and money are placed in the pouch. The pouch is sealed with the security seal and inserted through the night-safe slot.

The pouch is retrieved and normally opened in the presence of two bank officials the following day. The money is counted and lodged to the business account specified on the lodgement slip.

Lodging Money Using the Express Lodgement Facility

An express lodgement box is available within the bank to lodge money during banking hours. The money and completed lodgement slip are placed in a special lodgement envelope. The envelope is sealed and deposited in the Express Lodgement box.

Withdrawals

Money can be withdrawn from bank accounts in a variety of ways:
1. by filling in a withdrawal slip at the bank
2. using the ATM machine
3. cheques
4. Electronic Funds Transfer (EFT).

Withdrawal counterfoil

Withdrawal slip

Electronic Funds Transfer (EFT)

Electronic Funds Transfer is a safe and convenient method of paying bills or transferring funds from one account to another automatically. Common methods of transferring money or paying bills using EFT are standing orders and direct debits.

A *standing order* is used to make payments of a *fixed* amount from one account to another account on a regular basis, eg, monthly. Standing orders are typically used to: pay insurance premiums, mortgage repayments, or to make regular lodgements to other bank accounts. This facility ensures that payments are made on time.

A *direct debit* is used to make payments of *variable* amounts from one account to another account on a regular or irregular basis. For example, telephone bills and ESB bills must be paid regularly, but are of irregular amounts. A standing order/direct debit facility is set up by completing the appropriate form (mandate) stating:

◆ the name and bank account details from which payment is being made
◆ the name and bank account details of the account receiving the payment
◆ frequency of payment, date of each payment and the amount of payment (for standing orders).

A business may offer the facility of paying bills by EFT by sending its customers the appropriate mandate to complete. The business account details will be pre-printed on the mandate. There is a set-up fee and a transaction fee on each standing order/direct debit.

Standing orders/direct debits are cancelled only upon the written instruction of the customer to their bank.

Example

The Gas Company sends the customer a direct debit mandate to complete. The customer signs the form, giving their account name, number and bank details and returns the direct debit form to the Gas Company.

The Gas Company sends the direct debit mandate to the customer's bank authorising the bank to debit the amount of the gas bill from the customer's account.

The Gas Company is credited with the amount of the bill.

Details of the direct debit transaction are shown on the customer's bank statement.

Advantages of Standing Orders/Direct Debits

1. Payments are automatically deducted from the customer's current account and paid into the account named on the mandate.
2. Safe method of ensuring payment is made on time.
3. Details of the transaction are shown on the bank statement.
4. Special discounts may be obtained by paying bills on time.

Foreign Exchange

Since the introduction of the euro on 1 January 2002, the exchange to foreign currency is necessary only when travelling to non-euro-zone countries. Non-euro-zone countries quote daily buy and sell rates as determined by the central bank and the world trading markets.

The *sell rate* is the rate at which the bank will sell foreign currency to the customer. The *buy rate* is the rate at which the bank will buy foreign currency from the customer.

Purchasing Foreign Currency

When a customer is purchasing foreign currency the banks' 'sell rate' is used to calculate the amount of foreign currency sold for €1. The euro quantity is multiplied by the sell rate.

Example

Miss Carty wishes to holiday in the US and has a budget of €3,000. If the banks' 'sell rate' is US$1.75, how many US$ can she buy? (Assume no commission.)

Solution

For every euro purchased, Miss Carty will receive US$1.75

For €3,000, Miss Carty receives US$5,250, ie, €3,000 multiplied by US$1.75.

Selling Foreign Currency

When a customer is selling back foreign currency to the bank, the 'buy rate' is used. The foreign currency amount is divided by the buy rate.

Example

Miss Carty returns from her holiday and discovers a US$50 note in her handbag. The buy rate is €1.24. How many euros does she receive in exchange for US$50? (Assume no commission.)

Solution

Miss Carty will receive €40.32 for her US$50 note, ie, US$50 divided by €1.24.

Traveller's Cheques

When travelling abroad it is advisable to use traveller's cheques rather than carry cash. Traveller's cheques are pre-printed cheques of a fixed value which can be exchanged in most countries for purchases or local currency. Traveller's cheques are purchased from a bank in most strong currencies, ie, euro, sterling, dollars, yen, etc. Traveller's cheques should be ordered in advance of travel.

When purchasing traveller's cheques, the cheques are signed at the bank by the customer. The customer is presented with a list of the cheque numbers. This list should be kept separate from the cheques (ie, at home) and is used to secure a refund in case of theft.

When purchasing an item with a traveller's cheque, the customer must countersign the cheque and personal identification is required (eg, passport). Change is given in local currency. A commission may be charged.

Unused traveller's cheques can be sold back to the bank at the current exchange rate or kept for future use.

Electronic Banking

Customers can now access their accounts 24 hours a day, 7 days a week, by using Internet banking or telephone banking.

The customer must complete the appropriate registration form to take advantage of these services and will receive a registration code and a Personal Access Code (PAC) from the bank. When accessing the Internet banking or telephone banking service, the customer will be prompted to enter both codes to access their account.

Internet banking and telephone banking allow the customer to:
◆ check their account balance
◆ review recent transactions (eg, lodgements, withdrawals, standing orders, direct debits, etc).
◆ check balance on credit-card accounts and review recent transactions
◆ transfer funds to other registered accounts, eg, from a current account to a deposit account
◆ pay bills (eg, utility bills, credit cards, etc.)
◆ order a new cheque book
◆ request a statement
◆ change PAC
◆ 'top up' mobile phone credit.

Internet banking allows the customer greater transparency compared with telephone banking, as the customer can view their account while carrying out their banking transactions. The customer should ensure that there is no unauthorised access to their account and should:
◆ never reveal the registration number or PAC to anyone
◆ ensure that the bank has a secure website for transacting business. A secure address would display https// as distinct from http (notice the 's')
◆ exit from the website when finished accessing the service or when leaving the desk, even for a short period.

Short Questions

1. List the EU member states that are participating in the euro zone.
2. List the 3 original EU member states that have not joined the euro zone.
3. State four benefits of the euro to Ireland.
4. What is the role of the Central Bank in Ireland?

5. Outline the facilities offered by commercial banks to customers.
6. List and briefly distinguish the four facilities available on one 'basic card' issued by the banks.
7. List four services available through an ATM machine besides the withdrawal of money.
8. Outline the information required by the bank before a current account can be opened.
9. What is a cheque? Explain the three parties to a cheque.
10. What is the effect of crossing a cheque? Distinguish between the various types of crossing.
11. What does endorsing a cheque mean?
12. Distinguish between a cheque and a bank draft.
13. List the checks carried out when accepting a personal cheque for payment.
14. Explain the following terms: open cheque, stale cheque, post-dated cheque.
15. Outline the procedure to follow when preparing money for lodgement.
16. Describe briefly four methods by which a lodgement can be made.
17. Explain the term EFT.
18. Distinguish between a standing order and a direct debit.
19. State four advantages of a standing order/direct debit.
20. Distinguish between a credit card and a debit card.
21. Outline the procedure to follow when accepting a debit card or a credit card for payment.
22. Convert:
    a) €500 into US$ assuming a 'sell rate' of US$1.57
    b) US$70 into euros assuming a 'buy rate' of €1.50.
23. Explain the procedure involved in purchasing and exchanging traveller's cheques.
24. Distinguish between telephone banking and Internet banking, outlining the services available.
25. Explain why the balance on a bank statement may not be the 'true balance'.
27. What documentation is necessary to carry out a bank reconciliation?

Chapter 4 — Legislation in the Workplace

Since joining the EU, Ireland has introduced legislation that protects the rights of employers and employees at work and provides for a safe working environment. Workplace legislation includes laws governing: terms and conditions of employment, employee welfare and the protection of personal information held by a business.

Ireland has also developed a number of State agencies, such as: the Labour Court, Labour Relations Commissions, Equality Officers, Employee Appeals Tribunal and the Rights Commissioners, to facilitate and mediate over disputes that arise between employers and employees. Typical cases brought to these agencies involve disputes over dismissals, discrimination, pay and working conditions.

Decisions from the above bodies are seldom legally binding. However, employers and employees attend these bodies with the intention of resolving disputes through independent facilitators and usually accept their recommendations. If both parties do not accept the recommendations made, the case can be taken to the civil courts.

Recent workplace legislation, as listed below, is discussed in this chapter in relation to: conditions of employment, employee welfare and data protection.

Conditions of Employment	Terms of Employment (Information) Act 1994; Minimum Notice and Terms of Employment Act 1973–2001; Protection of Employees (Part-time Work) Act 2001; Protection of Employees (Fixed-time Work) Act 2003; Redundancy Payments Acts 1967–2003; Employment Equality Acts 1998–2004; Organisation of Working Time Act 1997; National Minimum Wage Act 2000; Unfair Dismissals Acts 1977–2001
Employee Welfare	Maternity Protection Acts 1994–2004; Parental Leave Act 1998; Safety, Health and Welfare at Work Act 1989–2005
Data Protection	Data Protection Acts 1988–2003; Freedom of Information Act (FoI) 1997–2003

Conditions of Employment

Employment legislation includes Acts of law enacted to ensure that employees receive a contract detailing the terms of their employment, regulations controlling working hours, wages/salaries, as well as legislation to provide redress in cases of discrimination, unfair dismissal or redundancy.

Terms of Employment (Information) Act 1994

The *Terms of Employment (Information) Act 1994* applies to all employees who work more than 8 hours per week. An employee is entitled to a written statement of the terms and conditions of employment within 2 months of commencing work. This statement should include the following details:

◆ Name and address of employer and employee
◆ Title and description of job
◆ Date of commencement of job
◆ Place(s) of work of employee
◆ Nature and duration of contract — (ie, full-time, part-time, contract)
◆ Rates of pay
◆ Methods of payment and frequency of pay
◆ Conditions relating to holiday leave and sick leave
◆ Pension contributions and entitlements
◆ Period of notice required by employee and employer.

Other information such as grievance procedures, company rules and regulations, shift-work regulations and probationary periods are often included in this statement.

Minimum Notice and Terms of Employment Act 1973–2001

This Act entitles employees who are in employment for 13 continuous weeks to receive minimum notice of termination from their employer as outlined below:

Length of Service	Notice required
13 weeks–2 years	1 week
2–5 years	2 weeks
5–10 years	4 weeks
10–15 years	5 weeks
Greater than 15 years	8 weeks

Employers are entitled to receive at least one week's notice from an employee. The contract of employment may include a clause outlining the notice required to terminate the contract for both employers and employees. Both employers and employees can receive payment in lieu of notice. The minimum notice required does not apply to cases where termination was due to gross misconduct by the employee.

Protection of Employees (Part-time Work) Act 2001

This Act protects part-time employees, ie, those who have thirteen consecutive weeks' employment and whose normal hours of work are fewer than a full-time employee. Part-time employees should not be discriminated against in their terms of employment.

Protection of Employees (Fixed-term Work) Act 2003

This Act protects fixed-term contract employees who are entitled to the same benefits from legislation as full-time employees. Fixed-term contract employees should not be treated in a less favourable manner, in terms of conditions of employment, than comparable full-time employees. In addition, if an employee has been employed under a fixed-term contract that spans more than 4 years, and receives another contract of employment, that contract is deemed to be a 'contract of indefinite duration', ie, a permanent contract.

Redundancy Payments Acts 1967–2003

These Acts provide employees with statutory compensation payments in the event of dismissals due to redundancy. Employees between the ages of 16 and 66 years of age, with a contract of employment and with at least 104 weeks of continuous service, ie, 2 years, are entitled to receive a lump sum based on length of service calculated as:

◆ (two weeks' gross pay) x (the number of years in continuous service) plus
◆ an additional one week's gross pay.

If an employee has worked more than an exact number of years, the excess days are credited as a proportion of a year. For example, John worked for ABC Ltd for 10 years and 73 days or 10.2 years (73 days / 365 days = 0.2). His weekly gross wage on redundancy was €350. His statutory entitlement is: [(2 weeks x €350) x 10.2 years + €350] = €7,490.

The employee is entitled to two weeks' notice, with time off during the notice period to look for other employment.

The *Protection of Employment Act 1977* requires the employer to consult with employee representatives (eg, trade unions) before redundancies take place.

Employment Equality Acts, 1998–2004

These Acts incorporate the *Anti-Discrimination (Pay) Act 1974*, which entitles men and women to equal pay for equal work. The *Employment Equality Acts 1998–2004* state that:

◆ The employer must not discriminate against employees in relation to: access to employment, conditions of employment, training, promotion and classification of positions.

◆ The employer must not discriminate against employees, in relation to: age, sex, marital status, sexual orientation, religion, colour, disability, nationality, ethnic origin or members of the travelling community.

◆ Conditions of work laid down by employers must be related to the job, be justifiable and not discriminatory.

◆ Employees should not be victimised for exercising their statutory rights.

◆ Sexual harassment cases can be brought under this Act.

Organisation of Working Time Act 1997

This act regulates working times for employees with regard to hours worked per week, hours worked at night, rest periods and holidays. The act states the following:

◆ The maximum number of hours an employee should work per week is 48 hours, which can be averaged over a 4-, 6- or 12-month period. For example, a hotel employee on a 6-month contract from May to October works the following hours per week: 60 hours during June, July and August and 20 hours during the off-peak months of May, September and October. Over the 6-month period (ie, 24 weeks) the employee worked 960 hours (12 weeks x 60 hours) + (12 weeks x 20 hours) which when averaged over 6 months (24 weeks) works out at 40 hours per week, which complies with the legisation.

◆ Employees who work at night (from midnight to 7 am) should not be expected to work more than 8 hours in any 24-hour period.

◆ Employees are entitled to a 15-minute rest break when more than 4.5 hours have been worked, and 30 minutes when more than 6 hours have been worked. However, many industry sectors have reached agreement on rest periods with employee unions and the labour court in cases where the statutory rest periods have implications for their industry.

◆ Full-time employees are entitled to 20 days' paid holidays in a year (ie, one week's paid holiday is given for every 3 months worked). A qualifying month requires the employee to work at least 117 hours per month, or 1,365 hours over a 12-month period.

◆ Part-time employees (who work fewer than 117 hours per month or 1,365 hours per year) are entitled to paid holidays based on 8 per cent of the hours worked.

◆ Holidays must be taken within a 12-month leave period or within 6 months of the following year. The timing of annual leave is determined by the employer, who should take due consideration of the employee's work and family commitments.

◆ Employees are entitled to paid public holidays. If the employee agrees to work the public holiday, s/he should receive another day's leave or an additional day's pay.

Where an employee is requested to be available for work and is then not required to work, the employee should be paid for 25 per cent of the time s/he was required to be available.

National Minimum Wage Act 2000

This Act sets minimum payment rates for all employees except apprentices, family members and the defence forces. The current minimum wage is set at €7.65 per hour for experienced adult workers (ie, a person over 18 years with at least 2 years' experience). An inexperienced adult is entitled to 80% of the minimum wage rate in the first year of employment, rising to 90% in the second year of employment, and should receive the full minimum wage rate in subsequent years. Employees bvetween 16 and 18 years of age and who have at least 1 year's continuous employment are entitled to receive 70% of the minimum wage rate.

Unfair Dismissals Acts, 1977–2001

These Acts apply to employees over 16 years of age with at least 1 year's continuous service. An Unfair Dismissal case can be taken by an employee through the Rights Commissioners, the Employee Appeals Tribunal (EAT) or the courts. The onus is on the employer to prove that there were substantial grounds for the dismissal. The claim must be made by the employee within six months of dismissal by sending a claim form (available from the Department of Enterprise, Trade and Employment, www.gov.ie) to the relevant body, ie, the Rights Commissioner, etc. A copy must also be sent to the employer. An employee can be fairly dismissed if:

◆ the employee was not qualified or competent to do the job s/he was employed to do

◆ the conduct of the employee contravenes company rules or is a danger to others at work

◆ the dismissal was due to unavoidable redundancy.

The dismissal is seen as unfair if it is shown that the reason for the dismissal was due to:

◆ religious or political beliefs

◆ gender or racial bias

◆ involvement of the employee in trade union activities

- pregnancy
- sexual orientation
- age.

Remedies for unfair dismissal

If it is agreed that the employee has been unfairly dismissed, the employer must:

- reinstate the employee to the original job, or
- re-engage the employee to an alternative similar position, and/or
- arrange financial compensation for the employee.

Employee Welfare Legislation

Employee welfare legislation includes Acts of law that are enacted to give rights to expectant mothers, to enable parents of children under five years old to take unpaid leave and to ensure that the working environment is a safe and healthy place to work.

Maternity Protection Acts 1994–2004

These Acts provide protection at work for pregnant women and for those who have recently given birth. The entitlements include:

- a minimum maternity leave of 18 consecutive weeks
- an option of an additional 8 weeks' unpaid leave
- time off from work for antenatal care, postnatal care and for breastfeeding, without loss of pay
- be reinstated to her original job if it is reasonable to do so. Her status and rights at work should not be affected by availing of maternity leave.

Maternity leave can be postponed in the event of the newborn child requiring hospitalisation after birth.

The employee must:

- notify her employer in writing of her intention to take maternity leave at least 4 weeks before the maternity leave begins
- present a medical certificate indicating the expected week of birth
- take at least 2 weeks of the maternity leave before the birth and 4 weeks after the birth of the child.

Should the nature of the job or working environment affect the health of the expectant mother, she is entitled to take 'health-and-safety leave' during pregnancy. This leave is in lieu of maternity leave and can be taken from the beginning of pregnancy to 26 weeks after the birth.

If the mother becomes ill during her additional unpaid maternity leave, she can transfer the unpaid leave to sick leave with the agreement of the employer. In this case, the mother forfeits any additional unpaid maternity leave not taken.

The father of the child is also entitled to time off work without loss of pay to attend antenatal classes and to be present for the birth of the child.

Parental Leave Act 1998

This Act enables both parents to take unpaid leave of 14 weeks per child up to the age of five where the employee has one year's continuous employment with his/her employer. (A 'bill' is currently in place for the age limit to be increased to 8 years, and up to 16 years if the child has a disability.) Parental leave is non-transferable between parents and 6 months' notice should be given to the employer in advance of the leave. The leave can be taken consecutively or in shorter periods with the consent of the employer.

Force Majeure Leave (emergency leave of 3 days in a 12-month period) is also provided for in this Act, ie, where an employee is entitled to take leave in the case of injury/illness affecting an immediate family member.

Safety, Health and Welfare at Work Act 1989–2005

This Act places general duties and responsibilities on employers and employees to prevent accidents and to increase the safety levels at work. Manufacturers, designers and suppliers of materials also have a duty to ensure that the goods and materials produced will not interfere with the welfare of others.

The Health and Safety Authority (HSA) was established under this Act and is responsible for enforcing the legislation, devising codes of practice and industry regulations, providing guidelines for safety statements and advising businesses on safety and welfare matters.

Employers have a duty to:

◆ provide and maintain a safe place of work with safe access to and egress from the building
◆ provide and maintain safe machinery
◆ prevent and/or reduce risks by implementing, providing and maintaining safe systems of work
◆ employ competent employees
◆ provide information, training and supervision to ensure safety standards are met
◆ provide and implement a *safety statement*, outlining safety procedures and emergency plans
◆ provide welfare facilities.

Employees have a duty:

◆ to take reasonable care to perform duties safely so that the health, safety and welfare of others are not affected

◆ to cooperate with employers in matters of safety by following procedures and using any protective clothing and safety guards provided

◆ to report unsafe conditions/practices to a supervisor or the Safety Representative

◆ not to interfere with, misuse or damage anything in the workplace that could endanger others

◆ not to engage in improper conduct that could endanger themselves or others at work

◆ not to be under the influence of alcohol or drugs, and to undergo testing for intoxicants if requested by an employer.

Safety Representative

Every business should have at least one employee safety representative who will negotiate with management on behalf of employees on safety and welfare issues and to ensure that safety measures are being adhered to. S/he can inspect the workplace to identify unsafe conditions/practices and can make oral or written submissions to management. The safety representative can also investigate accidents and can accompany the HSA inspector on an inspection tour of the premises. Management must provide the safety representative(s) with information and training to enable them to carry out their duties effectively.

The Safety Statement

The Safety Statement is management's written commitment to safety. Every business must have a safety statement that specifies how health and safety will be provided and implemented. Safety statements are normally prepared by a consultant, in conjunction with employers and Safety Representatives. The employer is primarily responsible in ensuring that the safety statement is implemented. The Safety Statement should be reviewed annually.

A *risk assessment* should be carried out in the preparation of the Safety Statement in order to identify and assess the risk of potential hazards in the workplace. This involves examining the structure and layout of the building, equipment, work practices and other physical elements such as noise and dust levels, light and heat levels, that may have a negative impact on the health and welfare of employees. Common causes of accidents in the workplace include slippery floors, faulty/loose electric cables, frayed carpets and cluttered work areas.

The Safety Statement should specify:

- the identified hazards and the levels of safety required
- resources necessary to implement and maintain safety standards
- precautions that should be taken to prevent accidents
- the level of cooperation expected from employees in maintaining safety
- names, departments and responsibilities of elected safety representatives
- procedures for consultations between employer and employees
- reporting procedures for accidents

All incidents at work resulting in minor injuries should be reported internally. Accidents that result in more than three days' absence from work must be reported to the HSA.

Organisations with 3 or fewer employees can fulfil their Safety Statement obligations by adopting a Code of Practice designed by the HSA advisory body for that industry.

Data Protection Legislation

The Data Protection Act (DPA) 1988–2003

The *Data Protection Act (DPA) 1988–2003* applies to organisations that maintain information on individuals, in manual or electronic format. For example, a personnel file will contain details of the employee's contract of employment, pension contributions, etc. The file may also hold sensitive information regarding an employee, such as: health, family circumstances, disciplinary details, etc. Breaches of the Data Protection Act can result in a fine or a conviction.

The DPA Acts regulate the collection, processing, storage and disclosure of personal information through:

1. *A Data Protection Commissioner:* who enforces the legislation, investigates complaints, develops codes of practice for information-sensitive industries and maintains a register of *Data Controllers*, ie, the organisations or individual that controls the contents and use of personal data.
2. *The Data Controller,* who must ensure that data is:
    - obtained lawfully, ie, the individual should be aware of why the data is being collected, where it will be stored and for what purpose it will be used
    - used for the purpose for which is was collected
    - not used or disclosed for any unspecified or unlawful purposes
    - kept safe and secure to prevent unauthorised access or alteration
    - accurate and as up to date as possible
    - complete, relevant and not excessive
    - not stored longer than is necessary.

The Data Controller may be instructed to disclose personal information relating to an individual by the Gardaí or a Government Minister, where the information is required to investigate tax or criminal cases to prevent injury, serious loss or damage to others.

3. *Giving rights to the Data Subject:* ie, the person affected by the information. The Data Subject:
   ◆ can request a copy of the information held and must receive that information within 40 days, unless the Government instructs the Data Controller to withhold the information
   ◆ has the right to rectify any incorrect information.

Freedom of Information Acts (FOI) 1997–2003

The Freedom of Information Acts 1997–2003 place an obligation on public bodies (ie, public authorities and government departments) to publish information on their activities and to make personal information on an individual available upon request by that individual.

Every public body is obliged to produce a Freedom of Information Manual that outlines general duties and services provided by the body, a description of the records held and how members of the public can access these files if required.

Under the Acts, an individual has a legal right to:
◆ access information kept by public bodies and government departments
◆ have official information relating to him/herself amended where it is incomplete, incorrect or misleading
◆ obtain reasons for decisions relating to him/herself. For example, in the case of an individual not being successful at a job interview with a public body, the individual can obtain the results of his/her interview.

An application for information must be made in writing to the public body and the request must refer to the FOI Acts. The request should be as specific as possible, to allow the Information Officer of the public body to search for the information required. A request for information should be responded to within 4 weeks or the request is deemed to be refused. The individual can then appeal the refusal to a senior staff member in the public body and, if still not satisfied, can appeal to the Office of the Information Commissioner, which was set up under the FOI acts to investigate complaints and to carry out independent reviews on public bodies that do not comply with FOI legislation.

Short Questions

1. List four agencies available in Ireland that mediate over employment disputes in the workplace.
2. List six details that should be included in an employee's terms of employment.
3. List four conditions that are covered under the *Employment Equality Acts 1998–2004*.
4. State the entitlements of employees under the *Organisation of Working Time Act 1997* in relation to: rest periods, holidays, total hours worked and night-time work.
5. What is the national minimum rate per hour for a 19-year-old with one year's experience?
6. Under the *Unfair Dismissals Act 1977–2001*, state three cases where a dismissal is regarded as fair and three cases where a dismissal is regarded as unfair.
7. What should:
   a) an employee do, if s/he has been unfairly dismissed?
   b) an employer do, if it is found that the employee had been unfairly dismissed?
8. John started work at 16 years and has worked with the same company for 26 years. His gross weekly wage at the time the company closed down was €650. Calculate the statutory redundancy payment to which he is entitled.
9. Under the *Maternity Protection Act, 1994–2004*, state:
   a) three rights of the expectant mother
   b) three duties of the expectant mother.
10. State two entitlements that are covered under the *Parental Leave Act 1998*.
11. State four duties of employers and four duties of employees under the *Safety, Health and Welfare at Work Act, 1989–2005*.
12. Explain the function of the HSA under the *Safety, Health and Welfare at Work Act 1989–2005*.
13. What is a 'risk assessment'?
14. What is a 'safety statement'? State four points that a safety statement should specify.
15. Outline the role of the Safety Inspector and the Safety Representative under the *Safety, Health and Welfare at Work Act, 1989–2005*.
16. State four duties of the Data Protection Commissioner under the *Data Protection Acts, 1988–2003*.
17. State four obligations imposed on the Data Controller under the *Data Protection Acts, 1988–2003*.
18. State two rights given to individuals under the *Data Protection Acts, 1988–2003*.

19. Explain the obligations placed on public bodies under the *Freedom of Information Act, 1997–2003*.

Summary

Typical legal forms of business are sole trader, partnership, company and co-operative. Each business form is specific in terms of set-up, control, ownership and the liability of the members. Once the business is formed it is generally necessary to divide the business activities according to business function, such as: marketing, finance, human resources and production.

The *marketing* function is generally responsible for sales, market research and product promotion. *Finance* is responsible for preparing accounts and budgets, accounts payable, accounts receivable and cost control. *Human Resources* is responsible for manpower planning, recruitment and selection, employee and management development, employee welfare and industrial relations. *Production* is the function responsible for producing the product to suit the market. However, as a business grows it may be necessary to reorganise the business activities according to product, geographic location or a combination of both. An *organisation chart* depicts the structure of a business by outlining the business functions and formal lines of communications.

The administration office is central to every business. It is often the first point of contact with customers and is the central point for collecting, processing, recording, storing and communicating information. Once the location of the office is decided upon, the Office Manager must decide what office activities will be centralised, or whether it will be necessary to duplicate services throughout the business. The latter may typically occur where the business is organised according to geographic location. The layout of the workstations and the location of the office equipment must be carefully organised to allow an efficient flow of work.

Equipment typical to an office includes: workstations, photocopiers, telephones, desktop equipment (stationery items), filing cabinets, fax machines, binders and laminators. Generally an *open-plan* office is preferred to a *corridor-style* office, because it utilises space efficiently and facilitates the sharing of resources. Some offices adopt a combination of both styles — a *landscaped* approach, where furniture and partitions can be arranged to allow some element of privacy. Where the office is dealing with the public, an open plan is generally preferred, with a counter dividing the public from the work area.

All businesses utilise a range of banking services, such as: current accounts, electronic funds transfer, credit-card and debit-card facilities and foreign exchange. Traditionally businesses settle their accounts by cheque. While this is a safe and trusted method of paying bills (especially when the cheques are crossed), it does take time to prepare and process the payment.

Modern banking facilities such as electronic funds transfer (EFT) and electronic banking (telephone banking and Internet banking) enable the business to pay its bills directly to the creditors' accounts, ensuring bills are paid on time with minimum effort. Using electronic banking the business can track its transactions at any time, day or night. International trading has also changed significantly, as businesses can now compete with their euro-zone partners without experiencing fluctuations in foreign currency.

Every business must be aware of current legislation regarding conditions of employment, health, safety and welfare of employees at work. Agencies such as the Rights Commissioners, Equality Officers and the Labour Court help to resolve disputes between employer and employees. While the majority of decisions of these agencies are not legally binding, both parties approach these bodies in the hope of resolving the issue without going to court. Disputes generally involve terms and conditions of work, pay issues, unfair dismissals and equality issues. Much of the current legislation (ie, Acts relating to Unfair Dismissals; Terms of Employment; Data Protection; Health, Safety and Welfare; Maternity and Paternity) is a result of directives issued by the EU and reflects the changing work patterns in Ireland today.

Assignments

1. Using information from a local small/medium business (fewer than fifty employees) draw up an organisation chart showing the departments and key positions in the business. Write a brief description of the activities carried out in each department.
2. John and Joe are setting up a new recruitment business but are undecided as to whether to set up the business as a partnership or a private company. Write a report explaining the advantages and disadvantages of each and recommend one form, justifying your choice. Outline the necessary steps, involved in setting up your chosen form of business.
3. The Marketing team is launching a new detergent. What promotion techniques would you recommend to the Marketing Manager and why? Remember, this product must be differentiated from similar products on the market.
4. Assume that an organisation is divided into four departments — production, finance, sales/marketing and human resources. Write a one-paragraph summary on each department, detailing the types of activity that would be handled by each of the four departments.
5. The Office Manager in a Travel Agent has been informed that the office is being relocated to a bigger site. S/he has asked the office staff for suggestions to design the best layout. Write a report to the Office Manager outlining how the office should be designed. State whatever

assumptions you wish regarding the building structure. Include drawings of the new office, indicating workstations, equipment, doorways, etc.

6. You have been asked to purchase for the office a new photocopier that is capable of handling complex jobs and a large workload. Research three different models that meet this specification. In your report document the features of each model and highlight the differences between the models. Recommend one photocopier, stating why you think it is most suitable for the office requirements.

7. There are various types of credit card on the market at present. Compare and contrast three credit cards in terms of annual cost, interest rates, credit periods, bonuses such as travel insurance, etc.

8. In your business, bills such as telephone and ESB are paid by cheque and are often overdue. Suggest three alternative methods of payment that your business could use to ensure these bills are paid on time.

9. Compare the Internet banking services of the Irish commercial banks. Which bank offers the most suitable services and rates for you?

10. What currency is used in the following countries? Using the current rate of exchange, calculate how much €500 is worth in:
    a) Bulgaria
    b) Saudi Arabia
    c) South Africa
    d) the US.

11. The *Safety, Health and Welfare Act, 1989–2005* have made people more aware of safety levels at work. Look around your classroom (or your home) and identify five potential hazards; assess the risk level of injury (high, medium or low), and recommend how you could make that environment safer.

12. Examine the various state agencies and chart the different options an employee has if they wish to take a case for unfair dismissal against their employer.

13. Explain the implications of the *Data Protection Acts, 1988–2003,* for the Human Resources department of a business.

Unit 2 — Office Duties

Introduction

Unit 2 provides an overview of the typical office duties carried out by the receptionist and office administrators. It examines in detail the procedure and documentation involved in a business transaction (ie, the buying and selling of goods), and it concludes with an overview of the types of formal meeting that an organisation must convene. Unit 2 is divided into four chapters:

Chapter 5 — Receptionist Duties

Reviews typical receptionist duties and examines procedures for dealing with visitors and operating the switchboard:
- Maintaining the Reception Area
- Receiving Visitors
- Dealing with Complaints
- The Switchboard and Features
- Operating the Switchboard
- The Answering Machine and Voicemail
- Telephone Charges
- Making National and International Calls

Chapter 6 — Administration and Accounting Duties

Discusses the typical administrative and accounting duties. It provides guidelines on how work can be planned and organised to ensure its completion in time for deadlines. Guidelines on how to deal with petty cash and the preparation of wages are also provided. Topics include:
- Planning and Organising Work
- Arranging Appointments
- Arranging Travel
- Preparing for Meetings and Conferences
- Accounting Activities
- Wages and Salaries

Chapter 7 — Business Transactions

Examines the documentation involved in a business transaction, from the initial enquiry to the final payment for the goods. Stock control is also examined, ensuring that every item of stock moving to and from the warehouse is accounted for. Topics include:

◆ Stages of a Business Transaction
◆ Procedure for Dealing with Incoming Orders (Supplier)
◆ Procedure for Dealing with Incoming Goods (Purchaser)
◆ Statement of Accounts
◆ Overview of Stages in Business Transactions
◆ Stock Control

Chapter 8 — Meetings

Discusses formal meetings in a company and the duties of the secretary and chairman in relation to the preparation and conduct of the meeting. Topics include:

◆ Types of Formal Meeting
◆ Convening Company Meetings
◆ Documentation for Meetings
◆ Duties of the Chairman and Secretary

Chapter 5 — Receptionist Duties

Large businesses will employ a receptionist to operate the switchboard and receive visitors. Often the receptionist will assist with clerical work such as filing and dealing with correspondence during quiet periods.

As the receptionist is often the first point of contact with the business, a smart personal appearance and good interpersonal and communication skills are essential.

The reception desk should ideally be placed facing the door, so that visitors are seen when entering the building. However, the reception desk should be some distance away from the waiting area, so that work can continue while visitors are waiting, but the receptionist should be able to view visitors at all times. The reception desk should not be left unattended.

The main duties of the receptionist are as follows:

1. Maintaining the reception area
2. Receiving visitors
3. Dealing with complaints
4. Operating the switchboard.

Maintaining the Reception Area

The reception area should be kept neat and tidy and should have a no-smoking policy in keeping with recent legislation. Comfortable seating should be provided for the visitor, with reading material available. If it is policy to offer refreshments, these should be kept close at hand. The receptionist should keep at hand:

◆ telephone message pad
◆ appointments book
◆ diary
◆ visitor log book and visitor badges
◆ telephone and fax directories, internal telephone lists and emergency numbers (eg, doctor, guards, fire brigade, etc)
◆ stationery
◆ calendar
◆ first-aid kit.

Receiving Visitors

As the receptionist is the first point of contact with the company, it is his/her duty to welcome and screen visitors. The receptionist should always be pleasant but not too familiar with visitors, and should greet the expected visitor formally: eg, 'Good morning, how may I help you?'

If the receptionist is busy with a telephone call or another visitor, s/he should acknowledge any visitor approaching the desk and invite them to take a seat while they are waiting.

The following procedure may be used when dealing with expected visitors:

◆ Greet visitor pleasantly and check their name, the business they represent and whom they wish to see, with the details recorded in the appointments diary.

◆ Request the visitor to sign the visitor log book both on entering and exiting the building. (This is a security precaution in case of an emergency, so that the receptionist will have a record of who is in the building.)

◆ Distribute a visitor badge, if policy. This may be necessary to allow the visitor access to restricted areas. The badge should be returned on departure.

◆ Inform the person concerned by telephone that the visitor has arrived.

◆ Depending on company policy, direct the visitor to the appropriate office or call an office junior to accompany the visitor to the desired location.

Power Ltd, Main Street, Wexford						
Name	Company	Date of arrival	Time of arrival	Referred to	Signed	Time of departure
G Larkin	Glen Ltd	June 10	1000 hrs	L Kiernan	K Shea	1200 hrs
L Flynn	Carbury Products	June 10	1500 hrs	A O'Connor	K Shea	1510 hrs
G Deegan	ACT Ltd	June 12	1550 hrs	V Shanahan	K Shea	1640 hrs

Visitor log book

Even though appointments are made in advance, emergency situations may occur that cause delays or even prevent the appointment from taking place. The receptionist should be discreet when dealing with this situation. The receptionist should:

◆ apologise for the delay and inform the visitor of the approximate waiting time

◆ offer to reschedule the appointment, if the visitor is unable to wait or the appointment cannot be met

◆ if the visitor decides to wait, offer some reading material and refreshments if appropriate.

Often the receptionist will encounter visitors who do not have an appointment. These visitors may be:

♦ important clients who happen to be in the area
♦ sales representatives 'cold calling' in the hope of obtaining new business
♦ a customer with an urgent message or problem
♦ a personal emergency.

Whatever the reason for the visit, the receptionist must use his/her initiative and assess the urgency of the caller. In an emergency situation, inform the person concerned of the visitor immediately. Sometimes the manager may not wish, or is unable, to meet unexpected visitors. The experienced receptionist will judge whether or not s/he can deal with the visitor. The receptionist should be polite at all times and should:

♦ greet the visitor and obtain his/her name, name of organisation and reason for his/her visit
♦ if s/he cannot deal with the enquiry, invite the visitor to sit in the waiting area, while s/he checks to see if the person requested is free to meet the visitor
♦ if the person required is unavailable to meet the visitor, suggest another appropriate person, or arrange another suitable time, or record the query for the person concerned.

Dealing with Complaints

The receptionist will often have to deal with complaints. In situations like this, the receptionist must retain his/her composure and be polite at all times. Even though the nature of the complaint will differ from business to business, a general procedure to deal with complaints is to:

♦ listen attentively to the caller and avoid unnecessary interruptions
♦ carefully record details of the complaint
♦ neither agree nor disagree with the complaint
♦ offer assistance or refer the problem.

The receptionist should keep the caller informed on progress, as appropriate.

The Switchboard and Features

The telephone is perhaps the most important means of communication. A business will operate a switchboard to cater for the volume of incoming and outgoing calls and to enable calls to be transferred to the appropriate person.

A switchboard is a private local exchange used in businesses that have a large volume of incoming and outgoing calls. The switchboard is connected to the public telephone network and is used to direct incoming calls to the appropriate person's telephone extension. As the telephone extensions are not **directly** connected to the public telephone network, the switchboard reduces the number of telephone lines required in a business, thus making it possible for a telephone to be on everybody's desk.

The switchboard allows a number of incoming calls to be received at the same time and permits telephone extensions to make outgoing calls if a line is free. Extension users make external calls by dialling a single-digit code or pressing a line number that is free.

Special switchboards can be linked to cordless telephone extensions, allowing calls to be made and received as long as the user stays within the coverage area of the switchboard. Cordless telephones are particularly useful where employee mobility is important, such as in hospitals, large factories, building sites, garages, airports and large stores.

Features of a Switchboard

All the features and facilities of a switchboard are under software control and can be easily customised. Switchboards vary in their degree of sophistication, but will include some or all of the following features:

Hold and transfer: Calls are received through the switchboard and are routed to the appropriate telephone extension. The receptionist puts an incoming caller on hold and dials the appropriate telephone extension number to transfer the call. Sometimes, music is played to the caller while they are on hold. The person at the telephone extension can also transfer the incoming call directly to another extension if appropriate.

LCD (liquid crystal display): A panel on the telephone which displays the number dialled and the duration of the call.

Call status display: Coloured lights are displayed to indicate whether the calls are internal or external, transferred, picked up or forwarded.

Hands-free operation: Calls can be made without lifting the handset. The conversation is carried out via a built-in microphone and loudspeaker. A useful feature if information needs to be checked while on the telephone or if more than one person needs to hear the conversation.

Memory recall: Also known as 'last number redial'. By pressing a special key the *most recently* dialled number is dialled again. A useful feature when the number dialled is engaged.

Speed dialling: The switchboard can be programmed to store frequently used telephone numbers alphabetically by surname, business name, etc. The assigned name is then dialled rather than the full telephone number.

Clear last digit: A function to erase a misdialled digit while entering a telephone number.

Call forwarding: Also known as 'follow me'. A diversion facility which diverts all incoming calls to another telephone number (internal or external). This facility could be used in the evening, when the switchboard operator is off duty.

Call waiting: A facility which alerts a person on the telephone to the presence of another incoming call. S/he can then put the call on hold, deal with the incoming call and return to the on hold call.

Call barring: Telephone extensions can be prevented from making specific calls such as national, international or mobile calls.

Call logging: A metering facility to record the origin of incoming calls and the destination and duration of outgoing calls by extension number.

Call pickup: Allows a telephone extension to answer a call ringing on another telephone extension. This is useful if the person requested is not at their desk and the call can be dealt with by someone else in the office.

Camp on busy: Allows automatic redial of an engaged telephone extension. This saves time trying to contact individuals and avoids the pitfall of forgetting to redial. When an extension number is engaged, the caller enters a code. When the extension becomes free, the caller's telephone will automatically ring. When the caller lifts the receiver, the extension number previously dialled is automatically redialled and the call can be completed.

Conferencing: A number of telephone extensions and, if required, a number of exchange lines can be connected. This allows more than two people to be involved in a conversation.

Voicemail: A facility that sets up an answering machine for each extension user. Using special software, extension users are given their own personal answering machine called a 'mailbox', where messages can be stored.

Direct dial in (DDI): A facility that allocates DDI numbers for each telephone extension, allowing a caller to dial directly to an extension without going through the switchboard, thus reducing the pressure on the switchboard. If the person is unavailable, features such as voicemail, call forwarding or call pickup could be implemented, ensuring that all incoming calls are answered.

Uniform call distribution: Allows incoming calls to a listed directory number to be evenly distributed over a given number of lines. Useful for distributing calls on a 'helpline' or a 'call centre'.

Detailed switchboard

Operating the Switchboard

When dealing with enquiries over the telephone, the receptionist must always be pleasant, friendly and efficient and must speak clearly.

Handling Incoming Calls

◆ Keep a pen and telephone message pad close at hand by the telephone.

◆ Answer the telephone as soon as possible (eg, on the second ring).

◆ Greet the caller pleasantly and identify the business by name, eg, 'Good morning, Power Products Ltd, how may I help you?'

◆ Obtain the caller's name, business name and to whom they wish to speak. Sometimes the receptionist will make further enquiries as to the nature of the call, as s/he may be able to deal with the issue him/herself.

◆ Ask the caller to 'hold' (while connecting to the appropriate person).

◆ Dial that person's extension number and inform him/her of the caller's name, nature of the call and the telephone line number.

◆ If the call cannot be taken, return to the caller and inform him/her that the person is unavailable at present and offer to take a message or to leave a 'voicemail'.

◆ If the person concerned is on another telephone call (as seen from the 'call status' feature), the receptionist should ask the caller if they wish to 'hold'. The call can then be put through when that line is free. The 'call waiting' facility could also be used to alert the person on the telephone call that another caller is waiting.

◆ If the caller is waiting longer than expected, the receptionist should return to the caller and offer to take a message.

◆ When taking a message, record the caller's name, organisation, telephone number, date and time of call and details of the message. Repeat essential details to the caller, such as telephone numbers and dates, to ensure accuracy.

◆ Distribute the message to the person concerned as soon as possible.

On-line message pads can be set up, allowing the message to be transferred electronically to the recipient's e-mail account.

Telephone Message Pad

Date: _____   For: _____

From: _____   Tel No: _____

Returned call: ☐   Will call again: ☐   Please call back: ☐

Message: _____

_____

Taken by: _____   Time: _____

Example 1

Receptionist: Good morning, Print Technology Ltd.

Caller: Hi, I want to speak to Mr Walsh please.

Receptionist: Who shall I say is calling?

Caller: Oh, this is Barry O'Brien.

Receptionist: Barry O'Brien — from?

Caller: Oh — from Highway Wholesalers.

Receptionist: (Checks the switchboard and sees that Mr Walsh is on another call.)
    I'm sorry, but Mr Walsh is on another call. May I help you?

Caller: I'm ringing in connection with my account from last month.

Receptionist: Ms Ryan also deals with accounts; would you like to speak to her?

Caller: Yes, thank you, I need to get this problem sorted out immediately.
    (The receptionist should inform Ms Ryan of the caller's name and nature of his business.)

Receptionist: I'm putting you through to Ms Ryan now.

Example 2

Receptionist: Good morning, Fitzgerald Insurances — Margaret speaking.

Caller: Hi, I wish to speak with Mary Drohan, please.

Receptionist: Who shall I say is calling?

Caller: This is Mrs Cooney.
    (The receptionist checks to see if the person required is available and returns to the caller.)
    I'm sorry, Mrs Cooney, but Mary is with a client; would you like to hold?

Caller: No thanks.

Receptionist: Can I take a message?

Caller: Yes, I'm calling to see if my motor policy is ready yet.

Receptionist: I believe that that policy is ready, but may I take your telephone
    number, and Mary will call you back when she is free?

Caller: OK, the number is 35475 and I'll be here for another 20 minutes.

Receptionist: That is (writing down) Mrs Cooney at 35475. I'll give Mary the
    message and if she can't contact you this evening she will telephone you
    tomorrow morning.

Caller: Thank you.

*Note in this example, the name and telephone number of the caller are repeated to
ensure that the receptionist heard the details correctly.*

The Answering Machine and Voicemail

A telephone answering facility is an essential business tool today; allowing telephone messages to be received, when there is no one available to answer the telephone.

An answering machine is built into modern telephones or one may be attached to the telephone. Where the answering machine is based on digital technology the facility to leave messages is known as 'voicemail'.

In general, the answering machine/voicemail operates as follows:

1. When an incoming call is received, the telephone automatically switches to the answering machine/voicemail after a certain number of rings.
2. A recorded message is played inviting the caller to leave a message after the tone.
3. Messages are recorded and can be played back from that telephone or can be accessed from a remote location, using a PIN to access the messages.

Recording an Outgoing Message

1. Write down your message in advance, keeping it short.
2. Record the message in a quiet area; speak slowly and articulate each word.
3. The message should do the following:
    ◆ Greet the caller and state the name of the business.
    ◆ Apologise that there is nobody available to take the call.
    ◆ Ask the caller to leave their name, number and message after the 'tone'.
4. Play back the message, to ensure that it is audible. If not, delete it and repeat the process.

Example 1 — Message Recorded

You have reached the office of O'Flynn, Solicitors. We apologise that there is no one available to take your call. Please leave your name, number and message after the tone and we will contact you as soon as possible.

Example 2 — Message Recorded

Hello, High Flyers Ltd. We regret that our office is closed. Opening hours are 9.00 am to 1.00 pm weekdays. Please leave your name, number and message after the tone.

In the above message, the opening hours of the business are stated. This is not usually required, but as the opening hours are not standard, it does provide the caller with useful information. 'Hello' is used as the greeting, as it is suitable for all times of the day.

Leaving a Message

1. Speak slowly and clearly, giving the following details:
   ◆ state who the message is for
   ◆ give your name, business name and telephone number.
   (It is not necessary to state the date and time of the call, as this is automatically recorded on a modern answering machine.)
2. If the message is short, state your message. Spell out any words or figures that may be confusing. For example, the number '15' could sound like '50' and some foreign names are difficult to comprehend.
3. Do not leave a message if it is long and complex or confidential; just ask to be called back at a specific telephone number.

Example 1 — Leaving a Message

Good morning, this is Michael Carty from Shape-Up. Message is for Harry Smith, Sales Department. Please add two more boxes of All-Green Shampoo to my order. If you need further details, contact me at 234987 up to 6.00 pm. Thank you.

Here the caller leaves a message. This is very efficient as the receiver can act on the information and may not need to contact the caller again, saving time and money.

Example 2 — Leaving a Message

Good afternoon, this is Joe. Message is for Nora Shannon, Public Relations. Please call me at your earliest convenience.

In the above message, the caller's full name, business name and number were not given. This is acceptable if the receiver knows the caller very well. The caller does not state a message, maybe because it is too complex, private or the receiver is familiar with the issue from an earlier conversation.

If the answering machine is located and managed in the general office, incoming messages should be played back and the details transcribed. The messages should be given to the appropriate person as soon as possible.

Advantages and Disadvantages of Answering Machines/Voicemail

Advantages	Disadvantages
1. Messages can be received when there is no one in the office.	1. They are impersonal; people do not like talking to machines.
2. Messages can be picked up remotely.	2. The person leaving a message may forget to state their name and telephone numbers making the message redundant.
3. Forward contact numbers can be left.	
4. Calls can be screened. The receiver can cut in on urgent calls.	

Telephone Charges

Since deregulation of the telecommunications industry, Eircom no longer has a monopoly on providing fixed-line telephone calls. Eircom's main competitors are from telephone call providers such as: Esat (BT), Smart Telecom and Tele2.

The charge for local, national, international and calls to mobile phones can vary significantly from different telephone call providers. Therefore, in selecting a telephone call provider, a business should study the type of call most commonly made during a billing period. For example, a business dealing mainly with local markets could make significant savings by selecting the telephone call provider that offers the best rate for local and national calls. For all telephone call providers:

♦ Calls are charged at different rates during daytime, evenings and weekends.
♦ Prices quoted are on a per-minute basis; however, the telephone call is charged on a per-second basis, subject to a minimum charge.
♦ Prices include VAT at 21%.

A simple comparison of telephone charges from fixed lines is given below, based on two telephone call providers: Eircom and Tele2.

EIRCOM RATES FOR CALLS FROM FIXED LINE (MIN. CHARGE 6.34C)						
	Local	National	UK	Vodafone	02	Meteor
Day: Mon–Fri 8am–6pm	4.93c	8.17c	15.35c	23.07c	23.07c	29.19c
Evening: Mon–Fri 6pm–8am	1.26c	4.92c	14.44c	19.46c	19.46c	19.46c
Weekend & Public Hols: Fri 12 midnight–Mon 8am	1.26c	1.26c	12.44c	11.5c	11.5c	15.23c

TELE2 RATES FOR CALLS FROM FIXED LINE (MIN. CHARGE 6.35C)						
	Local	National	UK	Vodafone	O2	Meteor
Day: Mon–Fri 8am–6pm	3.49c	3.49c	5c	21.9c	21.9c	22.99c
Evening: Mon–Fri 6pm–8am	1.1c	1.1c	5c	16.9c	16.9c	18.99c
Weekend & Public Hols: Fri 12 midnight–Mon 8am	1.1c	1.1c	5c	10.4c	10.4c	14.99c

Telemarketing and Premium Services

Telemarketing services are used by businesses to generate sales. The business pays the full cost or balance of the telephone charge, depending on the number(s) they choose.

CALLS TO TELEMARKETING SERVICES		
Number	Charge to Caller *from anywhere in Ireland*	Business Pays
FreeFone — 1800 CallSave — 1850 LoCall — 1890	FREE at all times 6.34c for any duration at all times Same cost as a local call	The total telephone charge The balance of the telephone charge The balance of the telephone charge

Premium services are used by businesses that provide an information service to the public, ie, news, weather, sports results, horoscopes, entertainment, advice, etc, generally 24 hours a day, 7 days a week. The cost of the call, which is paid totally by the caller, depends on the number called, which can range from 1520 to 1590.

CALLS TO PREMIUM SERVICES			
Number	Charge to Customer	Number	Charge to Customer
1520	15c per minute at all times	1560	€1.25 per minute at all times
1530	32c per minute at all times	1570	€1.75 per minute at all times
1540	60c per minute at all times	1580	€2.40 per minute at all times
1550	95c per minute at all times	1590	€2.90 per minute at all times

Costing Telephone Calls

All calls made from fixed-line telephones are charged on a per-second basis, subject to a minimum charge which depends on the telephone provider.

The cost of a telephone call will be the higher of the:
1. minimum call charge
2. duration of call multiplied by cost per second.

Example 1 — National Call

Cost a call made from Waterford to Cork on Tuesday at 5.00pm for 3 minutes 22 seconds, using Eircom as the telephone provider.

This call is charged at the daytime rate, which is 8.17c per minute. The call is of 202 seconds duration, ie, (3 minutes × 60 seconds) + 22 seconds. Every second costs 0.136c (8.17c ÷ 60 seconds), therefore the cost of the call is 202 seconds × 0.136c = 27.50c.

Example 2 — Local Call

Cost a local call made on Saturday at 11.30pm for 4 minutes, using Eircom as the telephone provider.

This call is charged at the weekend rate, which is 1.26c per minute. The call is of 240 seconds duration. Every second costs 0.021c (1.26c ÷ 60 seconds), therefore the cost of the call is 240 seconds × 0.021c = 5.04c. However, this is less than the minimum charge of 6 c, so the **actual** cost of the call is 6.34c.

Example 3 — International Call

Cost a call from Dublin to the UK made on a public holiday at 5.30pm for 12 minutes, using Tele2 as the telephone provider.

This call is charged at the weekend rate, which is 5c per minute. Every second costs 0.083c (5c ÷ 60 seconds). The duration of the call is 12 minutes or 720 seconds; therefore the cost of the call is 720 seconds x 0.083c = 60c.

Outgoing Calls

Before making a telephone call, the receptionist should:

◆ locate the telephone number from the telephone directory or other source, ie, letterhead or telephone operator

◆ plan the telephone call and identify the person or department s/he wishes to contact

◆ keep files and correspondence nearby for easy reference.

Making National and International Calls

Making Telephone Calls within Ireland

Ireland is divided into a number of telephone zones which are represented by an STD code (subscriber trunk dialling), eg, the STD code for the Dublin area is 01. To make a local telephone call (ie, dialling within the same STD code), the number to dial is simply the local number.

To make a telephone call outside the local STD area, the STD code for the zone is dialled first, followed by the local number. The STD codes are listed in the telephone directory.

Example

Joan is on her way from Waterford to Cork Airport. When she gets to Cork city, she discovers that she has forgotten her passport and needs to telephone home for it to be sent by courier. Her local number in Waterford is 382111. To dial from Cork, Joan dials the STD code for Waterford, followed by the local number: (051) 382111.

Making International Calls from Ireland

When making an international telephone call from Ireland, an **access code** and an **area code** are required. The access code is necessary to enable the caller to **dial out** of Ireland. The access code from Ireland to all other countries starts with **00**. The area code is the code necessary to **dial into** another country. The area code will differ for every country. The access codes and area codes are listed in the telephone directory.

To make an international telephone call, dial the number in the following order:

access code + **area** code + **local number**

> **Example**
>
> You are requested by your boss to contact a supplier in Great Britain. She has given you the number of the company, which is based in Manchester. The local number is 4410700, but when you dial this number you discover that the number is incomplete. What do you do?
>
> **From the Telephone Directory locate:**
> the access code for Great Britain — 0044
> the area code for Manchester — 161
> The number you should dial is 0044 161 4410700.

Making International Calls to Ireland

When making an international telephone call to Ireland, the access code is 00353. If the STD code begins with **zero**, the caller should omit the first zero from the STD code when making an international call to Ireland. For example, if dialling from France to Cork, the procedure is:

The number to dial will be 00353 21 + local number (omitting first zero from STD code).

Short Questions

1. List four duties of the receptionist.
2. When scheduling an appointment, state the essential information that must be recorded by the receptionist.
3. Outline the procedure for dealing with expected visitors to the business.
4. How would you deal with a client/visitor who arrived without an appointment?
5. Outline a procedure for dealing with complaints.
6. Describe the following features of a switchboard:
   a)   speed dialling
   b)   camp on busy
   c)   uniform call distribution
   d)   voicemail.

7. Distinguish between the following features of a switchboard:
   a) call forwarding
   b) call pickup
   c) call logging
   d) call status display.
8. Explain what DDI is and how it operates.
9. Outline the procedure for dealing with incoming calls via a switchboard.
10. Design a telephone message pad suitable for use in the reception area.
11. List the essential points that an outgoing message on an answering machine/voicemail should contain.
12. List the essential points that should be dictated when leaving a message on an answering machine/voicemail.
13. State four advantages of an answering machine/voicemail.
14. Outline the procedure for making outgoing international calls.
15. Differentiate between telemarketing and premium services.
16. Explain the difference between the following telemarketing telephone numbers: 1800, 1850 and 1890.
17. Outline the range of codes that must be dialled when dialling from:
    a) Ireland to Paris, France
    b) Paris to Dublin.

Chapter 6 — Administration and Accounting Duties

With the speed of technological developments, the role of the secretary/administrator has changed from that of a decade ago. The administrator is expected to be competent in the use of computers and modern office technology.

The administrator should be:
◆ pleasant and courteous
◆ skilled in oral, written and electronic communication
◆ efficient and professional at all times
◆ tactful and discreet, especially when dealing with complaints
◆ willing to assist and show initiative.

Classifications of Administrator include:
◆ **Personal Assistant (PA):** A personal assistant to a senior executive in the business is responsible for the day-to-day organising of events that take place in the executive's working day. The personal assistant becomes a specialist in his/her area. For example, the PA to the Marketing Manager may be responsible for preparing sales presentations and processing orders from the sales representatives. The PA deals with confidential correspondence, arranges the executive's appointment schedule, prepares travel itineraries and often has to deal with queries on behalf of the executive.
◆ **Junior Office Assistant:** Most offices will employ a junior assistant to carry out general office tasks, such as: word processing, handling the post, operating the switchboard, filing, photocopying and other general administration duties.
◆ **General Administrator:** The duties regularly carried out by general administrators are:
  1. Planning and organising work
  2. Arranging appointments
  3. Arranging travel
  4. Preparing for meetings and conferences.

Planning and Organising Work

As the administrator's normal working day involves the preparation of work for a future date, it is vital that plans are made. Generally the administrator will plan in the short term, ie, on a day-to-day basis, but s/he will also make arrangements for dates in the future, for example, organising meetings, booking appointments, arranging travel or planning conferences.

However, even the best-made plans can go wrong in a dynamic office environment. Emergencies occur, new priority work may emerge, deadlines may change, but the routine work must also get finished. The administrator must therefore be organised to deal with these situations as efficiently as possible. S/he must **plan,** but must also be **flexible** to rearrange plans if necessary. To help plan the work, the administrator may use some of the following, either using a manual or an electronic version:

◆ **Diary:** used to record details of appointments or meetings for some date in the future.

◆ **'To-do' List:** used to list work that needs to be completed that day.

◆ **Calendar:** essential to identify days, dates and months when planning for future events, such as: meetings, arranging travel, conferences, staff holidays, etc.

Diaries

The administrator may use a manual or an electronic diary.

◆ **Manual Diary:** When selecting a manual diary, the administrator should choose one with appropriate space to record the necessary details. For example, in a doctor's surgery, a one-page-per-day appointments diary may be sufficient, with times specified and space allocated to allow the administrator to write the appropriate details when scheduling appointments.

APPOINTMENTS MONDAY				JANUARY 12
	Patient	**Telephone no**	**Doctor**	**Doctor**
0900	Mrs Joan Doyle	45394	Dr Byrne	
	Mr Tom Dawson	39641		Dr O'Sullivan
1000				
1100	Miss Nora Gaffney	53684	Dr Byrne	
1200				
1300				
1400	Mr Tadgh Coakley	49865		Dr O'Sullivan
1500	Mr Paul Cooney	49655	Dr Byrne	
1600	Miss Patricia Doherty	82101	Dr Byrne	

A one-page appointment diary for doctor's surgery

◆ **Electronic Diary:** Is normally managed from a desktop computer, usually via an e-mail system such as MS Outlook, which also contains scheduling functionality. The main advantage of an electronic diary is that it can be easily shared with others on the network, thereby significantly reducing the time taken to arrange meetings. For example, a simple check of the electronic diary will indicate when personnel are available.

An electronic diary generally contains the following planning tools: an address/contacts book, a diary, a 'to-do list' and a calendar. It can be viewed in different formats, eg: daily, weekly, monthly or yearly, to facilitate future planning. There are no space restrictions as in a manual diary, as new pages can be added as required. Reminders can be set in advance to notify the user of priority appointments/tasks. Different levels of access can be set up, for example, 'read-only' access may be granted to allow certain groups of users to view but not edit any entry in the diary.

Information on the desktop diary can be transferred to a handheld electronic diary, generally known as a 'personal digital assistant' (PDA) and vice versa. Sophisticated PDAs can connect to the business network and the Internet via a high-speed wireless network, thus enabling employees to monitor the 'desktop diary' from off-site locations.

Handheld Computer (PDA)

How to plan

1. Record all known deadlines in a diary.
2. Estimate the time required to complete each task and record the start and completion dates in the diary. The administrator may plan to complete the task before the deadline, to allow for changes in the workload that may take priority.
3. The administrator should consult with his/her manager each day (if possible) to arrange a 'To-do' list. Entries on the 'To-do' list will include: unfinished tasks that must be completed, routine tasks and the new entries taken from the diary for that day.
4. The tasks on the 'To-do' list should be prioritised, ie, placed in order of importance. For example:
   ◆ urgent work that must be completed immediately
   ◆ routine tasks that must be done, eg, dealing with correspondence
   ◆ work that will soon become a priority unless completed
   ◆ routine tasks that are less important and can be completed at some later stage.
5. As new work comes in, the order of the tasks on the 'To-do' list may change as the new work may take priority.
6. When tasks are completed, they are ticked off the list.
7. Tasks not completed on the day will be:
   ◆ listed on the 'To-do' list for the following day if it is a high-priority task, or
   ◆ listed in the diary and dealt with at a later date.

Arranging Appointments

In general, incoming appointments are arranged by telephone or the administrator may receive a written request for an appointment by post, fax or e-mail. The administrator should keep a diary at hand, to check free times and dates. The nature of the business will determine the appointment details taken by the administrator.

If the nature of the appointment is **in-house,** ie, a visitor is coming to the business premises, the administrator should record the visitor's name, the time and date, the telephone number and whom s/he wishes to see in the appropriate section of the diary.

Where clients are met **outside the premises**, eg, insurance representatives, auctioneers, etc, the administrator should take the client's name, telephone number and the address of the meeting point and, when arranging the appointment time and date, allow time for travel.

In some cases a general diary may not be sufficient to record non-standard details. In such cases a customised form is designed either manually (ie, typed) or electronically (ie, created from a database).

The Enquiry Form displayed below details the information required by the booking office of a coach business. The enquiry form is used to record the overall details; the date and summary details are recorded in the appropriate section of the main diary.

ENQUIRY FORM — COACH HIRE

Day:_____ Date of hire: _____

Destination: _____

Pick-up points:_____ _____ _____

Pick-up time: _____ _____ _____

Number of passengers (coach size): _____

Luggage capacity:_____

Special requests (microphone, disability facilities, etc): _____

Price (if quoted): _____

Contact name: _____

Booked by: _____

Date of booking: _____

Arranging Travel

Another duty of the administrator may be to arrange business travel. The administrator must identify:

◆ the destination
◆ the duration and purpose of the visit
◆ the date and time of departure/return
◆ the accommodation preferences (hotel, guesthouse)
◆ the preferred mode of transport, (eg, air, rail, bus, sea or car).

If the person is travelling by air, then it is likely that the business has already established a working relationship with a reputable travel agent. If no arrangement exists, the administrator should consult with more than one travel agency to ensure the best value is obtained, in terms of both finance and quality of service. The administrator may need to arrange for transport to and from the point of arrival, ie, it may be necessary to hire a car or a taxi.

Booking Accommodation

When the type of accommodation required is identified (eg, hotel or guesthouse, single or double room, *en suite*, Internet facilities, etc) the administrator should research a variety of accommodation providers, using approved accommodation websites, guidebooks or the local tourist office. Once accommodation has been identified, the administrator should:

◆ telephone, fax or e-mail the accommodation providers to find a room that suits the requirements of the business traveller. If the accommodation is satisfactory a provisional booking will be made.

◆ request details of the booking to be forwarded (ie, e-mail, fax, post).

◆ check the details received to ensure that the dates, room type, etc correspond to the initial booking requirements.

◆ confirm the booking.

◆ contact the accommodation provider a day or two before the person is due to arrive to ensure that the accommodation details are in order and remind the receptionist of any special requests.

Preparing an Itinerary

If the person travelling has a series of appointments to attend, an itinerary is prepared by the administrator. An itinerary is a concise schedule generally produced on one page, outlining the details of meetings, contact information and travel arrangements for the duration of the trip.

Relevant correspondence, confirmation of bookings and the final itinerary should be given to the person travelling and copies should be retained in a travel file and kept by the administrator for reference purposes.

TRAVEL ITINERARY

MR JAMES RYAN — Trip to England 13–14 November 2005

Mon 13 November	
0830 hrs	Check in at Dublin Airport — 0830 hrs.
1000 hrs	Depart Dublin Airport for Manchester — Flight No. IE 113.
1130 hrs	Arrive Manchester — Meet Ms Jane Carty at Terminal 2, Gate No. 11. Leave airport for Hilton Hotel, Stoke-on-Trent.
1400 hrs	Collected by Ms Carty at hotel to go to Wedgwood plant to meet senior executives. Tour of plant.
1600 hrs	Presentation to senior executives — Strategic Planning.
Tues 14 November	
0900 hrs	Depart hotel by taxi to manufacturing plant.
1100 hrs	Meet production managers — Demonstrations of new techniques.
1400 hrs	Depart factory for Manchester Airport — check in 1600 hrs.
1700 hrs	Depart Manchester Airport for Dublin.

Travelling Abroad

When employees are travelling abroad on business, the administrator should allow time to organise the following:

◆ check whether a visa is necessary
◆ advise the person travelling to update their passport if necessary
◆ check whether medical vaccinations are required before travel and make appointments if required
◆ arrange company credit/debit cards and foreign currency if required
◆ prepare any documentation necessary for meetings
◆ check that tickets are correct for the travel arrangements
◆ arrange car hire and insurance cover if necessary
◆ finalise accommodation arrangements
◆ prepare an itinerary for the person travelling.

Calculating Travel Expenses

Travel expenses are paid to employees who travel on behalf of the business. The business will pay for the employee's meals, accommodation, costs of transport and other costs associated with the travel.

Some businesses will give employees expenses before they travel, while other businesses will reimburse employees on their return. To claim travel expenses, the employee completes a Travel Expense Form and attaches receipts for expenditure incurred.

When processing the claim form, the administrator must ensure that details are correct (ie, dates, number of days away, distance travelled) and that the claim form is signed by someone in authority, usually a department senior.

Mileage charts detailing the official distances between main destinations in Ireland are found in most road maps and on relevant travel websites.

Example 1

Employees are paid 72c per kilometre for business travel. The expense form for Mr O'Donnell shows he travelled from Tralee in Kerry to Cork city and returned that evening. Calculate how much should be paid to Mr O'Donnell for miles travelled. Use mileage chart below.

1. Check the mileage chart and locate Cork and Tralee on the grid.
2. The intersection point of Cork and Tralee is the distance travelled. Tralee to Cork is 117 km.
3. Mr O'Donnell travelled a return trip, so 117 km by 2 = 234 km travelled. He should receive €168.48 as his travel expenses (ie, 234 km × 72c).

Mileage and Kilometre Chart

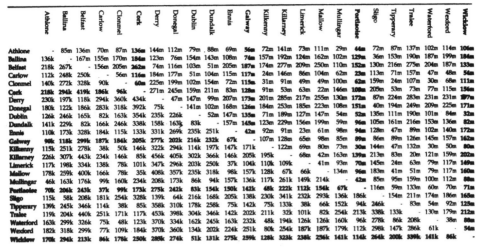

Mileage chart

Preparing for Meetings and Conferences

In many cases, the administrator will be expected to organise a conference or meeting on behalf of the business. This may involve:

◆ booking an appropriate hotel or conference centre, keeping in mind the size and layout of the room, audiovisual facilities, communication facilities (eg, Internet access, fax) and refreshments

◆ preparing and issuing booking forms for attendees

◆ obtaining literature on the local area for delegates, eg, lists of accommodation, tourist maps and other local information. This information may be enclosed with the booking form

◆ preparing a checklist to confirm the number of delegates attending

◆ booking accommodation for delegates if required

◆ preparing essential paperwork for the conference (ie, speaker's notes, copies of presentations, reports, etc)

◆ arranging name/title badges for delegates

◆ co-ordinating social programme for delegates

◆ arranging for a representative to meet delegates on arrival, if required

◆ handling queries that may arise during the conference

◆ for future reference, the administrator should carry out a post-conference evaluation of how the conference was organised.

Videoconferencing

Meetings or conferences can also be carried out remotely by using a videoconferencing system. A videoconferencing system consists of a screen, camera, microphone, loudspeakers and videoconferencing software. One videoconferencing system is connected to another either via an ISDN telephone line, or utilising Internet technology.

To use a videoconferencing system, a business may hire the conferencing studio available in most business hotels. However, owing to improved technology and affordability of web cameras that include videoconferencing software, videoconferencing for small groups most often takes place from a standard computer (ie, a desktop or portable), thus enabling a business with branches in various locations to conduct meetings virtually face to face.

Advantages

1. It allows meetings to take place face to face without the participants having to be in the same place.
2. It saves on travelling time and cost and enables people with conflicting schedules to 'meet'.
3. Remote expertise can be brought into a business, eg, guest speakers can provide their presentation through videoconferencing.
4. It can be used to interview potential employees.
5. It can be used in distance-learning courses.

Desktop videoconferencing system

Accounting Activities

The administrator may carry out accounting-type activities such as: maintaining the petty cash book, preparing lodgments, bank reconciliation statements and wages/salaries.

Petty Cash

A petty cash box is maintained in the office for purchasing or reimbursing employees for sundry items such as travel expenses, emergency stationery supplies, refreshments, etc. Petty cash operates on an **imprest system** where an imprest (ie, a float) is received at the beginning of the petty cash period, usually weekly. The float is restored to the original amount at the end of the period. The procedure is:

a) An initial amount of cash is received from the Accounts Department for the petty cash float. The float is the opening balance on the petty cash book.

b) When there is a request for money from petty cash, a petty cash voucher is completed giving details of the amount, item purchased and date of expenditure. Receipts for expenses incurred are usually required and are attached to the petty cash voucher. The voucher is signed by both the recipient of the money and the person authorising the petty cash payment.

c) The vouchers are used to write up the petty cash book at the end of the petty cash period.

d) The petty cash book is totted and balanced at the end of the petty cash period. More cash is requested to restore the imprest to the original amount for the next period.

PETTY CASH VOUCHER		
Voucher no 34 **Date** Aug. 7 '05		
Details	**Amount**	
	€	c
Stamps	2	54
Signed by *Carol Ryan*	_____	
Authorized by *Jack O'Reilly*	€2	54

Example

The imprest at the beginning of the petty cash period is €50. During the week, three vouchers were signed for:

stamps (€2.54)

stationery (€4.62)

cleaning agents (€6.38).

The total spent for the week was €13.54, leaving a balance of €36.46. €13.54 is required to restore the imprest to €50.

The petty cash book

The petty cash book analyses each petty cash transaction, which is displayed on the right-hand side of the petty cash book. The left-hand side of the book records the money received. The balance on the petty cash book is the original amount of imprest minus the total of the petty cash vouchers. This balance should match the amount of cash remaining in the petty cash box. The sum €13.54 represents the amount of money received to restore the imprest to €50 for the next period. The petty cash book for the above example is written up as follows:

PETTY CASH BOOK

Received	Date	Details	Voucher no	Total payment	Post	Stationery	Travel	Sundries
50.00	Aug 1	Bank						
	Aug 1	Stamps	34	2.54	2.54			
	Aug 2	Stationery	35	4.62		4.62		
	Aug 4	Cleaning	36	6.38				6.38
		Cash		€13.54	€2.54	€4.62		€6.38
	Aug 5	Balance c/d		€36.46				
€50.00				€50.00				
€36.46		Balance b/f						
€13.54	Aug 8	Bank						

Wages and Salaries

A common duty of the accounts clerk is to prepare wages and salaries for all the employees. Every employee is entitled to a wages slip from their employer, detailing how net pay is calculated and showing the various statutory and voluntary deductions.

Employees who are paid a **salary** receive a fixed amount of money on a fortnightly or monthly basis. Employees who are paid a **wage** may be paid on the following basis:

♦ **a basic hourly rate:** employees are paid a basic rate per hour. Any hours worked above the standard week (ie, 38 hours) are paid at overtime rates, ie, a rate higher than the basic rate. Businesses will generally have a range of overtime rates, for shift work, bank holidays and Sundays. Typical overtime rates are time and a half, double time and triple time.

♦ **a basic wage plus commission:** employees are paid a basic wage (ie, a standard week of 38 hours) and can earn more depending on their performance, eg, sales representatives are often awarded commission on the volume of sales over a specific target.

♦ **a piece rate:** employees are not paid a basic wage, but according to the quantity of output produced.

Calculation of Wages

The procedure for calculating tax on an employee's wage/salary is based on the tax credit system. An employer needs a *Certificate of Tax Credit and Standard Rate Cut-off Point* for each employee, which details the weekly/monthly 'tax credit' and the weekly/monthly 'standard rate cut-off point'.

♦ The *'tax credit'* reduces the amount of tax to be paid for each week/month and is based on an employee's personal circumstances (ie, single, married, widowed, etc) and relief for certain expenses such as: rent relief, tuition fees, service charges and trade-union subscriptions.

♦ The *'standard rate cut-off point'* is the amount of income each week/month to be taxed at the low rate of tax (known as the standard rate – currently 20%). Any income above the *'standard rate cut-off point'* is taxed at the higher rate of tax (currently 42%).

If an employer does not have this Certificate for an employee, s/he will deduct tax at the emergency rates as obliged by law. Therefore, the employee will pay more tax than is necessary and will remain on emergency tax until the employer receives the Certificate. Any overpayment of tax is refunded.

Obtaining a Tax Credit Certificate

a) If an employee has just started work, s/he must complete **Form 12A** (obtainable from the Tax Office or can be downloaded from the Revenue website, www.revenue.ie) giving details of income, personal circumstances, ie, single, married, age, disabilities, etc and certain expenditure such as: rent paid, tuition fees, trade-union subscription and service charges. The tax office then calculates the tax credits and the standard rate cut-off point which will be issued to both the employee and the employer.

b) A P45 is given to employees on termination of their employment. When an employee takes up a new job s/he should give the new employer the P45, which states the 'tax credits' and the 'standard rate cut-off point'.

Before looking at how wages are calculated, it is important to understand the following terms:

◆ **Gross pay:** consists of the total income earned by the employee *before* any deductions are made. If the employee is paid according to hours worked, the gross pay is calculated by multiplying the total hours worked by the rate per hour.

Example 1

James worked a total of 38 hours at €9.50 and 3 hours' overtime paid at time and a half. His weekly gross wage is:

38 hours × €9.50	=	361.00
3 hours × €14.25	=	42.75
		€403.75

◆ **Superannuation Contribution (SAC):** Many employees contribute to an approved pension fund at work, known as a superannuation contribution. SACs are not subject to tax, therefore the contribution is deducted from gross wages *before* the tax rates are applied.

◆ **Taxable Income:** is the amount of income on which an employee is taxed. It is calculated by deducting SAC from Gross Pay.

◆ **Gross Tax Liability:** is the **sum** of the tax calculated on *taxable income* by applying the standard rate of tax to the weekly/monthly standard rate cut-off point. Any balance of income is subject to the higher rate of tax.

◆ **Net Tax Liability:** is the *gross tax liability* minus the weekly/monthly tax credits.

◆ **Net Pay:** consists of Gross Pay minus all deductions. It is the employee's take-home pay.

Example 2 — Calculation of Net Pay

John's gross monthly pay is €3,000. He pays €100 per month into an approved Superannuation fund. His monthly Standard Rate Cut-off Point is €1,200 and he is entitled to Tax Credits of €650 per month.

Gross Pay	3,000	3,000
Less SAC	100	
Taxable Income	2,900	

Taxed as:

€1,200 @ 20%	240	
€1,700 @ 42%	714	
Gross tax liability	954	
Less Tax Credits	650	
Net tax liability	304	

Less Deductions

Tax	304	
SAC	100	
Total Deductions	404	404
Net Pay		**€2,596**

John will pay tax of €304. His take-home pay will be €2,596.

Pay related social insurance (PRSI)

An employee must contribute to a social insurance scheme to provide funds to the Government for its social programmes, ie, unemployment benefits, medical cards, etc. Different PRSI rates apply to certain classes of employment. Employers also pay a PRSI contribution for every employee. PRSI is calculated on 'Taxable Income' (ie, Gross Pay less SAC).

We will now calculate John's PRSI deduction and net pay. Assume John pays PRSI at 5%; how much PRSI does he pay and what is his take-home pay?

Example 3 — Calculation of Net Pay (continued)

Gross Pay	3,000		
3,000			
Less SAC	100		
Taxable Income	2,900		
Taxed as:			
€1,200 @ 20%	240		
€1,700 @ 42%	714		
Gross tax liability	954		
Less Tax Credits	650		
Net tax liability	304		
Less Deductions			
Tax		304	
SAC		100	
PRSI (at 5% of Taxable Income)		145	
Total Deductions		549	549
Net Pay			**€2,451**

John will pay PRSI of €145 and this reduces his take-home pay to €2,451.

Deductions from wages

An employer will deduct two types of deduction from gross pay. These are:

a) *Statutory deductions:* deductions that an employee is obliged to pay by law from wages, ie, tax (known as PAYE or **P**ay **A**s **Y**ou **E**arn) and PRSI.

b) *Voluntary deductions:* deductions that the employee is not obliged by law to pay from wages. However, many employees subscribe to group schemes to pay VHI contributions, to donate money to charities, to save or to pay their trade-union subscriptions *directly* from their wages.

The accounts clerk should ensure that s/he has a signed form from the employee authorising voluntary deductions to be made from the wage/salary.

We will now calculate John's net pay assuming he pays the following voluntary deductions: VHI contributions of €24, contribution to saving scheme €20.

Example 4 — Calculation of Net Pay (continued)

Gross Pay	3,000	3,000
Less SAC	100	
Taxable Income	2,900	
Taxed as:		
€1,200 @ 20%	240	
€1,700 @ 42%	714	
Gross tax liability	954	
Less Tax Credits	650	
Net tax liability	304	
Less Deductions		
Tax	304	
SAC	100	
PRSI (at 5% of Taxable Income)	145	
VHI contributions	24	
Saving scheme	20	
Total Deductions	593	593
Net Pay		**€2,407**

Payslip

Most payslips are produced using computerised payroll packages. The details necessary for calculating pay are entered once, ie, name of employee, employee work number, PPS (Personal Public Service) number, SAC contribution, standard rate cut-off point, tax credits and the voluntary deductions.

At the end of each week/month, the accounts clerk only enters the standard and overtime hours worked and the payroll package automatically calculates the total gross pay, PAYE due, PRSI due, total deductions, net pay and provides a running total of the pay to date since the start of the tax year.

Every employee is entitled to receive a payslip which summarises the calculations of take-home pay. The payslip for John would read as follows:

PAYSLIP	APPLEWOODS SUPPLIES		PPS No. 6743212 S	
John Creedon 0008976			Tax Period 10	
Date: 31 August 2005				

Gross Pay Analysis		**Deductions**		**Year To Date**	
Basic Pay	3,000.00	PAYE	304.00	Gross Pay	30,000.00
O/T		PRSI	145.00	Taxable Income	29,000.00
Holiday Pay		Superannuation	100.00	Standard Rate	
Other				Cut-off Point	12,000.00
		VHI	24.00	Tax Credits	6,500.00
		Savings Scheme	20.00	Tax Paid	3,040.00
Total Gross Pay	€3,000.00		593.00	PRSI Paid	1,450.00
Hourly Rate					
Hrs @				Tax credits per month	650.00
Hrs @					
				NET PAY	€2,407.00

Short Questions

1. Briefly describe three classifications of administrator.
2. List four main duties of a general administrator.
3. Describe three aids used by an administrator in planning and organising work.
4. List four main features of an electronic diary.
5. Outline a procedure for planning and organising work, taking into account: events in the future, day-to-day activities and unexpected urgent activities.
6. When taking appointments/messages, state the essential information that must be recorded.
7. Why is a general appointments diary not suitable for all appointments? Give an example.
8. What steps would you follow when booking accommodation for your manager?
9. What is an itinerary and what details are generally recorded?
10. List the main duties an administrator may have when arranging for a conference to be held in another location.
11. Describe how videoconferencing operates.
12. List three advantages of videoconferencing.
13. Why is a petty cash system maintained? What document is used to record money issued?
14. Distinguish between wages and salaries.

15. In the payment of wages, distinguish between a piece rate and a basic rate plus commission.
16. What is Jane's gross wage if she is paid a basic hourly rate of €10.00 and works a standard week of 38 hours, plus 3 hours overtime paid at time and a half?
17. Briefly describe the tax credit system.
18. Distinguish between Form 12A and a P45.
19. Distinguish between the following:
    a) gross pay and net pay
    b) gross tax liability and net tax liability
    c) statutory deductions and voluntary deductions.

Chapter 7 — Business Transactions

A business transaction takes place between two organisations, one of which is purchasing goods or services, the other selling. From the time of the initial enquiry to the dispatch of the goods, several **stages** are involved in the process.

In a small business the whole process may be carried out by one person. For example, in a sole trader or partnership one person may be responsible for monitoring stock levels, procuring an order, assessing quotations and placing the **order**. When the goods are received the same person may be responsible for checking the goods received against the **delivery document** that comes with the goods. S/he will also cross-check the goods received against the copy of the order to ensure that the goods were actually ordered. When the business is billed for payment by means of an **invoice**, the invoice will be checked against the record of the goods received to ensure that the goods have actually been received before payment is made and that the correct amount has been charged.

In a large business this process will be split among several individuals who work in different departments.

Stages of a Business Transaction

The stages of a business transaction are as follows:

Purchase Requisition

A purchase requisition form is used when there is an **internal request** for goods to be purchased. It is signed by the head of a department and sent to the Purchasing department. If details such as supplier's name, catalogue number and price are not known, a brief description of what is required is recorded. The purchasing department will source the information required.

In the purchase requisition shown here the supplier's name, price and catalogue numbers are unknown.

Distribution of Purchase Requisition:
- Original to Purchasing department
- Copy in the Department's file.

PURCHASE REQUISITION			Ref No. AB231	
Department **Admin Department**				
Supplier's name (if known)				
Address				

Qty	Details	Cat. No.	Unit Price
20	Reams of A4 laser printer paper (White)		
10	Copier transparencies (Box 100)		
2	Toner cartridges (black)		

Signature	Date
John Murray	**12 October 2005**

Purchase requisition form

Letter of Enquiry

The buyer in the purchasing department sources the supply and the price of goods by contacting appropriate suppliers. The buyer can track down possible sources of supply by looking up the items in particular directories, for example, the Golden Pages, trade journals and files on past suppliers. Details for the enquiry are taken from the Purchase Requisition.

A letter of enquiry is a written request from a buyer to a seller requesting a quotation and terms of trade such as: trade discounts, cash discounts, delivery dates and whether delivery costs are paid or not. All the terms and conditions received from various suppliers will be compared before any particular supplier is decided upon.

Distribution of Letter of Enquiry:
◆ Original to various suppliers
◆ Copy in Buyer's File.

Office Supplies Ltd
34 Main St
Blackrock   **Tel No: 01 2875640**
Co. Dublin   **Fax No: 01 2876543**

12 October 2005

Photocopy Ltd
Wexford Industrial Estate
Wexford

Dear Sir/Madam

We would like you to quote for the following items which we will
need on a regular basis:

20	Reams of A4 laser printer paper (White)
10	Copier transparencies (Box 100)
2	Toner cartridges (Black) Model Express 30

Please send me your catalogue and a quotation for the above items
including your most favourable terms and delivery arrangements.

Yours faithfully

Brendan Kelly
Purchasing Dept

Letter of enquiry

Quotation

The letter of enquiry will be handled by the **Sales Department** of the
supplier, who will send a quotation in reply.

A quotation is an offer to supply goods at the stated price and under the
terms and conditions stated in the quotation. An order form is generally sent
with the quotation.

Distribution of Quotation:
◆ Original to Customer
◆ Copy in File (Sales Department of Supplier)

Quotation No. 1460

Photocopy Ltd
Wexford Industrial Estate
Wexford

Tel No: 053 564396
Fax No: 053 564987

VAT No: 159 4321 67

16 October 2005

Attention of Mr Brendan Kelly

Office Supplies Ltd
34 Main St
Blackrock
Co. Dublin

In reply to your enquiry dated 12 October, we have pleasure in quoting as follows:

Qty	Description	Cat. No.	Unit Price
20	Reams of A4 laser printer paper (White)	B2345	€10.00
10	Copier transparencies (Box 100)	B3347	€34.65
2	Toner cartridges (Black) Model Express 30	F1037	€150.23

VAT — Standard Rate of 21%

Terms: Trade Discount   25% for orders over €380 (before VAT)

               Cash Discount   5% for payment within 10 days of invoice date

                                     $2^1/2$% within 1 month

Delivery: by our van within 7 days of receipt of order — carriage paid

We look forward to receiving your order.

Quotation

Terms and Conditions of Trade

The terms and conditions of trade stated on business documents may include: trade discount, cash discount, transport costs (such as carriage paid and carriage forward) and methods of payment such as cash with order (CWO).

◆ **Trade discount:** an allowance given by a seller to a buyer for bulk purchasing to encourage customers to buy in large quantities. It is deducted on the invoice before VAT and **does not** depend on the time of payment.

◆ **Cash discount:** an allowance given in **addition** to trade discount to encourage prompt settlement of an account. Cash discount is offered as it improves the cash position of the supplier, enabling the supplier to pay its debts on time. The supplier may offer different rates of cash discount for accounts settled within a stated period. For example, s/he may offer 5% for accounts settled within 10 days of the invoice date and $2^1/2$% for accounts settled within 1 month. It is deducted by the buyer when payment is being made.

If the terms of sale were stated as **net two months**, this means that no cash discount will be given and payment must be made within two months.

◆ **Carriage paid:** cost of transporting the goods to the purchaser's premises is included in the price quoted, ie, it is paid by the supplier.

◆ **Carriage forward:** cost of transporting the goods is **not** included in the price quoted, ie, it is paid by the buyer.

◆ **CWO (cash with order):** The purchaser must forward the payment with the order before the order will be processed.

◆ **VAT number:** Registered businesses must quote their VAT (value-added tax) registration number on **all** business documents. The trader submits a VAT return to the Government every two months detailing the VAT on sales and the VAT on purchases. If the VAT on sales exceeds the VAT on purchases the trader pays the difference, otherwise a refund is claimed.

◆ **Reference number:** a unique number placed on business documents which is used to trace correspondence. For example, if a business has placed many orders with the same supplier, a query about a particular order can be traced immediately by quoting the order reference number.

◆ **E&OE:** means 'errors and omissions excepted'. This means that the seller has the right to correct the information stated on the documentation. For example, if there is an error in arithmetic or if an item has not been charged for, the seller can send a supplementary invoice to correct the mistake.

Order

When the purchasing officer receives the quotations from the various suppliers, s/he will evaluate them. The cheapest may not necessarily be the best. Quality and the terms and conditions of trade are other important factors to take into account. An order will be placed with the supplier that offers the best overall package.

The buyer will use the supplier's order form if available (manual or on-line) or an order form will be prepared. The order is sent by the buyer in the Purchasing Department to the Sales Department of the supplier. The order gives full details of the goods to be supplied including catalogue references, quantity, quality, colour, size, unit cost and total cost.

Distribution of Order:
- ◆ Original to the Sales department of the supplier
- ◆ Copy in buyer's file (Purchase department)
- ◆ Copy to stores (of the Purchasing business) — notification of goods to be received, for checking with Delivery Note.

Order No. A221

Office Supplies Ltd
34 Main St
Blackrock
Co. Dublin

Tel No: 01 2875640
Fax No: 01 2876543

VAT No: 284 3455 89

Quotation No: 1460

20 October 2005

Photocopy Ltd
Wexford Industrial Estate
Wexford

Please supply the following:

Qty	Description	Cat. No.	Unit Price	Total Price
20	Reams of A4 laser printer paper (White)	B2345	€10.00	€200.00
10	Copier transparencies (Box 100)	B3347	€34.65	€346.50
2	Toner cartridges (Black) Model Express 30	F1037	€150.23	€300.46
				€846.96

Terms of Sale: As on quotation no. 1460
Trade Discount   25% for orders over €380 (before VAT)
Cash Discount   5% within 10 days of invoice date
                 $2^1/2$% within 1 month

Carriage paid

Brendan Kelly
Purchasing Department

Order form

Procedure for Dealing with Incoming Orders (Supplier)

When an order is received a credit check is normally run on the buyer's credit status. When dealing with a new customer, the seller may request references from a bank or an existing supplier of the customer. The seller may request payment from a new customer by one of the following means:

(i)   requesting cash with the order (CWO)

(ii) submitting a pro-forma invoice, which is an imitation invoice rather than a real invoice. It is used to request payment in advance of delivery from a first-time customer or where no credit facility is allowed. (A pro-forma invoice is also used when goods are sent 'on approval', eg, in a mail-order business. If the goods are retained, payment is made in accordance with the pro-forma invoice.)

(iii) requesting the buyer to furnish a percentage of the cost of the order before delivery is made and the balance on delivery.

Preparation of Invoice

If the order is approved, an invoice is prepared by the Sales department in duplicate form for distribution. An invoice is a bill requesting payment; it is sent by the Sales department of the supplying firm to the Accounts department of the purchasing firm. It is usually sent **after** the dispatch of the goods, though in some cases the invoice is enclosed with the goods. An invoice will contain the following information:

◆ name and address of both the buyer and the seller
◆ date and VAT registration number
◆ quantity, description and catalogue/reference number of product
◆ the unit cost of each item, the total cost of each item and the overall total cost
◆ trade discount
◆ the VAT rate and VAT amount shown separately
◆ terms of sale such as cash discounts, carriage details as quoted on quotation
◆ E&OE at the bottom of the invoice.

Distribution of Invoice:
◆ Original to buyer (Accounts department)
◆ Copy held in Sales department to answer queries
◆ Copy to Accounts department to record the sale on the customer's account
◆ Copies to Stores omitting price details.

Stores will keep one copy as proof of authorisation to release the goods. The other copies, known as a delivery or an advice note, are sent with the goods.

Delivery Note

Delivery Note No. D1675

Photocopy Ltd
Wexford Industrial Estate
Wexford

Tel No: 053 564396
Fax No: 053 564987

VAT No: 159 4321 67

Order No: A221

27 October 2005

Office Supplies Ltd
34 Main St
Blackrock
Co. Dublin

Qty	Description	Cat. No.
20	Reams of A4 laser printer paper (White)	B2345
10	Copier transparencies (Box 100)	B3347
2	Toner cartridges (Black) Model Express 30	F1037

Not Examined

Received by: *John Hegarty*

Delivery note

A delivery note contains the same details as the invoice except that the price details are omitted.

A two-part delivery note accompanies the goods and the delivery person requests the customer to sign the delivery note. The top copy is given to the customer and the other copy is returned as proof of delivery.

Before signing, the customer (Stores department) checks the goods against the delivery note, ensuring that all goods listed on the delivery note are received. If the goods are found to be faulty or goods are missing, this is recorded on the delivery note before signing.

It is rarely possible to examine goods in detail immediately they are delivered. The most that can normally be done is to check that the correct number of boxes are received and that there is no obvious damage. In this case 'not examined' should be recorded on the delivery note.

Distribution of Delivery Note:
- Top copy given to customer
- Duplicate copy held by delivery person who returns it to the business.

Advice Note

An advice note contains the same information as a delivery note. An advice note may be sent in advance of the goods, to inform the buyer that the goods are being dispatched, detailing carriage arrangements, expected time of arrival (ETA), etc. The buyer can use this information to track the delivery via the Internet. An advice note may also be sent when the goods are not sent by the supplier's transport, for example, the goods are sent by post or rail. It is packed with the goods to enable the receiver to check them upon arrival. It does not have to be signed.

Procedure for Dealing with Incoming Goods (Purchaser)

When the goods are delivered to the Stores department, the following procedure is carried out:
1. The contents are checked against the delivery note or advice note.
2. The goods are then checked against the copy of the order to ensure that the goods received were ordered, and also that all the goods ordered were received.
3. A goods received note is prepared by the Stores department.

Goods Received Note

When the goods are received a goods received note is prepared by the Stores department, noting any discrepancies such as shortages, damages or incorrect goods received. A copy will be sent to the Accounts department to be compared with the incoming invoice before payment is processed.

Distribution of Goods Received Note:
- Original to Accounts department (to check against incoming invoice)
- Copy held in the Stores department to update stock records.

Goods Received Note No: 12343

Office Supplies Ltd

Supplier: Photocopy Ltd
Date Received: 27 October 2005
Delivery/Advice Note No: D1675

Order No.	Description	Qty Received
A221	Reams of A4 laser printer paper (White) Copier transparencies (Box 100) Toner cartridges (Black) Model Express	20 10 2

Received by:	Date:	Entered in stock by:	Date:
D. Foyle	27/10/05	P. Connolly	27/10/05

Inspected by: Harry Dineen	Date: 27/10/05

Shortages:
Damage recorded:
1 ream of A4 laser printer paper damaged

Goods received note

Checking Invoice Received

The invoice is usually sent **after** the dispatch of the goods, though in some cases the invoice is enclosed with the goods. When the invoice is received by the Accounts department of the purchasing firm the following checks are made:

1. Check invoice against the goods received note (from Stores) to ensure that goods have actually been received before making payment.
2. Check all calculations, total unit cost, trade discount and total cost.

If errors are discovered on the invoice, the Accounts department will contact the supplier, who will rectify the error by sending a credit note or a debit note as appropriate.

Cash discount is deducted at the appropriate rate and the payment is sent to the Accounts department of the supplier before expiration of credit period, to claim the discount.

Distribution of Received Invoice:
◆ Original held in Accounts department.

Invoice No. 1675

Photocopy Ltd   **Tel No: 053 564396**
Wexford Industrial Estate   **Fax No: 053 564987**
Wexford

                                                     VAT No: 159 4321 67

Delivery Note No: D1675
Order No: A221

28 October 2005

Office Supplies Ltd
34 Main St
Blackrock
Co. Dublin

Qty	Description	Cat. No.	Unit Price €	Total Cost €
20	Reams of A4 laser printer paper (White)	B2345	10.00	200.00
10	Copier transparencies (Box 100)	B3347	34.65	346.50
2	Toner cartridges (Black) Model Express 30	F1037	150.23	300.46
				€846.96
	Deduct: 25% Trade Discount			211.74
	Net goods value		**Sub Total**	635.22
	ADD: VAT @ 21%		**VAT**	133.40
			Total	**€768.62**
	Terms: 5% within 10 days			
	$2^1/_2$% within 1 month			
	Net 2 months			
E&OE	Carriage Paid			

Invoice

Calculating Cash Discount

To claim the cash discount, the invoice must be paid within the time specified by the terms of trade. The date is taken to be the date of the invoice.

Example

Calculate how much Office Supplies Ltd will pay, if they pay Invoice No. 1675 on:

a) 4 November 2005
b) 25 November 2005
c) 10 January 2006

Solution

a) As the invoice is paid on 4 November, which is within 10 days of the invoice date, Office Supplies Ltd are entitled to deduct a discount of five per cent. They will therefore pay €768.62 less five per cent, which is €730.19.

b) As the invoice is paid on 25 November, which is within one month of the invoice date, Office Supplies Ltd are entitled to deduct a discount of 2½ per cent. They will therefore pay €768.62 less 2½ per cent, which is €749.41.

c) As the invoice is not paid until 10 January, which is after the date when the invoice should be paid (ie, net 2 months), Office Supplies Ltd pays the full amount owing of €768.62. Under the Prompt Payments Act 1997 suppliers who are not paid on time are entitled to charge interest at the rate of 2½ per cent per month on unsettled accounts.

Credit Note

A credit note is sent by the seller to the Accounts department of the purchasing firm when goods were overcharged, goods were charged for but not received, goods are returned or packing cases are returned. The credit note reduces the original invoice charge, ie, the buyer pays the original invoice less the amount of the credit note.

Distribution of Credit Note:

◆ Original to Customer (Accounts department)
◆ Copy to Sales department
◆ Copy held in Accounts department to record on customer's account.

Credit Note No. C2343

Photocopy Ltd　　　　　　　　　　　　**Tel No: 053 564396**
Wexford Industrial Estate　　　　　　　**Fax No: 053 564987**
Wexford

　　　　　　　　　　　　　　　　　　　　VAT No: 159 4321 67

Invoice No: 1675
Order No: A221

30 October 2005

Office Supplies Ltd
34 Main St
Blackrock
Co. Dublin

Qty	Description	Cat. No.	Unit Price €	Total Cost €
1	Reams of A4 laser printer paper (White)	B2345	10.00	10.00
	Deduct: 25% Trade Discount			2.50
	Net goods value		**Sub Total**	7.50
	ADD: VAT @ 21%		**VAT**	1.57
			Total	**€9.07**
E&OE				

Credit note

Debit Note

An error in an invoice resulting in an **undercharge** is corrected by means of a debit note. It is sent by the seller to the Accounts department of the purchasing firm for the additional charge. It has the same effect as an invoice, so businesses generally just send a revised invoice for the additional charge instead of a debit note. For example, assume that the VAT rate on Invoice No. 1675 was charged at 18% instead of 21%. There is an undercharge of €19.07 (€635.22 × 18% = €114.33. €133.40 – €114.33 = €19.07).

Distribution of Debit Note:
◆ Original to Customer (Accounts department)
◆ Copy held in Accounts department to record on customer's account.

Debit Note No. D343

Photocopy Ltd
Wexford Industrial Estate
Wexford

Tel No: 053 564396
Fax No: 053 564987

VAT No: 159 4321 67

Invoice No: 1675
Order No: A221

30 October 2005

Office Supplies Ltd
34 Main St
Blackrock
Co. Dublin

Ref.	Description	Amount €
Invoice No. 1675	VAT charged at 18% instead of 21% Undercharge	€19.07
E&OE		

Debit note

Statement of Accounts

At the end of the month the Accounts Department of the supplier firm sends a Statement of Account to the customer. The statement of account is a copy of the customer's account in the sales ledger, also known as the debtor's ledger. These details are entered from source documents such as invoices, credit notes and debit notes sent to the customer and cheques received from the customer. (The customer is known as a debtor — a person who owes you money.)

The statement does not contain particulars of the goods supplied but will show the balance at the beginning of the month, all transactions during the month (ie, invoices, credit notes, cheques received) and the balance due.

Statement

Photocopy Ltd   **Tel No: 053 564396**
Wexford Industrial Estate   **Fax No: 053 564987**
Wexford   **VAT No: 159 4321 67**

---

31 October 2005

Office Supplies Ltd   Shows all increases in   Shows all decreases in
34 Main St   amounts owed, eg,   amounts owed, eg,
Blackrock   invoices, debit notes.   credit notes and
Co. Dublin   cheques received.

Date	Ref. No.	Details	Debits €	Credits €	Balance €
28 Oct	1675	Invoice	768.62		768.62
30 Oct	C2343	Credit Note		9.07	759.55

Statement

When the statement is received by the Accounts department of the purchasing firm the following checks are made:

1. Details of the statement are compared with the details entered for the creditor in the purchaser's ledger.
2. Calculations on the statement are checked.
3. The balance on the statement is paid, less the appropriate cash discount on invoices listed, if those invoices are paid within the time period to avail of cash discount.

Overview of Stages in Business Transactions

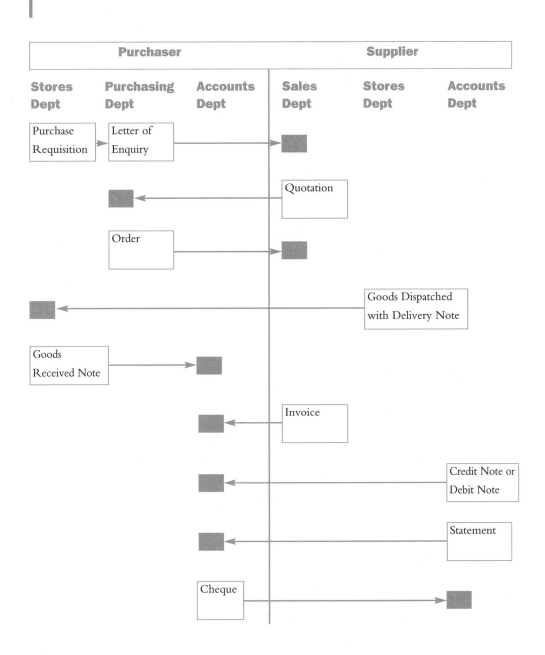

Stock Control

Stock control means controlling the level of stock held in a business. It is used to ensure that the business has sufficient stock to meet anticipated needs, while at the same time not holding more than is necessary.

No business wants to hold large stocks of items. Stock represents money tied up in the business. It also costs the business in terms of insurance, storage space (ie, rent) and security. Indeed, some stock items may go out of date, lose their value or deteriorate. On the other hand, having insufficient stock available ('stock-out') when it is needed is also unsatisfactory. Delays ('bottlenecks') will occur in production, which may result in customer orders not being processed on time. What is needed is a balance between these two extremes.

In a small business the stock of stationery and supplies may be the responsibility of the administrator. S/he will be responsible for monitoring stock levels, ordering supplies and dealing with incoming supplies. In a large organisation, stock control will be the responsibility of the Stores department which will monitor stock levels and notify the Purchasing department, via a purchase requisition, when new supplies are required.

Stock Control System

A business will set a minimum stock level, a re-order level and a maximum stock level for each item of stock, based on the rate at which stocks are used over a given period and the time it takes for the order to be processed. Mathematical formulae may be used in complex situations to determine the economic order quantity (EOQ).

Minimum stock level: Stock cannot safely be allowed to drop below this level. To avoid this happening, a 're-order level' is set above the minimum stock level. The minimum stock level is the 'buffer stock' and it is used in case of emergencies. It is set at a level so that an order will be received before the buffer stock is depleted.

Re-order level: When stock falls to the re-order level an order is placed. The quantity ordered is the difference between the re-order level and the maximum stock level. It is set at a level such that the order will be received before the minimum stock level is reached.

Maximum stock level: This is the maximum amount of stock that should be stored. Above this level it is uneconomical to hold stock.

For example, illustrated overleaf is a stock control card for inkjet printer cartridges. The firm has set the maximum level at 30 cartridges, the re-order level at 10 cartridges and the minimum level at 7 cartridges based on knowledge of usage and the **lead time**. (Lead time is the time it takes from ordering the stock to the actual delivery of the stock.) The unit size of 1 means that the cartridges can be ordered as a single item.

The balance on 1 July was 17 cartridges. On 3 July and 10 July, cartridges were issued to departments, reducing the stock to 9 cartridges on 10 July. As 9 cartridges is below the re-order level, an order was placed to replenish the stock. The quantity ordered was 20 cartridges which is the difference between the re-order level of 10 and the maximum level of 30. The stock was received on 15 July and brought the stock level to 29 cartridges. Another issue took place on 17 July. This system ensures that the business holds an economical amount of stock.

Stock Control Card

Item:	Inkjet Printer Cartridges			
Code No:	D0034		**Maximum Level:**	30
Unit Size:	1		**Re-Order Level:**	10
Location:	A34		**Minimum Level:**	7

Date	Issued to/ received from	Quantity issued	Quantity received	Balance
1-7-05				17
3-7-05	Marketing Dept	3		14
10-7-05	Accounts Dept	5		9
15-7-05	Johnstown Supplies		20	29
17-7-05	Office Admin	1		28

Stock control card

To avoid losses due to obsolete or perished goods, the First In First Out (FIFO) system of issuing stock is used. The FIFO system operates by distributing the goods according to the earliest date at which they were delivered.

For example: assume 20 items were received on 4 June and 25 items on 28 June. If a requisition for goods was received on 8 July for 25 items, the stock will be issued from the delivery received on 4 June first, and the balance of 5 items will be issued from the later delivery.

Computerised stock control

Today, the stock control procedure is normally automated using an accounting/stock control computer package. This package will display stock control cards for each item of stock in a manner similar to the manual system.

The accounting/stock control package will be set up initially with details of each stock item and the minimum, re-order and maximum levels entered. The issue and receipt of stock are entered from the source documents (ie, requisition form, goods received note) received by the Stores department and the balance of stock is automatically calculated. The system will indicate when the re-order level or the minimum level is reached.

Stock control systems can be incorporated at the point of sale. This type of control system is used typically in supermarkets, where there is a high volume of stock passing through the point of sale. All stock received is entered on the computer and as each item is purchased, the amount of related stock decreases. This is achieved by a bar code scanner linked to a computer. Thus an up-to-date list of the amount of stock remaining can be obtained on demand. Computerised stock control systems simplify the process of stocktaking, as a complete list of all items in stock can be printed.

Stocktaking

While a stock control system ensures that the business holds an economical amount of stock and will not suffer a stock-out, procedures also need to be put in place to check that the amount of stock stated on the records actually is in stock. To confirm the accuracy of the stock records a stocktake is carried out.

A stocktake is simply a physical count of the stock that remains in the storeroom. A stocktake is carried out once a year or more frequently, depending on the nature of the business and value involved. The business may operate a constant stocktake where areas of stock are checked periodically throughout the year, or it may operate random 'spot checks' on certain items of stock to ensure that stock records are being maintained properly and to reduce the risk of pilfering.

When a stocktake is carried out, the physical stock is counted and recorded on a **stock list**. The stock list will have the following information pre-recorded: reference number of stock item, item description, location of stock item and value of the item. The stocktaker records only the **actual count** of each stock item. This information is then entered into an accounting/stock package, where the value of stock remaining is automatically calculated. If a manual stock control system is in use, the stocktaker will also calculate and record at a later date the total value of each stock item for financial accounting purposes.

The quantity of stock recorded for each item is compared to the balances stated on the individual stock control cards. Discrepancies are investigated; these can arise for the following reasons: (a) stock was stolen; (b) stock was issued and not recorded; (c) stock was received and not recorded; (d) breakages or spillages were not recorded.

Rally's Mail Order Ltd
Main Street
Wexford

Stock of Stationery as at 17 July 2005

This column is completed by the stocktaker.

This column is completed by the stocktaker or automatically calculated by the computer.

Ref. No.	Item Description	Location	Quantity in stock	Value per item €	Total value €	Signature
P675	A4 Bond Paper	A45	40	7.50	300.00	
D0034	Inkjet Printer Cartridges	A34	28	38.00	1,064.00	
E89	DL Envelopes	B23	30	4.50	135.00	
	etc					
total						

Stocktake list

Short Questions

1. Outline the main stages of a purchasing transaction, from the initial enquiry to the time when the goods are paid for.
2. Outline the main stages of a selling transaction, from the receipt of the enquiry to the time when payment is received.
3. List four common terms of trade offered by a supplier to a buyer when sending a quotation for goods.
4. Distinguish between trade discount and cash discount. What does 'net one month' mean?
5. Explain what the following terms mean:
   a) carriage forward
   b) CWO
   c) E&OE.
6. A buyer is offered goods by the two suppliers below. What does each term mean, and what factors will the buyer have to take into account in deciding which of the quotations to accept?

Supplier 1	Supplier 2
15% trade discount	25% trade discount
Ready delivery	1 month delivery
Cash — one month net	5% cash discount within 10 days

7. Distinguish between:
   a)   a purchase requisition form and an order form
   b)   an invoice and a pro-forma invoice.
8. Distinguish between:
   a)   a delivery note and an advice note
   b)   a credit note and a debit note.
9. What checks are made on an incoming invoice?
10. An invoice shows a total amount of €3,500. A cash discount of 5% is offered if the invoice is paid within two weeks and 2% if paid within one month. Calculate the amount a customer should pay if s/he pays:
    a)   within two weeks
    b)   within one month
    c)   after one month.
11. What is a 'statement of account'?
12. What is the relationship between the following in a stock control system:
    a)   minimum stock level
    b)   re-order level
    c)   maximum stock level?
13. Distinguish between stock control and stocktaking.
14. Explain the term FIFO. Give an example.

Chapter 8 — Meetings

Formal Meetings are conducted according to specific rules relevant to the form of business. For example, club and society meetings are governed by the club or society Charter, while company meetings are governed by the Companies Acts and the individual company's Articles of Association.

Types of Formal Meeting

The main types of formal meeting are:
- ordinary meetings
- extraordinary meetings
- class meetings (or specific group meetings)
- annual general meetings (AGMs).

Ordinary Meetings

Ordinary meetings are regular meetings to discuss routine issues that must be dealt with in the normal course of the business; for example, a meeting with Department Heads at the beginning of each month to discuss budgets, production plans and sales.

Extraordinary Meetings

Extraordinary meetings are convened to discuss urgent, non-routine business matters. Companies have a legal requirement to extend specific notice of an extraordinary meeting to shareholders, along with any information that may be deemed necessary to allow the shareholder make an informed decision on a resolution.

Class Meetings

Within a company, there may be several classifications of shareholder, eg, Ordinary Shareholders and Preference Shareholders, each with different voting rights attached. Class meetings are meetings that are specific to a certain class of shareholders.

Annual General Meetings

Companies have a legal obligation to hold an Annual General Meeting (AGM) within six months of the end of their accounting year. The main business of the AGM is to:

- ◆ consider the audited accounts
- ◆ consider the directors' and auditors' reports
- ◆ appoint directors to the Board
- ◆ appoint auditors and decide their remuneration
- ◆ consider whether a dividend should be declared.

Convening Company Meetings

Company meetings are convened by the chairman of the Board of Directors, in accordance with the Companies Act and the Articles of Association. Shareholders can also request the directors to call a meeting. If a meeting is not properly convened, ie, if improper notification is given to shareholders, or if information necessary to consider a *special resolution* is not given, then any business carried out at the ensuing meeting may be considered null and void.

If the Board of Directors refuse to call a meeting, the Minister can intervene and direct that the meeting be held.

Quorum

Every meeting must have a quorum, (ie, a specified number of members present) before the meeting can start. The quorum for the meeting is determined by the Articles of Association. The normal quorum requirement is three members present for public-company meetings, two members present for private-company meetings and one member present for a single-member company. If the appropriate quorum is not present, and the meeting goes ahead, the business of the meeting may be declared null and void. If a quorum is not present after thirty minutes of the due commencement time of the meeting, the Chairman can adjourn the meeting.

Resolutions

Resolutions are motions that are voted upon by shareholders. There are two types of resolution: **Ordinary** and **Special**. An Ordinary resolution requires a simple majority vote to succeed (ie, over 50% of the votes cast), while a Special resolution requires a 75% majority vote to succeed.

Voting at Meetings

At a company meeting, the voting rights of the shareholder are determined by the classification of shares held. Voting may be carried out by a show of hands, secret ballot or shareholders may call for a **poll** (ie, where votes are cast according to the number of shares held). In clubs or societies normally each member has one vote only.

Shareholders who cannot be present at a meeting may be allowed to vote on a resolution by **proxy**. This means that they can nominate another person, usually the chairman, to vote as directed by them at the meeting.

Documentation for Meetings

1 — Notice of Meeting

A Notice of Meeting must be sent out to everyone who is entitled to attend the meeting. The notice may be issued in hard-copy or electronic format (ie, posted, sent by e-mail or put on a website). If the meeting is an annual general meeting (AGM), then 21 days' notice is required to be given to members. The same period of 21 days' notice is also required when a 'special resolution' is to be passed. For all other meetings, 14 days' notice of the meeting is normally sufficient, unless a shorter term is agreed by the members.

The Notice of Meeting should contain the date, day, time, location and type of meeting called. It is usual to send out an Agenda with the Notice of Meeting and any extra information that members may need to decide on resolutions. A proxy form may be included if the member is entitled to appoint a proxy to vote at the forthcoming meeting.

Example of Notice of Meeting

Springclean Ltd
14 Manor West
TRALEE
Co. Kerry

31 May 2005

Notice is hereby given that the Annual General Meeting of Springclean Ltd will take place on Wednesday 16 June 2005 at the Grand Hotel, Tralee, at 8.30 pm.

AGENDA
1. Apologies
2. Minutes from previous meeting
3. Matters arising from the Minutes
4. To receive and consider the Financial Statements and Reports of the Directors and Auditors for the year ended 31 December 2005. (Resolution 1)
5. To consider a declaration of a final dividend. (Resolution 2)
6. To reappoint the following Directors who retire by rotation in accordance with Article 34 of the Articles of Association. (Resolution 3)
   Mr J. Hegarty, Mr J. Creedon, Mr M. Connors
7. To authorise the Directors to fix the Auditors' remuneration. (Resolution 4)
8. Any other business (AOB)
9. Date and time of next meeting

Dervilla Spring
Company Secretary

2 — Agenda

The Agenda sets the order of business for the meeting. The Chairman must deal with the items on the Agenda in that order, unless agreement is reached by the meeting to change the order.

Normally, apologies from members who cannot attend the meeting is the first item on the agenda. Minutes from the previous meeting are read by the Secretary and any matters arising from those minutes are dealt with at this point. The meeting continues in accordance with the items on the Agenda. If a member wishes to raise an issue that is not on the Agenda, s/he may do so under Any Other Business (AOB). The meeting may deal with the issue then, or decide to place the issue on the agenda for the next meeting.

When the meeting is concluding, a date and time for the next meeting may be decided. This may not always be possible, so the Chairman may decide the time and date of next meeting and notify the members in due course.

3 — Proxy Form

A proxy form may be sent with the notice of meeting to allow the shareholder to nominate another shareholder and to direct him/her to vote on their behalf in their absence.

Springclean Annual General Meeting Form of Proxy

Name (in full): _____

Address: _____

I/We being an ordinary shareholder of the above-named company hereby appoint the duly appointed shareholder to be Chairman of the meeting:

_____

As my/our proxy to vote for me/us on my/our behalf at the Annual General Meeting of the company to be held at 8.30 pm on 16 June 2005 at the Grand Hotel, Tralee, and at any adjournment thereof. I/we direct my/our proxy to vote on the resolutions set out in the notice convening the meeting as instructed below and in respect of other resolutions that may arise at the meeting as the proxy thinks fit.

		For	Against
Resolution 1	To adopt the Accounts	❏	❏
Resolution 2	To declare a dividend	❏	❏
Resolution 3	To re-elect the directors (as named)	❏	❏
Resolution 4	To authorise Directors to fix auditors' remuneration	❏	❏

Signature: _____ **Date:** _____

---

4 — Minutes

The Minutes of the meeting are the legal evidence of events that take place at the meeting. It is vital that the Secretary correctly transcribes the details of the meeting. Every company is required by law to keep records of Minutes and Resolutions at their registered office for a period of 10 years. The documents may be kept in hard-copy or electronic format and can be inspected by the shareholders at any time.

When the Minutes of the previous meeting are agreed by the meeting, it is normal to have members to propose and second the Minutes. The Chairman can then sign the Minutes as being a true record of the events of that previous meeting. The Minutes now become a legal record and cannot be adjusted without the consent of the meeting. A resolution is normally required to amend the Minutes.

Example of Minutes

Springclean Ltd

Minutes of the AGM of Springclean Ltd held on the 16 June 2005 at the Grand Hotel, Tralee, Co. Kerry.

Present

K. Woods (Managing Director)	J. Creedon (Director)
D. Spring (Company Secretary)	M. Connors (Director)
J. Hegarty (Director)	D. Browne (Auditor)
and 30 shareholders	

1. **APOLOGIES FOR ABSENCE**
   Apologies were received from Mr O'Donnell (Director).

2. **MINUTES OF THE LAST MEETING**
   The minutes read by the Company Secretary, proposed by Mr M. Connors and seconded by Mr J. Creedon, approved by the meeting and signed by the Chairman as being a correct record.

3. **MATTERS ARISING FROM THE MINUTES**
   There were no matters arising from the minutes.

4. **AUDITOR'S REPORT**
   Ms D. Browne outlined the financial position of the company to the shareholders for the past trading year, stating that the accounts had been prepared in accordance with normal accountancy standards and practice.

5. **DIRECTOR'S REPORT**
   Mr Woods outlined the activities of the company during the year. The company had succeeded in reaching its target growth of twenty per cent with the acquisition of Brightclean Ltd in September. This has proved to be extremely advantageous in obtaining lucrative cleaning contracts in the hospitality industry. As a result, the company is intending to expand its employee base by ten during the next quarter. Each shareholder was given a full copy of the Director's Report.

6. ELECTION OF DIRECTORS

It was proposed by Mr Woods and seconded by Ms O'Neill, that Denise O'Connell be elected as a Director to the Board. This resolution was passed by the meeting.

7. APPOINTMENT AND REMUNERATION OF AUDITORS

It was proposed by Mr M. Connors and seconded by Mr J. Creedon that Ms D. Brown be retained as auditor to the company with a two per cent increase in remuneration. This was agreed unanimously by the meeting.

8. DIVIDEND

Mr Woods recommended a dividend of five per cent on ordinary shares which was agreed by the meeting.

9. ANY OTHER BUSINESS

There were no other issues raised and the meeting was closed by Mr Woods at 10.30 pm.

Chairman: _____   Date: _____

Duties of the Chairman and Secretary

The Chairman

The Chairman has a duty to control the meeting, to manage discussions fairly and to abstain from influencing any debates. A Chairman must ensure that the timing of the meeting is adequate, so that each issue is discussed in an equitable fashion. A realistic Agenda should be set and sufficient time allocated for any debate that may ensue at the meeting. In the case of a debate, the Chairman should allocate equal opportunities to both parties to air their opinions, rule on 'points of order' (queries regarding correct procedures) and must decide when to call for a vote. The Chairman usually abstains from voting, but in the event of a tie, will have a casting vote.

The Chairman can adjourn the meeting if a quorum is not present or where there is unruly conduct at the meeting.

The Secretary

The Secretary sends out notices of the meeting, prepares documentation, will book the venue and make any other arrangements necessary for the smooth running of the meeting. At the meeting, the Secretary is responsible for taking the Minutes.

Short Questions

1. What regulations govern formal meetings conducted at clubs or societies and companies?
2. List four main types of formal meeting.
3. Distinguish between an ordinary general meeting and an extraordinary general meeting.
4. What is a class meeting?
5. List four obligations on companies in relation to convening an AGM.
6. List four items that are usually dealt with at an AGM.
7. What is a quorum and what are the consequences of an insufficient quorum?
8. What is a resolution? Distinguish between an ordinary and a special resolution.
9. Distinguish between the terms 'poll' and 'proxy'.
10. List three documents that are normally sent out with the notice of a meeting.
11. Outline the format of the minutes of a meeting.
12. List three duties of the chairman and three duties of the secretary in relation to meetings.

Summary

Office personnel include the receptionist, administrators, accounts clerk and office juniors. As the receptionist is often the first point of contact with a business, it is vital that a professional impression is given when taking telephone calls, greeting visitors and receiving complaints. The receptionist's main task is to operate the switchboard and distribute messages. This has been made easier with facilities on the switchboard such as DDI, that allow callers to dial directly to an extension without going through the switchboard; if the person required is not available the 'voicemail' answering service is activated.

Technology has also affected routine administrative tasks. Correspondence is made easier by word-processing packages and messages can be circulated internally and externally by e-mail. Arranging appointments can be made easier by using an electronic diary that allows the administrator to view and book time slots for appointments. Arranging travel can create quite a lot of paperwork, for example, forms authorising travel, quotations for 'best price', expense forms and receipts which must be compiled before calculating the appropriate expenses. This procedure can be automated by users completing an on-line form and e-mailing the completed form to the administrator — expenses can then be calculated by using an electronic mileage chart and calculator.

The administrator may also be responsible for maintaining Petty Cash. Petty Cash is usually maintained using the imprest system, where a float is obtained at the beginning of every petty cash period and cash is issued on receiving a completed voucher and the receipt for the expense incurred.

The accounts clerk in the office is responsible for accounts payable, accounts receivable and payroll. While most offices will have a computerised payroll package, it is necessary to understand how wages are calculated and the appropriate statutory deductions that must be paid to the Revenue Commissioner, such as PAYE and PRSI.

In every organisation, formal meetings must take place to discuss the business of the organisation. In relation to the forms of business, a company must hold an Annual General Meeting to outline the activities of the company over the past year to the members and interested parties. Other types of meeting that the company may have to convene are: Ordinary, Extraordinary and Class meetings.

When convening a meeting the secretary of the company must send out notification of the meeting, and usually an agenda is attached and a proxy form if necessary. At the meeting the chairman controls the conduct of the meeting and the secretary takes the 'minutes' which are a record of the events of the meeting. This is a legal record and cannot be altered once approved by the meeting and signed by the Chairman. Rules and regulations regarding the running of the meeting (eg, voting procedures, resolutions, quorums, etc) are determined by the Companies Acts and the Articles of Associations in the case of a company, and by a Charter in the case of a club or society.

Assignments

1. You work in Kerry and you are responsible for arranging a trip for a senior executive who must make a presentation to head office in Grafton Street, Dublin city. The meeting starts at 10 am Monday and the executive must attend another meeting in Dublin on Tuesday which ends at 5.30 pm.
   a) Outline the best means of transport for this trip. Use appropriate references to source this information.
   b) Review three hotels in Dublin city and check price and availability of a single en suite room for the Monday night. Choose one of these hotels and prepare a fax or e-mail as a provisional booking request.
   c) Prepare an itinerary for the executive detailing his departure time, connect time for other transport, the meetings he is attending and the return departure time.
2. Mr Buckley travels on a daily basis from Limerick city to Waterford city on business. At the end of the week he submits a claim form for

mileage. However, on checking his claim form, his mileage is incorrectly calculated. Use a mileage chart to calculate his total mileage expenses for five days of travelling, assuming he is paid 70c a kilometre.

3. Your company is hosting this year's annual conference. You are assigned full responsibility for arranging the whole weekend. Fifty delegates are expected. Design a plan to cope with all aspects of the weekend — both formal and social. Make any assumptions you wish.

4. Write up procedures for a new junior receptionist for the following:
   a) maintaining the reception area
   b) handling incoming telephone calls
   c) receiving visitors.

5. The following is a record of a telephone conversation between a junior administrator, Niamh Kelly at Health Care Products Ltd, and Mr Griffin, an important client from Shape Up Ltd:

Administrator:	Hello.
Mr Griffin:	Is that Health Care Products Ltd?
Administrator:	Ya.
Mr Griffin:	Is Mr Shannon there please?
Administrator:	Hang on, I'll check.... No, sorry, he seems to have taken an extended lunch.
Mr Griffin:	What time do you expect him back?
Administrator:	He should be back shortly.
Mr Griffin:	Can I leave a message please?
Administrator:	Sure, just a second while I get a pen.
Mr Griffin:	Tell him I can meet him tomorrow as arranged and to call me.
Administrator:	(Writing down) OK, all right. Thanks. Bye.

   a) State where you think the administrator went wrong in the way she handled this call.

   b) Rewrite the telephone conversation in the way it should have been handled by the administrator. You may adjust Mr Griffin's responses based on what the administrator states.

   c) Draw up a typical telephone message form and enter on it the message which you would pass to Mr Shannon.

6. Compare the costs of making a telephone call from a fixed-line telephone in Kerry to: (a) Dubai (b) Finland and (c) Galway, during office hours, using the following telephone providers: (a) Eircom (b) Tele2 (c) Smart Telecom and (d) Esat-BT.

7. Mary earns €8.00 per hour for a 35-hour week. The overtime rate is double time. Her Tax Credit is €60 per week. She pays tax at 20%, PRSI at 5% and pays €7 per week into an approved pension fund. She also contributes €2.50 per week to the company social fund. This week

she worked 38 hours. Calculate Mary's:

a) basic pay

b) gross pay

c) taxable income

d) net tax liability

e) take-home pay.

8. Prepare a petty cash book for the following sundry cash transactions. Decide the columnar headings. The imprest from accounts is €50. Balance the petty cash book on 30 June.

June 1   €2.60 for stationery

June 3   €5.80 for fax paper

June 6   €4.50 for office staff bus fares

June 8   €13.50 for cleaning

June 15   €6.90 for canteen supplies

9. You work as the company secretary in an Irish-based Internet company called 'WhereEire.com' which supplies the tourist market with local tourist information. The Director has asked you to prepare the documentation for the first AGM. Make whatever assumptions you wish, prepare the Notice of Meeting and the Agenda for the AGM.

10. Assign the roles of chairman, secretary, directors and shareholders to class members and using the documentation prepared in the previous question, let the meeting take place according to the agenda. Remember the secretary should write up the minutes after the event.

Blank documents are provided at the back of the book for the following exercises. These should be photocopied.

11. Joan Butler is employed as an office clerk in M & M Construction Ltd, Dundrum, Co. Dublin. She requests the following items to be purchased by the Purchasing Department:

2 packs Sigma Purchase Orders

1 pack Sigma Delivery Notes

1 pack PaperMate 2000 Fine (Blue).

a) Complete the necessary document she will send to Michael McGrath, the Purchasing Officer.

b) Complete the order (Order No. O231) sent by the Purchasing Officer, Michael McGrath, to Collins Stationery Supplies Ltd, Monasterevin, Co. Kildare. (Refer to price list in Question 18.)

12. From the information provided compile the quotation that is sent by Mr John Doyle, Sales Dept, Stationery Supplies, 44 White Street, Cavan in reply to a letter of enquiry received from Ms Jane Hanley, Purchasing Dept, 5 High Street, Cavan.

Quotation number Q531

Cat No. 231	40 lever-arch files @ €3.50 each
Cat No. 235	20 box files @ €6.00 each
Cat No. 211	10 boxes of manilla folders at €8.50 per box

Delivery 1 week from receipt of order

Cash discount 5% within 1 week.

13. (i) Show how the following items will appear in a statement of account dated 30.5.05.

1/5/05	Balance b/f	€55
4/5/05	Sales Invoice — 008	€975
15/5/05	Credit Note — Returns	€70
27/5/05	Cheque	€55
28/5/05	Sales Invoice — 009	€1,420

(ii) If the terms of sale on invoice 009 are: Cash Discount: 3% within 2 weeks, net one month, state how much the cheque payable will be if a cheque is sent:

within 2 weeks;

after 2 weeks but within 1 month;

after 1 month.

14. On 11 March, Printer Supplies Ltd, 12 Main Street, Kildare, supplied to Copypress, Westgate, Wexford, the items ordered on Order No. O451. On 18 March, Copypress returned 1 can of damaged cleaning fluid.

Order No. O451

10 cans of cleaning fluid at €5.50 per can excluding VAT of 21%.

Terms of sale were: 10% trade discount and 2½% cash discount within 1 month.

---

a) Complete the invoice number I231 sent on 11 March.

b) Complete the credit note number C390 sent on 20 March.

c) Complete the statement of account number S200 sent on 31 March.

d) How much will Copypress pay if the statement is paid on 27 April?

15. Joseph Moran is the manager of the Purchasing department in MEC Office Supplies Ltd. He receives the following quotation on 3 August 2005.

Quotation
Curragh Supplies Ltd, Kilcullen, Co. Kildare

Tel: 045 852329   **VAT Reg No:** 883294U
Fax: 045 852330   **Date:** 3 August 2005

MEC Office Supplies Ltd
Industrial Estate
Co. Laois

Qty	Code	Description	Unit Price €
20	3000	Treasury tags (box size 100)	6.35
4	4012	Two-ring A4 binders (packet 10) 2.27	15.00
2	3002	Dl 8⅝" x 4¼" window gummed	19.00

VAT 21%

Terms: 5% 1 Month   Carriage Paid

---

a) Complete the delivery note sent with the goods by Curragh Supplies Ltd.
b) Complete the invoice sent by Curragh Supplies Ltd.
c) Complete the cheque that Joseph Moran sends on 20 August.

16. You work for Office Equipment Supplies Ltd and the following goods were ordered by Marcol Systems Limited.

Order No.: x11

Marcol Systems Limited
Eagle House
Naas
Co. Kildare

Tel: 045 852000   **VAT Reg No:** 659844d
Fax: 045 852001   **Date:** 13 October 2005

Office Equipment Supplies Ltd
Evin Blue Industrial Estate
Dublin 1

Qty	Code	Description	Unit Price €
5	1933	3.5" DS/DD IBM PS2	€12.32
3	1934	3.5" DS/HD IBM PS2	€11.30
5	1827	3.5" DS/DD Applemac	€12.32
1	1600	3.5" 3 Drawer Unit	€81.26

Terms: Trade Discount 15%, VAT 21%, Discount Cash 2^1/$_2$ % 1 Month, Delivery 14 days

a) Complete the invoice sent by you on 25 October. All goods ordered were delivered.

b) If the invoice is paid on 12 November, how much will the buyer have to pay?

17. The supplier is Shannon's Supplies Ltd, Kilrush, Co. Clare and the purchaser is Kathleen Carty, Church Street, Athlone, Co. Westmeath.

		€
Balance outstanding from last month		425.50
4 Mar	Goods supplied on Invoice P2341	70.15
6	Goods returned — Credit Note CN523	20.10
7	Goods supplied on Invoice P2352	60.05
9	Cheque received	425.50
16	Goods supplied on Invoice P2370	15.00
18	Cases returned — Credit Note	12.00
26	CN547 Goods supplied on Invoice P2381	45.00

Complete the statement sent on 30 March from the details above.

18. On 30 June 2005, Hegarty & Co. Ltd, Delgany, Co. Wicklow received a statement from Collins Stationery Supplies Ltd, Monasterevin, Co. Kildare. The balance due was €527.

On 2 July, Nuala Lennon, the Purchasing Manager for Hegarty & Co. Ltd, ordered the following goods from the price list she received.

10 packs Bic Crystal Medium (Black)

15 packs Bic Crystal Fine (Red)

20 packs Bic Crystal Medium (Blue)

5 packs Bic Clic Stic Ball Pen (Blue)

<table>
<tr><td colspan="3">

Price List

Collins Stationery Supplies Ltd
Monasterevin
Co. Kildare

</td><td>Means €7.30 for a pack of 50.</td></tr>
</table>

Code	Description		Unit Price €
0124	PaperMate 2000 Fine (Blue/Black)		7.30/50
0125	PaperMate 2000 Fine (Red)		1.70/12
0126	PaperMate 2000 Medium (Blue/Black)		7.30/50
0127	PaperMate 2000 Medium (Red)		1.77/12
0128	Zebra Ball Pen (Black/Blue/Red)		6.12/10
0129	Zebra Refills (Black/Blue/Red)		2.06/10
0130	Bic Clic Stic Ball Pen (Blue/Black/Red)		8.00/25
0131	Bic Soft Feel Stic (Blue/Black/Red)		4.25/12
0132	Bic Crystal Fine (Blue/Black/Red/Green)		3.10/20
0133	Bic Crystal Medium (Blue/Black/Red/Green)		3.20/20
0136	Pentel Fountain (Black/Blue/Red/Green)		18.70/12
0137	Pentel Ultra Fine (Black/Blue/Red/Green)		12.90/12
0200	Sigma Purchase Orders		6.86/50
0201	Sigma Delivery Notes		5.40/50
0202	Sigma Invoice Sets		5.40/50
0203	Sigma Statements		6.80/50
0204	Sigma Memos		6.25/100

All Prices are excluding VAT at 21%
Terms: Trade Discount 15%, Cash Discount 2% 2 weeks
Net 1 Month

Required:

a) Complete the order form sent by Nuala Lennon on 2 July.

b) Complete the delivery note sent by Collins Stationery Supplies Ltd on 6 July.

c) Complete the invoice sent by Collins Stationery Supplies Ltd on 6 July.

d) On 8 July, Nuala Lennon wrote to Collins Stationery Supplies Ltd stating that 2 packs of the Bic Crystal Fine (Red) were damaged. Complete the Credit Note sent to Hegarty & Co. Ltd.

e) Complete the cheque sent on 20 July by Hegarty & Co. Ltd to clear their account.

f) Complete the statement sent by Collins Stationery Supplies Ltd on 31 July.

19. The details for receipt and issue of compact disks are given below. The unit size is 1 packet (20 disks per packet). Draw up an appropriate stock card recording the details.

July 1	25	packets in stock
6	4	packets issued to Personnel Department
9	6	packets issued to Office
9	2	packets issued to Accounts Department
12	1	packet issued to Advertising Department
13	20	packets purchased
20	8	packets issued to accounts

20. You have just taken over a position as stationery clerk, and have found that your predecessor kept records on scraps of paper. Your job is to set up a stock control system. From the information recorded on the scraps of paper given below:

    a) show how you would record the details for overhead transparencies;

    b) state when you will place an order for more supplies.

    Inkjet overhead transparencies: min and max level — 5 and 25 boxes
    Unit size of 1 box (50 sheets per box)
    Balance on 2 June was 10 boxes
    1 box issued to Human Resources Department on 5 June
    5 boxes issued to Office Services Department on 9 June
    Received from Star Stationery Limited on 11 June — 20 boxes
    4 boxes issued to Marketing Department on 23 June.

21. a) An invoice was sent by Astra Business Systems to Ideal Office Supplies on 14 April 2005, for goods on Order No. A125. All goods ordered were delivered. You are required to **write up the invoice**.

    b) Ideal Office Supplies returned two Olivetti Inkjet JP370 printers which were damaged in transit. **Complete the credit note** that was issued on 20 April in response to these returns.

    c) An opening unpaid balance of €2,579.50 was brought forward on the statement from March. On 18 April a cheque for €2,450.52 was received from Ideal Office Supplies. Cash discount of 5% had been deducted from the amount owing. **Complete the statement of account** that was sent to Ideal Office Supplies on 30 April, showing details of **all** transactions that occurred during the month of April.

    d) A cheque was received from Ideal Office Supplies in full settlement of the balance due on the April statement. **Complete the cheque and the stub** dated 12 May 2005.

    [NCVA adjusted]

Order

Ideal Office Supplies **No. A125**
Silver Springs
Delgany
Co. Wicklow

To: **Date:** 2 April 2005

Astra Business Systems
Santry Hall Industrial Estate
Dublin 9
Please supply:

Qty	Code	Description	Unit Price €
3	672/1125	IBM Aptiva P75 Mini Tower computer	1,599.00
2	672/0755	Apple Performa 6200	1,329.00
5	671/2000	Olivetti inkjet JP370 printer	299.00
1	671/2017	Sharp JX 9200 laser printer	349.00

Terms: Trade Discount 15%, VAT 21%, Cash Discount 5% 1 month, Delivery 14 days.

Astra Business Systems

Santry Hall Industrial Estate
Dublin 9

Price List

Code	Description	Unit Price €
672/1091	IBM Aptiva Cyrix 586 computer	1,429.00
672/1125	IBM Aptiva P75 Mini Tower computer	1,599.00
672/0755	Apple Performa 6200	1,329.00
671/2031	Citizen ABC mono printer	119.00
671/1324	Citizen inkjet Projet 2c colour printer	248.50
671/2000	Olivetti inkjet JP370 printer	299.00
671/2017	Sharp JX 9200 laser printer	349.00

Terms: Trade Discount 15%, Delivery 14 days, VAT 21%, Cash Discount 5% 1 month.

Unit 3 —
Computers and Networks

Introduction

Unit 3 provides an overview of the components of a computer system and demystifies the terminology encountered when buying a computer. The features of business software and how these tools assist office workers are reviewed.

The various ways in which computers can be networked to facilitate communication within and outside the business, and a guide on how to use the Internet are provided.

The unit concludes with a discussion of Information Systems implemented by a business to assist in the decision-making process at the various levels of management.

Unit 3 is divided into four chapters:

Chapter 9 — Computer Basics and Peripheral Devices

Reviews the components of a computer system and the various peripheral devices on the market such as printers, scanners and storage devices (ie, disk, tape, CD, DVD and USB Flash 'disks'). It concludes with a guide to buying a computer:

◆ Components of a Computer System
◆ Storage Media
◆ Printers
◆ Scanners
◆ Guide to Buying a Computer

Chapter 10 — Computer Applications

Examines the features of common application packages such as: word processing, spreadsheets, databases and desktop-publishing applications that are widely used in a business:

◆ Word Processing
◆ Spreadsheets
◆ Databases
◆ Desktop Publishing
◆ Computer Viruses

Chapter 11 — Networks and the Internet

Reviews private and public networks, as well as explaining the differences among LANs, WANs, the Internet, intranets and extranets. It provides guidelines on how to use the Web and tips on how to make searching for information more productive:

◆ Types of Network
◆ The Internet
◆ The World Wide Web
◆ Understanding Web Addresses
◆ Finding Information on the Web
◆ Intranet and Extranet

Chapter 12 — Information Systems

Discusses the different levels of decision making from operative level to senior management level and the information required to make such decisions. It looks at information systems implemented by a business to capture, process and distribute information to enable timely and informed decisions to be made at the appropriate level of management:

◆ Levels of Decision Making
◆ Operational Support Systems
◆ Management Support Systems
◆ Designing an Information System
◆ Accessing External Databases

Chapter 9 — Computer Basics and Peripheral Devices

Components of a Computer System

The Basic Components of a Computer

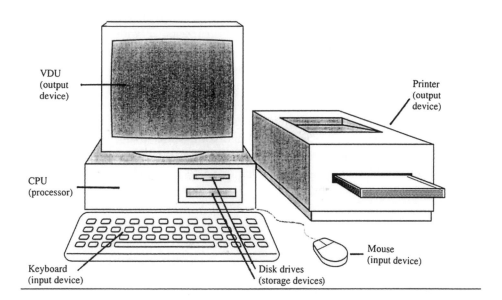

Basic components of a computer

◆ **Input Devices:** such as the keyboard, mouse and scanner, which accept data for processing.

◆ **Storage Devices:** such as the 'memory' for temporary storage, and magnetic and optical media for permanent storage, ie, tapes, disks, CDs and DVDs. The memory stores the data you are working on, which will be lost if the computer is turned off. Therefore, in order to keep your work for future use, it must be saved to a permanent storage device.

◆ **Central Processing Unit (CPU):** a microprocessor chip which is the core component of a computer and carries out the processing tasks by:

a) retrieving the software instructions and data from memory

b) processing the data as directed by the software

c) placing the results back into memory.

◆ **Output Devices:** such as the monitor or screen (known as the visual display unit — VDU) which displays the results of processing, and the printer which provides a printed copy, known as the 'hardcopy', of the information.

Software (ie, computer application packages) is necessary to operate the computer system.

The word **peripheral** refers to the components of a computer system other than the processor. It refers to equipment that could be added to a computer system to enhance its capability, such as a printer, scanner and extra storage devices. A keyboard, mouse, monitor and disk drives are also classified as peripheral devices, even though they are included with most computer systems.

Storage Media

Files are stored on: **magnetic** storage media (ie, disks and tapes), **optical** storage media (ie, CDs and DVDs) and **solid-state** storage media (ie, USB disks). The equipment that saves data to and retrieves data from the storage media is called a storage **device** or **drive**. For example, a DVD 'disk' is inserted into a DVD disk 'drive'.

Magnetic Storage Media

Magnetic storage media can be divided into two categories: **disks** and **tapes**. Disks are the most widely used as they provide **direct access** (also known as 'random access') storage. This means that the storage device can go directly to where the information is stored on the disk and retrieve it, ie, it does not have to read from the start of the disk.

Portable magnetic storage media is more prone to damage from incorrect storage and mishandling than optical or solid-state storage media. Portable magnetic storage media should not be stored near magnetic fields, ie, a telephone, TV or photocopier; or exposed to extremes of temperature, ie, heat/sunlight and cold/moisture.

Magnetic disk

The three most common types of portable magnetic disk are: floppy disk, zip disk and hard disk.

◆ **Floppy disks** are portable 3.5" disks with a capacity of 1.44 MB. Newer technologies (ie, optical and solid-state storage media) are decreasing the use of the floppy disk, owing to their limited capacity, unreliability and slower speed in retrieving data.

◆ **Zip disks** are portable disks, slightly larger than the 3.5" floppy disk. Zip disks are available in 100 MB, 250 MB and 750 MB capacity. Zip disks are read by a Zip drive of appropriate capacity, ie a 750 MB drive can read all disk sizes, a 100 MB drive can read only a 100 MB disk, whereas a 250 MB drive can read both 100 MB and 250 MB disks. Like the floppy disk, the zip disk is being replaced by new technologies.

◆ **Removable hard disks** are portable hard disks, that can be inserted and removed from a built-in drive much like a floppy disk or Zip disk. Removable hard disks increase the potential storage capacity of the computer. Hard disks are faster at locating and transferring data than a Zip or floppy disk; the speed depends on the technology behind the hard disk.

Magnetic tape

Magnetic tape is a **serial access medium**, which means that the tape drive cannot retrieve the file directly but must work its way through the tape until it reaches the file required (similarly to a music cassette). For this reason, magnetic tape is not used for on-line storage.

Magnetic tape was widely used in the past before optical storage media became popular for 'backup', ie, making a copy of the files stored on the hard disk in case they become corrupt or are deleted by mistake. A backup is carried out by attaching a tape drive to the computer and the software is set so that the selected files can be transferred from the hard disk to tape. The files can be transferred back to disk when required.

Optical Storage Media

Optical storage media can be divided into two categories: **compact disk** (CD) and **digital versatile disk** (DVD). Unlike magnetic media, it is not prone to damage from magnetic fields and is less prone to extremes of temperature.

Compact disk (CD)

There are three types of compact disk: CD-ROM, CD-R and CD-RW.

◆ **CD-ROM** (Compact Disk Read-Only Memory): A CD-ROM, like a music CD, contains data that is recorded on the disk when it is manufactured. It is a read-only storage medium, which means that the data can be retrieved and read, but no changes can be made to the data stored on the disk.

CD-ROMs are widely used in the office today; many reference manuals, catalogues, telephone directories, databases and training programs are available on CD-ROMs. Software also comes on CD-ROMs. A CD-ROM disk is read by a CD-ROM drive or a DVD drive. The capacity of a CD-ROM is 700 MB.

◆ **CD-R** (Compact Disk, Recordable): A **CD-R** is a blank disk used for recording data. However, once the information has been recorded it cannot be changed on that disk. CD-Rs can store up to 700 MB and are used for backing up the system and to archive data. A CD-R may also be referred to as a CD-WORM (Write Once, Read Many Times).

◆ **CD-RW** (Compact Disk, Rewritable): A CD-RW is a blank disk used for recording data, but unlike a CD-R the data recorded can be changed on that disk. They have the samecapacity as a CD-R, ie, 700 MB. CD-RWs are the way forward as regards data storage technology; however, they are more expensive than CD-Rs.

To *write* ('burn') to a CD-R or a CD-RW, a CD burner drive is needed. However, both types of disk can be *read* by most CD-ROM or DVD drives.

Digital versatile disk (DVD)

There are six types of digital versatile disk: a commercially produced DVD-ROM and five types of recordable DVD.

◆ **DVD-ROM** (Digital Versatile Disk Read-Only Memory): Like a CD-ROM, data is recorded on the disk when it is manufactured and cannot be changed or deleted from the disk. DVD-ROMs are used to distribute the same material as CD-ROMs, but unlike CD-ROMs, they are used to store movies, which can be played on a DVD player connected to a TV or through the DVD drive of a computer. DVD-ROM disks are read by a DVD drive — they cannot be read by a CD-ROM drive.

◆ **DVD–R and DVD+R** (DVD – Recordable): The DVD –R and +R are different formats of a blank disk used for recording data. Like a CD-R, once the information has being recorded on the DVD-R/+R, it cannot be changed on that disk.

◆ **DVD–RW and DVD+RW** (DVD Rewritable): The DVD –RW and +RW are different formats of a blank disk used for recording data, but unlike a DVD-R/+R the data can be changed, similarly to a CD-RW.

◆ **DVD–RAM** (DVD Random Access memory): Is a rewritable disk similar to DVD –RW/+RW. However, DVD–RAM is a competing technology requiring a DVD–RAM drive to read the disk. It is not as popular as DVD –RW/+RW.

The capacity of a DVD depends on the number of layers. For example, a single-layer disk has a capacity of 4.7 GB; a double-layer disk has a capacity of 8.5 GB (the second layer holds less information).

Modern DVD burners are capable of reading CDs and DVDs and writing to both CD and DVD recordable/rewritable disks. Such DVD burner drives are known as an 'all-in-one combination' and are generally stated as DVD +/–RW with CD-RW.

Solid-state storage media

Solid-state devices (abbreviated to SSD) consist of electronic, RAM-like chips, based on 'flash memory' technology. They contain no moving parts – hence the term 'solid state'.

There are many forms of SSD, such as the various sizes of 'memory card' used in electronic devices, for example: digital cameras, MP3 players, PDAs, etc. Here we are concentrating on the SSD device used as a portable storage device on a computer — called the USB disk which:

USB disk

◆ is more robust and reliable than magnetic or optical media, as SSDs have no moving parts.

◆ is small – about the size of a lighter or smaller

◆ can store from 20MB to 2GB of data, depending on the model

◆ has a faster access rate than magnetic or optical media, as the data can be randomly accessed as against waiting for a 'read/write head' to synchronise with a rotating disk

◆ has greater flexibility for transportation of files between computers. For example, files stored on a floppy disk, Zip disk or optical media can be accessed only on a computer with an appropriate drive. However, a USB drive can be used with any computer that has a USB port (which all computers have had since 1996)

USB disks are intended to be used as a transportation device from one computer to another, or as a back-up device. They are not intended to be used like a hard disk (or other forms of magnetic media) where information is constantly written to, as there is a restriction on the number of times information can be written to the disk. The restriction is very generous, however, allowing more than 100,000 writes. After that the disk may not function correctly and some data may be lost.

The correct use of an USB disk is to transfer the files to the hard disk before working on them, and then transfer the finished files back to the USB disk.

Printers

Printers are categorised into two groups according to their method of printing: impact printers and non-impact printers.

Impact Printers

An impact printer is an older technology and is generally not used in the office today, having been replaced by non-impact printers such as the inkjet and laser printers since the late 1990s. With an impact printer, the printhead makes contact with the paper and because of the contact, it is noisy. An example of an impact printer is the dot matrix printer.

Dot matrix printer

The dot matrix printer operates by a printhead pressing a combination of pins against a carbon ribbon as the printhead moves across the page. The characters appear as a matrix of dots. The greater the number of pins in the printhead, the better the quality.

Dot matrix printer

Unlike non-impact printers, dot matrix printers can print on continuous stationery and multi-part stationery. 'Continuous stationery' consists of pages joined together by perforations which can be separated easily when printed. 'Multi-part stationery' (also known as **NCR** — No Carbon Required) is the alternative to carbon paper used in earlier years. The output is printed once only, but two or more copies are produced at the same time. This is invaluable if the primary output is receipts, invoices and delivery documentation.

Non-impact Printers

The printhead does not make contact with the paper and because of the non-contact they are virtually silent. Examples of non-impact printers are inkjet printers and laser printers.

Inkjet printer

The inkjet printer consists of a printhead with a series of nozzles that squirt tiny drops of ink onto the paper to form each character.

Colour models are available, with some models using two cartridges (one for black and another for colour), while other models use one cartridge (for both black and colour). The one-cartridge model is cheaper to buy but very expensive to run, as the black ink is formed by mixing colours. Ink cartridges can be refilled but the quality may not be as good and the printer may not be guaranteed if the manufacturer's ink is not used.

The output produced is slightly moist, therefore the pages should be allowed to dry for a few seconds to avoid smudging.

Laser printer

A laser printer works much like a photocopier. The data to be printed is sent to the printer's memory where an image of the page is formed and printed.

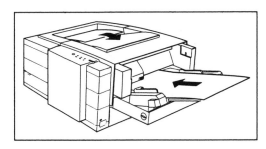

Colour models are very expensive and the cost is only justified where very high-quality colour output is required.

Laser printer

Both inkjet and laser printers are available with multi-functionality that incorporates a printer, fax, scanner and photocopier. A multi-function printer (MFP) is useful for small- to medium-volume output and is ideal for an office that does not have huge volumes of printing, faxing, scanning and photocopying.

Choosing a Printer

There are many different models of inkjet and laser printer available on the market. When selecting a printer consider the following points:

◆ Where will the printer be located? — consider the noise level and size of printer.
◆ What will the printer be used for? — consider fonts supported, colour capability, quality, paper types and sizes supported.
◆ Is speed important?
◆ What volume of work is expected from the printer per time period (ie, week/month)?
◆ What is the maintenance cost — ink, toner?
◆ Budget constraints?

Features of Non-impact Printers		
Features	**Inkjet**	**Laser**
Noise Level	Virtually silent	Almost silent
Initial Cost	Relatively cheap and middle of the range printer	Expensive and top of the range printer
Running Cost	Medium: replacement cost of ink cartridge	High: replacement cost of toner
Quality	Near-letter quality (NLQ) to letter quality	Letter quality
Speed	Prints one character at a time Relatively fast	Prints one page at a time Very fast
Colour Capability	Most models good quality and cheaper than a laser	Some models excellent quality but very expensive
Volume of Output supported	Medium workload	High workload

Scanners

A scanner takes an **image** of a page or object (similarly to a photocopier) and inputs it into the computer. A scanner eliminates the need for keying in data and thereby reduces the risk of input error. Any type of document can be scanned, ie, text, pictures, diagrams, etc.

The scanned image is known as a **bitmap** image and cannot be edited. To convert the bitmap image into a format that the computer can understand, and therefore to allow editing, the document is opened in special software known as *Optical Character Recognition (OCR)*. The OCR software 'reads' the scanned image and translates it into a text file that can be edited. OCR software can recognise a wide range of fonts and generally keeps the format of the document.

There are three categories of scanner available and the choice depends on the requirements of the user such as: the volume of data to be scanned, the quality required, the type of item to be scanned, (eg, single pages or pages from bound material, ie, books, magazines, etc):

◆ **Sheet feed scanner:** Consists of a document holder to store the page(s) to be scanned. As it can accommodate only single pages, articles from bound material must first be photocopied before scanning.

◆ **Flatbed scanner:** Consists of a glass plate similar to a photocopier, thus facilitating scanning from bound material.

◆ **Versatile scanner:** Is like a flatbed scanner with added attachments such as a document holder for batch scanning, as well as facilities such as double-sided scanning and negative scanning. It is used where the volume of scanning is high, ie, in an electronic document-management system (EDM).

Versatile scanner

Guide to Buying a Computer

Buying a computer can be very challenging, as advertisements list technical specifications describing the computer's components and features. The type of computer you buy depends on what you intend to use it for. Here we try to demystify some of the terminology involved, concentrating on the desktop Personal Computer (PC), ie, IBM-compatible computer.

Another type of desktop computer is the Apple Macintosh, known as the 'Mac'. Apple were among the earliest developers of a 'graphical user interface' (GUI) for a computer. A GUI displays: menu bars, buttons, icons (pictures), dialogue boxes, etc, enabling users to easily perform tasks. The PC in its early stage was difficult to operate, as the user had to type specific instructions (known as 'commands') to perform a task. However, in the late 1980s the PC industry caught up with the Apple Mac and developed its own GUI, known as the Microsoft 'Windows' operating system.

Common Units of Measures Used with Computers	
Storage Capacity	**Speed**
The unit of measurement for capacity is a byte	The unit of measurement for speed is a Hertz (Hz)
A *byte* is one character	A *Hertz* is one cycle per second
A *kilobyte* (KB) is approximately a thousand bytes	A *kiloHertz* (KHz) is a thousand cycles per second
A *megabyte* (MB) is approximately a million bytes	A *megaHertz* (MHz) is a million cycles per second
A *gigabyte* (GB) is approximately a thousand megabytes	A *gigaHertz* (GHz) is a thousand megaHertz
A *terabyte* (TB) is approximately a thousand gigabytes	

Processor

The processor is the core component in a computer and has a significant effect on price. For the latest processor, the price will be at a premium. However, for most users it is best to scale back a level or two and put the money into more memory. Advertisements generally indicate the processor manufacturer, the family name and a family number that indicates the features of a processor such as: architecture, speed and efficiency:

◆ **Manufacturer:** The two major manufacturers of PC processors are Intel and AMD. Intel is considered the industry leader, having led the development of the microprocessor.

◆ **Family Name**: Processors are assigned family names to identify their architecture. Intel produces the 'Pentium' and 'Celeron' families; AMD produces the 'Athlon' and 'Sempron' families. The 'Celeron' and 'Sempron' processors are intended for lower-cost computers; these processors are not available at the higher speeds of the 'Pentium' or 'Athlon' families.

The Pentium processor is currently at the family 'Pentium D'. The 'Pentium D' is a dual processor. With a 'dual processor', each processor can handle a different application (program), thus speeding up the task of switching between applications that require a lot of processing power, ie, applications such as video editing and 3D modelling.

The 'Pentium 4' family is a **single processor**, which uses a technology called '*Hyper Threading*' (HT). In effect it emulates a dual processor and is the current standard for users of general business applications.

◆ **Family Number**: Processors are assigned a number sequence within each processor family: for example, the 'Pentium D' 8xx, the 'Pentium 4' (7xx, 6xx or 5xx) and the 'Celeron' 3xx. The number sequence differentiates features within each processor family. For example, the processor number sequence 6xx has specific processor numbers of: 630, 640, 650, 660, etc). The 630 processor has the following features: 3.00 GHz Clock speed, 800 MHz FSB and 2 MB Level 2 Cache (explained below). This will be quoted in advertisements simply as:
'*Intel® Pentium® 4 Processor 630 with HT (3.00 GHz, 800 FSB, 2 MB L2 Cache).*'
The 640, 650 and 660 processors have similar features, but the clock speeds are different: 3.20GHz, 3.40GHz and 3.60GHz, respectively.

◆ **Features of a Processor:** As stated, the processor number indicates the features of a specific processor, which are: clock speed, bus speed (FSB) and cache:

Clock Speed: the onboard clock of the processor dictates the number of instructions it performs per second. The higher the clock speed, the faster the computer can perform instructions given from hardware components and software running on the computer. Clock speed is measured in gigahertz (GHz). Processor speed for the 'Pentium 4' ranges from 2.66 GHz to 3.8 GHz.

Front Side Bus (FSB): is the connecting path between the processor and other key components such as the memory. FSB speed is measured in MHz or GHz. Most desktop machines currently come with an 800 MHz FSB.

Cache: is special high-speed memory either built into the processor (known as Level 1 – L1) or mounted close to the processor (known as Level 2 – L2). Cache memory stores most recently or most frequently used data just before the processor needs it, and therefore improves performance, as the processor does not have to wait to retrieve the data from main memory. With today's computers, cache size is dependent on the processor family name and number, ie, the architecture of the computer.

Memory

The memory of the computer is the computer's temporary working area. Programs and data, which are generally stored on the hard drive, must first be loaded into memory so that the processor can process the data. Memory is also referred to as random access memory (RAM), as the processor can directly retrieve the data.

The amount of memory, type of memory and speed of transfer from memory to the CPU all have an impact on the computer's overall level of performance:

◆ **Amount of Memory**: Determines how quickly an application performs and how many applications can run concurrently. The minimum amount of memory recommended for a machine running Windows XP operating system, where more than one application will be running concurrently, is 512MB. For heavy business-application usage, ie, where several applications are running concurrently (ie, e-mail, Internet, and more than two other applications), 1 GB of memory is recommended.

◆ **Type of Memory**: In new systems this is generally DDR SDRAM (Double Data Rate-Synchronous Dynamic Random Access Memory) and transfers 32 bits of data *twice* every clock cycle, hence the term Double Data Rate (DDR). DDR2 SDRAM is the next step up from DDR SDRAM and transfers 64 bits of data. The machine is configured to accept one type of memory, so you can't later swap your memory from one type to another.

◆ **Speed**: Relates to how fast the data is transferred from memory to the CPU. It is measured in MHz and is often quoted in advertistements after the memory type *'512 MB Dual Channel DDR2 SDRAM at 533 MHz'*. 400 MHz is the minimum recommended memory speed.

Note: The terms 'Single Channel' and 'Dual Channel' are based on the design of the computer board (known as the 'motherboard'), rather than on a specific type of memory. In 'Single Channel' memory systems the memory chips are installed in the one channel; whereas with 'Dual Channel' memory systems the memory chips are installed in two independent channels, thus speeding up the data transfer.

If the computer does not have enough memory the machine will be slow, as the programs and data will have to be swapped from memory to the hard disk many times. When this happens, the computer is using so called **'virtual memory'**.

More memory can be added later up to a stated maximum dependent on the computer specification. However, it is advisable to get as much memory as you can afford with your initial purchase.

Visual Display Unit (VDU)

The visual display unit is the screen or monitor of the computer. The monitor is your main point of interaction with the computer, so it is important that the size and quality of the monitor match your requirements.

There are two types of monitor on the market today: the traditional monitor – 'CRT' (based on Cathode Ray Tubes technology) and the more modern model known as 'Flat Screen'/'Flat Panel' (based on LCD technology – 'Liquid Crystal Display'). A CRT monitor is big and boxy, while a Flat Screen monitor is slim and therefore saves a great deal of desk space.

CRT Monitor

Flat Screen Monitor

Generally the 'Flat Screen' is more expensive than the 'CRT', if purchased separately. However, many desktop systems now come with a 'Flat Screen' monitor as standard. Nevertheless, the 'CRT' monitor is still seen as indispensable for some computing tasks such as video-editing and games, owing to its ability to better handle fast-moving graphics. Factors that affect the readability of a monitor are: its size and resolution:

- **Size:** The recommended screen size is 17 inches. However, with a 'CRT' monitor the 'viewable area' of the screen will be smaller than the size specified, due to a black border around the screen. Advertisements may state the two measurements, eg, 17" (16" vis) monitor – ('vis' meaning viewable area). For a 'Flat Screen' monitor, the size specified is the actual size.

- **Resolution:** Characters and images displayed on the screen are constructed of dot patterns (dots of light) called **pixels**. The resolution is the number of pixels that can be displayed per inch on the screen and it affects the clarity of the display. At higher resolutions everything on the screen appears smaller but crisper, allowing more of the file to be displayed, thus avoiding horizontal scrolling. Advertisements generally state a monitor's maximum resolution. Newer models provide resolutions of 1600 x 1200 and higher.

The quality of the VDU display depends on the graphics card inserted in the computer. The amount of memory on the card (known as 'video memory') determines the maximum resolution and colour depth. A graphics card with 32 MB or 64 MB is fine for working with general business applications, but for the latest games and video applications at least 128 MB is recommended.

Hard Drive

The hard drive consists of a pack of disks stored inside the computer. As the hard drive is used as the main storage area for programs and data files, a high-capacity drive is recommended. Most computers today have at least a 120 GB hard drive as standard.

Apart from the size of the hard disk, the speed of the drive is also an important factor to consider. Speed is determined by both the *rotational speed* of the drive and the drive's *interface*:

- **Rotational speed**: is the speed at which the drive spins, measured in revolutions per minute (rpm). Rotational speed determines how *quickly* data can be retrieved, known as the *'access rate'* (ie, how quickly a file can be opened, an application started, etc). A hard drive with at least 7200 rpm is recommended for fast read/write capabilities.

- **Interface:** is the architecture of how the drive is connected to the computer. The interface determines the *amount* of data that can be moved from the hard disk to the computer per second, known as the *'burst rate'* or *'transfer rate'*. A 'Serial ATA' (SATA) 1.5 Gbs interface is recommended. The number 1.5 Gbs refers to the maximum burst rate at which the drive can pass data to the system. Other interfaces are: ATA/66 and Ultra ATA/100, transferring 66 MB or 100 MB per second, respectively.

Floppy Drive and Zip Drive

Computers today tend not to include a floppy drive or a ZIP drive as standard features, as these portable media for storing files have now almost been taken over by newer storage technologies, ie, CD, DVD and USB drives. Nevertheless, an external floppy drive or ZIP drive can be purchased to enable one to continue to use floppy disks or ZIP disks.

CD and DVD Drives

Most computers today come with a combination drive, generally known as 'CD-RW/DVD combo'. These drives can read both CD and DVD disks, but files can be copied only to a CD-R or CD-RW disk. These drives cannot copy to a DVD Recordable or DVD Rewritable disks.

Top-of-the-range computers come with a DVD/CD reader and burner drive, generally classified as a 'DVD +/−RW with CD-RW drive'. With this type of drive information can be read from a CD or DVD disk, and files can be copied to a CD or DVD 'recordable' or 'rewritable' disk.

A DVD reader/burner drive is recommended, because it is future-proofing your PC. In time, it is expected that the CD reader/burner drive will become obsolete.

The speed of the drive is confusing, as it is stated in terms of the advances in the technology. For example, the first CD drive had a data transfer rate of 150 Kilobytes per second (KBps), known as 1x. Nowadays, the speeds quoted are generally in the range of 40x , 48x and 52x, the maximum. A CD with a speed of 52x equates to a data transfer rate of 7.8 MB per second (ie, 150 KBps by 52x = 7,800 KB or 7.8 MB, as 100 KB equals 1 MB).

DVD drives are rated in the same way. The DVD's original 1x transfer rate is 1.385 MB per second. Speeds quoted today are generally in the range of 8x, 12x and 16x, the maximum. A DVD with a speed of 12x equates to a data transfer rate of a whopping 16.62 MB per second (1.385 MBps by 12x).

Sound

With the proliferation of multimedia applications, a sound system has become an essential piece of computing equipment. A basic computer sound system includes a sound card which is inserted into an expansion slot at the back of the computer and speakers which plug into the sound card.

The quality of the sound is a combination of both the sound card and speakers. Computer advertisements typically specify the sound card manufacturer and model. The models vary, but generally state: 'Sound Blaster compatibility' (the accepted standard).

Making the Purchase Decision

Computers generally are classified into three categories:

1. **Entry Level PC:** A budget machine capable of running Office applications, ie, word processing, database, spreadsheet, desktop publishing and the Internet.

2. **Multimedia PC:** A general purpose machine that can serve the immediate and future needs of small business or family.

3. **Top of the Range PC:** Aimed at the high-end multimedia and games market.

When purchasing a computer, decide which **category** suits your needs by reading reviews in magazines, talking to a sales assistant, etc. Once you have decided on a category, the comparison becomes more objective, ie, you are comparing like with like.

To help make your comparison, list out the main features in a chart. When making your comparison, pay particular attention to:

◆ processor manufacturer, family and number sequence

◆ memory

◆ monitor size and resolution

◆ hard drive.

Even with a high-performance processor, a computer system with a small hard drive and a small amount of memory is likely to be slow at tasks such as starting programs, loading files and scrolling through long documents. The final decision should not be made on price alone.

Short Questions

1. Describe the four basic components of a computer system.
2. What is a peripheral device? Give two examples.
3. Distinguish between magnetic storage media, optical storage media and solid-state storage media, giving an example of each.
4. Compare and contrast a floppy disk, Zip disk and hard disk using the following features: capacity, storage device required and speed of storage device.
5. How does magnetic tape differ from a disk? What is magnetic tape used for?
6. Distinguish between a CD-ROM, CD-R, CD-RW and DVD-RW/+RW.
7. Contrast the advantages of a USB disk (drive) as a portable storage media over portable magnetic and optical storage media.
8. What factors should be taken into account when selecting a printer?
9. Distinguish between an impact printer and a non-impact printer, giving examples.

10. Distinguish between continuous stationery and multi-part stationery.
11. Compare and contrast an inkjet and a laser printer, using the following features: noise level, quality, speed, running cost and volume of output supported.
12. Compare and contrast a sheet feed scanner, flatbed scanner and a versatile scanner using the following features: capabilities, quality and volume of output supported.
13. What is OCR software used for?
14. Distinguish between the measurement units a 'byte' and a 'Hertz'.
15. Outline what the following measurement units are: KHz, MHz, GHz, KB, MB, GB, TB.
16. Describe the term GUI.
17. List the family names of processors manufactured by both Intel and AMD. Distinguish between a processor family name and a family number.
18. What is the function of the onboard clock in a processor?
19. Distinguish between 'cache' and 'main memory', stating the function of each.
20. List and briefly describe three factors to consider when assessing the capability of the main memory of a computer.
21. Describe two features that affect the quality of a monitor.
22. What is meant by: '120 GB, 7200 rpm Serial ATA hard drive'?
23. Explain the marketing specification: '48× CD-ROM'.

Chapter 10 — Computer Applications

Computer application packages are software programs written to carry out specific tasks. These tools help to make office workers more efficient. For example, a business might store its rules and procedures manual or its price list on disk. When these documents need updating, they are retrieved from disk, updated, saved and printed or uploaded to a network.

Typical computer application packages used by businesses are: word processing, spreadsheets, databases and desktop publishing. Computer application packages vary in the functionality they offer depending on whether they are an integrated package or an application suite:

◆ **An integrated package** is **one program** which will have more than one application, normally word processing, spreadsheets, databases and graphics. More recent integrated packages offer additional applications to deal with personal finance, travel planning and photo editing, as well as an encyclopedia. Integrated packages cover the basics in each application and are suitable for small businesses or home users. An example of an integrated packages is MS Works Suite 2005.

◆ **An application suite** is a bundle of **single applications** from the same software developer sold together as one unit. A single application includes very advanced features not available in an integrated package. Single applications are generally sold as an application suite as it is more cost-effective, owing to the fact that the user interface is shared between applications. Examples of business application suites are:

  • *MS Office 2003 Standard,* which includes: MS Word (word processing), MS Excel (spreadsheet), MS PowerPoint (presentation package) and MS Outlook (e-mail and an electronic diary).

  • *MS Office 2003 Professional,* which includes MS Publisher (desktop publishing) and MS Access (database) in addition to the applications included in the standard version.

Word Processing

Word processing is a software application used for producing general office correspondence (ie, letters, memos, reports, etc), mail merges (ie, sending personalised letters to individuals on a mailing list) and for producing booklets, leaflets and newsletters. Examples of word-processing applications are MS Word and Word Perfect.

Features

Word processing provides editing, formatting and other features that enhance its functionality.

Editing features

Editing refers to making revisions and may involve:

◆ **Deletion and insertion** of text.

◆ **Moving or copying** text within a document or from one document to another.

◆ **Search and replace:** Used to locate and update text throughout the document, rather than scrolling through the document looking for the specific text to be changed.

◆ **Spellchecker:** Used to check the spelling of a document against an inbuilt dictionary. The operator can: ignore the word (if it is correctly spelt but not in the dictionary), add the word to the dictionary (useful for technical or legal words), or select the correct spelling from a suggested list.

◆ **Grammar:** Used to identify sentences that contain grammatical errors and to suggest ways to improve the sentence. The grammar rules can be set ranging from casual to formal English.

◆ **Thesaurus:** Used to find a different word with the same meaning (synonyms), eg, 'busy' can be interchanged with 'occupied', 'engaged' or 'employed'.

Formatting features

Formatting refers to changing the appearance and layout of a document and may involve changing:

◆ **Font appearance:** A font is a set of characters in a particular typeface, size and style. Different 'typefaces' can be selected, ie, Times New Roman, Arial,etc. The 'size' of the font can also be changed. Fonts are measured in **points**. There are 72 points to an inch, so a typeface with a font size of 12 points equals one-sixth of an inch.

A font style is used to emphasis particular words or to enhance the appearance of text. For example, <u>underline</u>, **bold**, *italics*, superscript (where the character is above the typing line, eg, 10°) and subscript (where the character is below the typing line, eg, H_2O).

◆ **WordArt:** Offers a variety of fonts, point sizes and unusual ways to position text on the page. For example, you can create a publication title in 48 point and position it vertically down the page, stretch the letters to make them wider or taller, add patterns, colours and shadows.

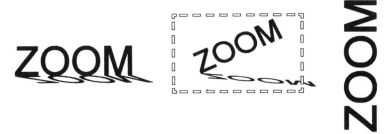

A sample of effects allowed with WordArt

◆ **Reverse Video:** Text is normally printed with black characters on a white background, but this can be changed (reversed) to white text on a black background. Other colours can be used.

◆ **Line spacing:** Spacing between lines of text can be adjusted to single, line-and-a-half, double or treble spacing.

◆ **Justification:** Refers to the alignment of the text on the page. There are four main types: left, right, full and centred, as illustrated below.

Left justification (also known as ragged right). Text is automatically aligned flush with the left margin producing a ragged right margin.	**Right** justification. Text can be aligned flush with the right margin, producing an even right margin but a ragged left margin. Generally used to draw attention to a small amount of text in a poster or flyer.
Full (even) justification. Text can be aligned flush with both the left and right margins, producing an even look. It is used in printed material.	**Centred** justification. Text is centred horizontally across the page. Used for displaying text, generally menus.

◆ **Bullets:** Symbols used to separate and emphasise items in a list. Examples of bullets are: • ⇨ ◆

- **Automatic numbering:** Items typed in a list are automatically numbered; if changes are made to the list, ie, deletion, reordering, etc the list will be automatically renumbered.
- **Tabs:** Are used to align columns of text. When the tab key is pressed, the cursor is taken from point 'A' to point 'B'. Four types of alignment are available:

Left	Right	Decimal	Centred
there	10,234	12.34	there
the	23	123.56	the

left — extends text to the right from the tab stop.

right — extends text to the left from the tab stop. Used to align non-decimal numbers.

decimal — aligns decimal numbers on the decimal point.

centred — centres text at the tab stop.

- **Table facility:** Used to align columns of text similar to tabs but with more flexibility. For example, columns can be moved, cells can be merged and minor calculations can be performed in the table.
- **Page layout:** The layout of the page can be changed, ie, the margins, the orientation of the paper (portrait or landscape) and the paper size (ie, A4, A5 etc).
- **Header/Footer:** A 'header' is text that is keyed in once and appears automatically in the top margin of every page, eg, chapter headings. A 'footer' is text that is keyed in once and appears automatically in the bottom margin of every page, eg, page numbers.

Other features

Other valuable features in word-processing programmes include the following:

- **Orphans/Widows:** An 'orphan' is a facility to ensure that the **first line** of a paragraph does not start at the end of a column or page. A 'widow' ensures that the **last line** of a paragraph is not brought onto a new column or page.
- **Templates:** Are preformatted documents into which you type your text. Most packages provide templates for several common types of document, such as memos, reports, curriculum vitae, business letters, invoices, faxes, etc. Templates can also be created to suit individual needs.
- **Style sheet:** The 'styles' used in a document are known collectively as the document's style sheet. A 'style' is a collection of formatting attributes (ie, typeface, size, indents, etc) defined by the user, named and stored.

When the named style is applied to selected text, the program applies all the formatting attributes in the named style to the selected text at once.

For example, a style could be stored to have all subheadings in the following format — Arial 14 point, underlined, bold and centred. When the style is selected, all of the above formats will be applied to the subheadings at once. This speeds up formatting, as each individual format does not have to be applied separately. In addition, any changes made to the style will automatically change all the paragraphs formatted with that style.

◆ **Table of contents:** When styles are created, a table of contents can be created automatically. A table of contents is used to give an outline of the contents in a book with the corresponding page numbers.

◆ **Clip Art:** A library of pictures incorporated into the application that can be imported into a document to add visual impact. Clip Art can also be purchased on CD-ROMs. Alternatively, the user can scan his/her own pictures to be inserted into the document.

◆ **Graphics facility:** To draw lines, boxes, circles, etc, which can be shaded using patterns and colour.

◆ **Image manipulation:** Images can be changed in shape and text can be positioned all around the image, over the image, down one side of the image, etc.

◆ **Mail Merge:** A facility used to create a series of personalised standard letters by combining the standard letter with another file which contains the names and addresses. Mailing labels for envelopes can also be produced from the file that contains the names and addresses.

◆ **Send To:** A facility to send a document directly from the word-processing program as an e-mail, an e-mail attachment or a fax. (The computer must have an Internet connection or a fax-capable modem.)

◆ **Save as Web Page:** A facility to save a document as a Web page, ie, the information is coded with instructions, known as XHTML tags, which instruct a Web browser how to display and lay out the page. This facility eliminates the need to manually code a document with XHTML tags.

Spreadsheets

A spreadsheet is a software package for financial modelling and analysis of results. For example, spreadsheets may be used for: preparing budgets and forecasts, job cost estimates and to carry out 'what-if' questions, such as, 'What effect will a 2% reduction in price have on profits assuming a 5% increase in sales?' Graphs such as pie charts, bar charts, etc can be produced to visualise the data entered in the spreadsheet.

Spreadsheets are essentially used for any documentation that requires a lot of computational work. The major advantage is the automatic recalculation of results when a number used in the calculation is changed.

Office work that involves dealing with numerical calculations such as managing budgets is simplified with the use of spreadsheets. Examples of Spreadsheet programs are: MS Excel, Lotus 123, QuatroPro.

Layout

A spreadsheet consists of rows and columns. Rows are numbered 1, 2, 3, etc, and the columns lettered A, B, C, up to Z. After Z, AA, AB, AC and so on are used. The intersection of a row and a column is known as a **cell**. Each cell is referenced by a column letter and a row number. For example, cell F3, as shown in Figure 10–1 represents the wages figure for May.

	A	B	C	D	E	F
1		January	February	March	April	May
2	Income				Cell F3	
3	Wages	900	900	900	900	900
4	Bonus	150	0	50	200	0
5	TOTAL INCOME	=SUM(B3:B4)	=SUM(C3:C4)	950	1,100	900
6						
7	Expenses					
8	Rent	400	400	400	400	400
9	Food	360	320	340	360	345
10	Clothes	50	15	10	30	0
11	Miscellaneous	80	20	25	50	55
12	TOTAL EXPENSES	=B8+B9+B10+B11	=SUM(C8:C11)	775	840	800
13						
14	SAVINGS	=B5-B12	145	175	260	100

Figure 10–1 Typical spreadsheet to manage income and expenditure

To perform calculations automatically, a **formula** is inserted in the cell where the answer is required. A formula is indicated by an equals sign and the cell references are used rather than the actual data in the cells.

For example, to add the expenses for January the cursor is placed in cell B12 (where the answer is to appear) and the **addition formula** =B8+B9+B10+B11 is entered. Therefore if the numbers in the cells are changed, the answer is automatically recalculated. For example, if the food expense figure for April were changed to €400, the total expenses figure for April would automatically be updated to €880 and savings for April to €220.

Spreadsheets also have built-in formulae called **functions**. The SUM function is used in cell C12; **=SUM(C8:C11).** This means add all the numbers in the range from C8 to C11 inclusive. This is similar to the addition formula of **=C8+C9+C10+C11** but a lot quicker to enter. The results of the formulae are actually displayed in the cells as in, for example, D5, E5, F5 and D12, E12, etc.

Features

The **editing** and **formatting** features as described under Word Processing are also available in a spreadsheet. Specific features of a spreadsheet include:

◆ **Automatic recalculation:** When rows/columns are inserted/deleted or figures are changed, the formulas automatically adjust to take account of the changes.

◆ **Copying formulae:** A formula entered for one column or row can be copied to other columns or rows and the cell references in the formulae will adjust automatically. For example, in Figure 10–1 if the formula for the January savings =B5-B12 is copied to February, it will read =C5-C12. This is known as a **relative reference** as the formula adjusts when it is moved.

◆ **Protect facility:** A command that allows cells to be protected from unauthorised or accidental alterations. For example, the formulas in the spreadsheet (Figure 10–1) can be 'locked' while the other cells may be left unlocked for updating.

◆ **Charting facility:** Graphs such as pie charts, bar charts, etc can be created from the data entered in the spreadsheet. Displayed below and overleaf are pie charts and a bar chart that are created from the spreadsheet in Figure 10–1.

A pie chart is generally used to show:

a) the *breakdown* of **one** category of information over **one** time period, eg, Figure 10–2 shows the breakdown of the expenses for January; or

b) the *relationship* of **one** item of information within a category over **numerous** time periods, eg, Figure 10–3 shows the relationship of the miscellaneous expenses between January and March.

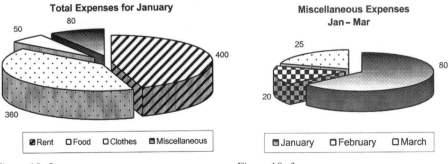

Figure 10–2   *Figure 10–3*

A bar chart is generally used to show:

a) the *breakdown* of **one** category of information over **numerous** time periods, ie, the breakdown of the *expense* category showing the amounts spent on rent, food, clothes and miscellaneous items for January to March; or

b) the *relationship* between categories of information over **numerous** time periods, eg, Figure 10–4 shows the relationship of the income, expenses and savings for the months January to March.

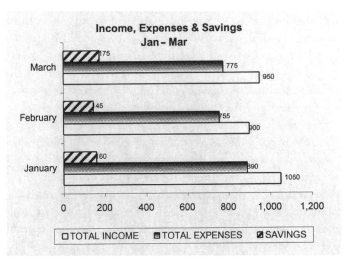

Figure 10–4

Databases

A database is a computerised filing cabinet storing a collection of related records. A database program provides a structure for storing data in such a way that it can be manipulated, ie, searches can be performed for specific information, or the information can be sorted by a specific category, ie, surname, country, etc. For example, a business could search a database of customers by county or age to target a specific segment of the market to promote its products. Other uses of databases include: telephone directories, library databases, customer and supplier records and personnel records. Examples of databases in use are MS Access and Paradox.

It is important to understand the terminology used in a database. Shown opposite is the structure of a database to record information about staff.

```
┌─────────────────────────────────────────────────┐
│  PERSONNEL DATABASE                               │
│  Title:          Mr                               │
│  First Name:     Jerry                            │
│  Surname:        Kelly                            │
│  Address 1:      15 Main Street                   │
│  Address 2:      Blackrock                        │
│  County:         Dublin                           │
│  Date of Birth:  10/11/75                         │
│  Telephone No.:  01-2864532                       │
│  Position:       Sales Assistant                  │
│  Salary:         €45,000                          │
└─────────────────────────────────────────────────┘
```

Figure 10–5

Field: Each category of information in a database is known as a **field**. For example, in the personnel database, 'title' is a field, 'first name' is a field, etc. Each item of information is entered into a field to facilitate searching or sorting the database. For example, notice that the name information is split into two fields, First Name and Surname, rather than entering the whole name under one field. This is a design decision — the way the data is split up into specific fields determines the way the database can be manipulated. For example, the personnel database can now be searched and sorted by surname.

Record: A record is a collection of related fields; it consists of all the fields for one unit of information. The record for Jerry Kelly is shown in Figure 10–5.

Database: A database is a collection of related records. In the Personnel database, there will be many records giving similar details for all employees.

Features

The **editing** and **formatting** features as described in Word Processing are also available in a database. Specific features of a database include:

◆ **Queries:** A facility to search the database for specific information and display the results, eg, a search for all employees who live in Blackrock.

◆ **Reports:** A facility to construct professional reports from the information in the database. Reports are generally constructed from queries as the information has been filtered.

◆ **Multi-user:** Some database packages are multi-user, which enables many users on a network to view the database concurrently. The database is stored in one location, ie, on a server.

◆ **Security:** Multi-user databases are controlled via passwords and 'access rights'. Passwords are used to block access to the system. 'Access rights' are used to control what users can view or alter within the system, eg, controls can be set up so that particular users see only certain areas of the database.

◆ **Merging information:** Information stored in a database can be merged with other applications. For examples, names and addresses stored in a database can be merged with a word-processing package to produce personalised letters.

Desktop Publishing

Desktop publishing software takes word processing one step further by providing more sophisticated features to lay out, format and manage complicated publications, ie, books, magazines, newspapers, brochures, etc.

DTP techniques require the **layout of a page** to be planned in advance, by creating columns and 'frames'. Frames are drawn to separate sections of the page from the main article or story, eg, headlines, pictures and 'boxed' text.

Once the page layout has been designed, the data can be entered. In DTP, large amounts of text are not generally typed directly into the columns or frames; the text is imported from a file created in a word processor. This is because DTP is a page-layout program and is not designed as a primary typing program. In the publication of newsletters and magazines the text of the articles, cover stories, features, etc are generally supplied by somebody else as a word-processing file.

Creating a Publication Using DTP

To manage complicated productions such as newspapers and magazines three techniques are used:

1. **Master pages:** A master page is a page created containing *design elements* such as headers, footers and column grids that are common to most of the pages in the publication. New pages added to the publication can be based on a particular master page, thus avoiding the need to re-create the design elements. Master pages ensure consistency across pages in a publication.

2. **Style sheets:** Like those used in word processing, styles are set up for the various text elements in a publication, ie, headings, captions, body text, etc. Styles ensure consistency among similar text elements in a publication.

3. **Templates:** A template is a preformatted document into which you type your text. In DTP, the user generally designs his/her own template by saving the *master pages* and *style sheets* as a template, thus providing the structure for further publications.

For example, in the production of a magazine, a template with master pages and style sheets is created and saved. So when a new issue is required, the template is recalled and the new text, graphics, etc are inserted.

Features

All of the formatting and editing features offered by word processing packages are available in DTP. For example, headers/footers, control of typographical nuisances, (ie, widows/orphans, hyphen control etc), control of readability of text (ie, spellchecker and grammar checker), word art etc. Other features particular to DTP programs include:

◆ **Leading:** Refers to line spacing, ie, the amount of space between lines of type. In word processing, line spacing is generally limited to single-line, line-and-a half or double-line spacing. However, in DTP the spacing between lines is adjusted in points, allowing immense flexibility (72 points equals 1 inch).

◆ **Kerning:** Refers to letter spacing, ie, the amount of space between letters in a word. In word processing, letter spacing applies to the whole word. However, in DTP the spacing between selected pairs of letters can be adjusted to improve readability, especially at large point sizes. For example, the shape of some letter pairs, such as Wo, Ya, and Tu makes the space between the letters seem too big, while the shape of other letters, eg, Mi and Li, makes the letters seem too close together.

Computer Viruses

A virus is a program written with malicious intent by vandals, known as 'hackers', to corrupt or destroy data stored on computer disks. Computer virus programs can be designed to:

◆ destroy files on the hard disk

◆ corrupt data within certain files, eg, all MS Excel files

◆ cause failure in the operation of the computer, sometimes on the occurrence of some trigger event or on a specific date.

Viruses are spread through downloads from unsecured websites, e-mail attachments and exchange of infected disks. A virus can easily be transmitted. For example, assume you install a copy of a games program downloaded from the Internet onto your hard drive. Unknown to you the games program has a virus — now your hard drive is infected. You e-mail a file to a friend, unaware that your hard drive has a virus. Your friend brings the file to school to work on — so now the computer at school is infected. Another student at the school then uses the infected computer and saves a file to a floppy disk and brings the disk home to finish the work — now the home computer is infected. Unless everyone detects and cleans the virus from the computer and disks used, the virus will continue to be spread.

Installing up-to-date anti-virus software on a computer can control viruses. Anti-virus software scans the hard disk and disinfects any files found to contain a virus. Popular anti-virus software includes: Norton Anti-Virus and McAfee VirusScan. Because new viruses appear frequently, it is important that the anti-virus software is kept up to date so that it contains the information necessary to find new viruses as well as old ones. Updates can be downloaded from the Internet from the companies that publish the anti-virus software. It is recommended that the anti-virus software is updated about every three months.

Short Questions

1. Distinguish between an integrated package and an application suite.
2. Describe and give an example of usage of the following features in word processing:
   a) Search and Replace
   b) Justification
   c) Right Tabs.
3. Describe and give an example of how the following features in word processing are used:
   a) Clip Art
   b) WordArt
   c) Reverse Video.
4. Describe and give an example of usage of the following features in word processing:
   a) Mail Merge
   b) Send To
   c) Save as Web Page.
5. Distinguish between a font's typeface, point size and style.
6. Explain the difference between, and advantages of, a document template and a style sheet.
7. Distinguish between a spreadsheet formula and a function.
8. Describe what the following features in spreadsheets do:
   a) relative references
   b) protect facility
   c) charting.
9. Give an example of when it is more suitable to use a bar chart rather than a pie chart.
10. Distinguish between a field, a record and a database as used in a database program.
11. What is a multi-user database and what security measures are incorporated?
12. Distinguish between 'desktop publishing' and 'word processing'.
13. Distinguish between 'leading' and 'kerning'.
14. Distinguish between a master page, a style sheet and a template.

15. List four common computer software application packages and state the main use of each.
16. What is a computer virus? How are they controlled?

Chapter 11 — Networks and the Internet

A network is a collection of computers linked together via cables, a wireless link, the telephone network or satellite, depending on the geographical distance between computers. A network typically consists of a 'server' or 'hub', ie, a dedicated device that manages and distributes resources to network users.

A typical small network layout, where each computer is connected to a central 'hub' via cable, is shown below.

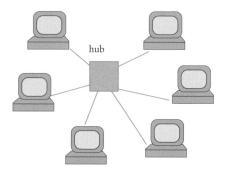

Graphical representation of a small network linked by cables

Types of Network

Networks can vary in size from a local area network (LAN), to a wide-area network (WAN), up to the worldwide network known as the Internet.

LAN — (Local Area Network)

A LAN is a network within a limited geographical area (ie, a single building or group of buildings) such as: a small office/home office (referred to as SOHO), office buildings, universities, airports, hospitals, or manufacturing complexes. A LAN allows the computers attached to the network to: share peripheral devices (ie, printers, scanners, etc) and communicate with each other via e-mail. A LAN is generally also connected to the Internet to enable users on the network to view websites and to communicate with others external to the organisation via e-mail.

A LAN can be built using either cables or a wireless connection, (referred to as Wi-Fi). A wireless LAN is abbreviated to WLAN, the 'W' standing for 'wireless'. Cable has been the traditional choice, but wireless technology is gaining popularity in office buildings and is well established for use in publicly accessible areas such as: airports, hotels, cafés, etc.

In both cases, an appropriate network card (ie, cable standard or Wi-Fi-enabled) is inserted into each computer to be used on the network. However, the difference lies in how the computers communicate with each other.

With a cable connection, cable is attached to the network cards to link the computers together.

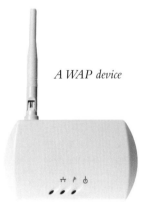

A WAP device

However, with a Wi-Fi connection a building is equipped with many Wireless Access Points (referred to as WAPs or APs — Access Points, known generically as 'Hotspots'). A WAP is a device equipped with an aerial/antenna, and a built-in radio transmitter which enables Wi-Fi-enabled computers to communicate with each other on the network via radio signals.

Wireless networks (WLANs) enable employees to be in regular communication with their business while travelling. For example, employees can access their business WLAN or the Internet from any place that is Wi-Fi-enabled, such as: hotels, cafés, etc, thus avoiding the need to return to the office to complete their work.

Security is vital in both LANs and WLANs to prevent unauthorised users accessing the network. The basic protection for all LANs is a password and 'firewall' software, which determines what access rights users have within the network, ie, which files they can view or update.

WAN — (Wide Area Network)

A WAN is a network which covers a wide geographical area, for example, one which spreads across a country or between countries. Communication is through the telephone network and satellites where necessary. A WAN may use either the public telephone line or a private telephone line. Private telephone lines are leased from a telecommunications provider (ie, Eircom), if the business requires a permanent connection between networks.

A WAN is installed where there is a high volume of inter-branch communication. For example, a business with many branches spread throughout the country may install a WAN to enable branches to: access the head-office database, transfer files between branches, send e-mail on a private network, etc.

A typical set-up for inter-branch communication could be as follows: each branch has a LAN installed and each LAN is connected to Head Office via a private telephone line, giving a permanent connection between networks.

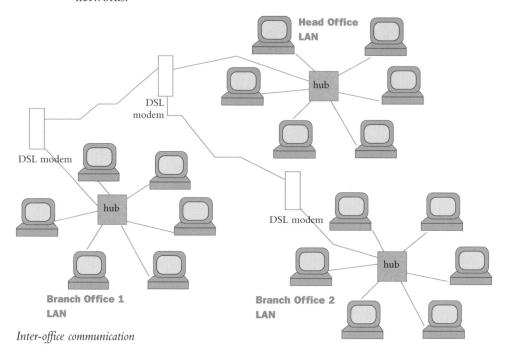

Inter-office communication

The Internet

The Internet is a worldwide network of computers. It is made up of many independent networks which are linked together through the telephone and satellite system. Every computer on the Internet is connected, **indirectly**, to every other computer on the Internet.

Think of the Internet in terms of the telephone system. Your telephone is not directly linked to another telephone; it is linked to your local telephone exchange. Your local telephone exchange is linked to other telephone exchanges, allowing calls to be automatically switched to the appropriate exchange so that a connection can be made.

Similarly for the Internet, an **I**nternet **S**ervice **P**rovider, or ISP, maintains a series of communication links for Internet data. These links interconnect at several points (like the road network) and another ISP will maintain a series of links from these points. For example, assume your local

ISP covers mostly Drogheda, Meath and Dublin and you want to view a website located on a server in London. Your local ISP network puts you on the quickest route to its exit point; and then you are switched to another ISP network.

Connecting to the Internet

Although you can access the Internet via the television using a cable modem or via a mobile phone, most people use the fixed-line telephone network to subscribe to an Internet Service Provider (ISP). This is similar to subscribing to a telecommunication company to use the telephone network. An ISP could be your telephone company (such as Eircom, ESAT, BT Ireland, etc) or a private company.

The two most common types of connection to the Internet for the home or business are: a '*Dial-Up*' connection or an '*Always-On*' connection, generally known as '*Broadband*'. In either case a modem is required. A modem is a device that connects a computer to the Internet via cable or a wireless link. The type of modem required depends on the connection type. As a modem often includes additional network functions, it may also be referred to as a '*router*'. Internet transfer speed is measured in 'bits per second', ranging from kilobits (K) to megabits (M).

A **Dial-Up** connection is an older technology based on the standard telephone line and a modem that transmits data at a maximum rate of 56K, which is very slow. It is known as 'Dial-up' because you must dial your ISP via software to make a connection to the Internet, and while connected you cannot make or receive telephone calls. The cost involved includes a monthly flat-rate fee plus a per-minute charge for the duration of time online — which can be expensive, especially if using the Internet for long periods in 'peak times'.

Broadband refers to faster Internet speeds of 256K and over and is available via cable, satellite and, most commonly, using the telephone line. A broadband connection via the telephone line is a newer technology based on ADSL (Asymmetric Digital Subscriber Line), which provides faster access to the Internet and allows telephone calls to be made or received while online, unlike with a 'dial-up' connection. Broadband is delivered through an existing telephone line using a special modem or router. Broadband speeds vary from 256Kbps to 4Mbps, depending on the broadband category purchased; categories available are generally classified as:

◆ *Entry-level*: Provides speed connections of either 256K or 512K and is suitable for browsing the Web and e-mailing.

◆ *Mid-range*: Provides speed connections of either 1Mb or 2Mb and is the choice recommended to download music, play games, watch video or view websites with a high multimedia content.

◆ *High-end*: Provides speed connections of either 3Mb or 4Mb, the fastest currently available in Ireland. Recommended for very heavy users and for business.

The cost involved includes a monthly flat-rate fee, but unlike a 'dial-up' connection you do not pay for the time spent online. However, some ISPs have a limit on the amount of data that can be transferred per month (generally an 8Gb allowance), after which you are charged for usage.

Broadband is the recommended choice of connection to the Internet as it offers faster speeds, use of telephone while online and it is generally cheaper for high-usage users, as there are no extra charges for the amount of time spent online.

The World Wide Web (WWW)

Many people mistakenly use the term Internet when referring to the World Wide Web (www) or simply the Web. However, the Internet is the communications network and the Web is one service provided over the Internet. Other services provided over the Internet are e-mail, newsgroups, chat and file transfer.

The Web is an information-retrieval and interactive system. It consists of files referred to as websites stored on computer servers connected to the Internet. Information is available on the Web on almost any topic, ie, business, investments, computers, education, government, health, arts and entertainment. Besides information websites, e-commerce websites that sell goods or services on-line are the major drivers of the popularity of the Web, bringing benefits to both consumers and suppliers.

An e-commerce website allows viewers to browse through an on-line catalogue of goods or services and select the products or services they wish to buy. Payment is usually by credit card; the buyer enters his/her credit-card number in the on-line form displayed on the screen. The on-line business delivers the goods or can arrange with a courier to have the goods delivered within a stated time period.

The information for the Web is written by anybody who cares to do so, ie, an organisation or any member of the public. The information is coded with instructions, known as **XHTML** (Extensible Hypertext Markup Language) tags. XHTML tags instruct a Web **browser** how to display and lay out the page(s)/website. Alternatively, a Web authoring package, such as Frontpage or Dreamweaver, could be used to write the XHTML code automatically. The user simply creates a document with text, images, etc (similar to creating a word-processing document), but behind the scenes the Web authoring package is inserting the XHTML tags.

Browsing the Web

The word 'browsing' or 'surfing' simply means viewing websites. To access websites, Web browser software is used, (ie, MS Internet Explorer, Netscape Communicator, etc). The Web address of the site you wish to visit is typed in the 'Address Bar' of the browser window.

E-mail Button

Search Button

Address Bar. The website address is typed here

The website for Gill & Macmillan, (the publisher of this book) is displayed above using the browser Internet Explorer. The website address is www.gillmacmillan.ie, which displays the website's **home page**. The home page is the opening page of the site; it identifies the site and provides a 'linked' list of topics covered in the site, similar to a table of contents in a book. A **link** (also known as a hyperlink) is a visual element on a Web page, generally recognised by an underline, which when clicked loads a specified Web page into the browser.

The **Back** button allows you to go to a page you have just visited; the down arrow beside the Back button is a quick way to select a Web page just visited. Once you have gone back, you can use the Forward button to go forward to the page you were reading.

If you frequently 'surf' particular websites, the Web addresses can be saved in the **Favorites** folder, thus facilitating quick access to these websites in the future. This is known as **Bookmarking** a website.

Understanding Web Addresses

Many of today's browsers assume that all Web addresses begin with http:// and therefore, this is generally omitted from the Web address. Web addresses generally start with a '**www.**' prefix.

Every computer that connects to the Internet has a unique number called an **IP address**, which is used by the network to send data to the correct location. An IP address is a set of four numbers between 0 and 255 that are separated by full stops. An example of an IP address is: 204.130.122.232. As numbers are difficult to remember, the IP addresses are mapped to names, known as **domain names**. For example, to view a website the user would enter the 'name' of the website, but the network will send the IP address of the computer being accessed.

Domain Names

Every website has a unique address, known as a **domain name**, usually in the format of **companyname.ie** or **companyname.com**. Domain names in Ireland generally end with the '**.ie**' suffix. Other suffixes you might see on Web pages are:

.com means a commercial site, usually based in America

.org means a non-profit organisation

.gov means a government office

.edu means an educational site

.uk means United Kingdom — some websites use the country code as their suffix.

Domain names are registered; so no two websites can have the same domain name. The domain name **gillmacmillan.ie** takes you to the website's 'home page'.

URLs

To go directly to a specific page on a website (as distinct from the home page), you need the 'full path' to the file, ie, the file name and the folder name where the file is stored. This is referred to as a URL (Uniform Resource Location); it is an address of a particular page on the website.

For example, consider the web page address: **www.rte.ie/2fm/ ryanshow/education.html.** This web page address is extended beyond the domain name **rte.ie**. It is locating the Web page named **education.html,** which is stored in a folder named **ryanshow,** which is a sub-folder of **2fm**. Basically, after the domain name, the URL could be a series of folders and the last part of the address is the file name — Web page.

Finding Information on the Web

If you don't know a Web address, or if you want to search for specific information, a **search engine site** or a **directory site** is used. Both constantly survey the Web (via a program known as a 'Web Bob' or 'Spider'), cataloguing and indexing information and maintaining a database of the addresses and topics they have found. There is no definitive search engine or directory of everything available on the Web, so you may need to search more than one to find the information you require.

Search Engines

The most common method of finding information is to use a search engine. Examples of popular search engines are: Google (www.google.com), Yahoo (www.yahoo.com) and AskJeeves (www.ask.com). A search for information on the Web is made by entering the search engine address in the 'Address Bar' of the browser window, or by clicking the **Search** button on the browser toolbar. (The Search button initiates a search using the default search engines set on the browser.) In either case, a search window will be presented with an input box where the search criterion is entered, ie, a keyword or words that help to locate the information required.

The search results appear as a 'link' list of topics that match the search criterion entered. Clicking on a link takes you to a particular website. If you are not satisfied with the search results, (ie, the topics listed are not exactly what you were looking for, or there are hundreds of topics listed), you need to redefine your search to make it more specific.

Directory Sites

A directory site such as Yahoo (www.yahoo.com) —— which is also a search engine site — provides a list of subject topics organised into major categories.

To find information using a directory site, you need to figure out which category a particular topic might be under. For example, when searching for information on flatbed scanners, the relevant major category to select might be computers. When the computer category is selected, a further sub-category is presented, maybe: hardware, software, terminology, etc. So unless you knew that a scanner was hardware, you would be searching under the wrong category and therefore would not find the correct information.

Tips on searching

If your search result yields hundreds of topics, use the following tips to produce the most relevant results:

◆ **Be as specific as possible with keywords:** ie, a search for *bicycles* is not specific; it will find Web pages that have the word bicycles in them, finding hundreds of irrelevant websites.

◆ **Use only lower-case letters:** unless you want your search to be case-sensitive. Lower-case letters will find all words with varying capitalisation. For example, a search for *multimedia* will find Multimedia, MULTIMEDIA, MultiMedia.

◆ **Use quotation marks:** to search for a phrase, otherwise Web pages with any of the words in the phrase will be found. For example, a search for *bicycle accessories*, will find Web pages with the word *bicycle* in them first, then it will find Web pages with the word *accessories* in them. However, enclosing the search words in quotation marks, ie, '*bicycle accessories*', will find Web pages that contain those two words together.

◆ **Use a plus sign (+):** in front of a word to require that word to appear in the results. For example, *multimedia +software* is more likely to produce useful results than a search for multimedia alone.

◆ **Use a minus sign (-):** in front of a word to exclude it from results. For example, to search for information about multimedia software, but not hardware, course, games, etc. try, multimedia +software -hardware -course -games.

◆ **Combine quotation marks with the plus sign:** for example, a search for '*raleigh bicycle*' *+gents* finds Web pages that have the words *raleigh bicycle* together, and the word *gents* somewhere on the page.

◆ **Order the keywords:** the order in which the words are placed will impact on the results. A search for *multimedia +hardware* will yield different results from a search for *hardware +multimedia*.

◆ **Use an asterisk (★) to broaden the search:** used to cater for plurals of words. For example, a search for '*raleigh bicycle★*' will find both *raleigh bicycle* and *raleigh bicycles*. The asterisk indicates that it will find words with any letters after the initial word you typed, ie, *gent★* will find gentlemen, gents, gentile, etc, so be careful about its use.

◆ **Keep in mind different spelling:** different spelling will yield different results, ie, labor/labour, color/colour.

You may find it difficult to implement these tips on your first search. However, once the results of the search are displayed, you can quickly figure out what keyword(s) you want and use the tips on searching to locate the required information.

Intranet and Extranet

An **intranet** is a 'private Web' generally implemented over a local area network (LAN), accessible by employees within an organisation and not by the general public. It is the implementation of Internet technologies.

An intranet is the organisation's information infrastructure, providing up-to-date information in a timely and cost-effective manner.

The primary use of an intranet is to publish, via a Web browser, internal information such as: the organisation's background and policy, health and safety guidelines, Human Resources department information, product literature, annual reports, newsletters, price lists, manuals, internal forms, current news about the business, forthcoming events — generally any information that was previously distributed via memos, leaflets or handbooks to employees.

In addition, an intranet may have a link to the organisation's database to enable employees to check names and addresses, inventory levels, status of orders, etc. An intranet generally also has a connection to the Internet. Like any network, controls are put in place to allow certain groups of employees to access specific information.

An **extranet** extends an organisation's intranet to a closed community outside the organisation such as business partners, suppliers and customers with special access permissions to certain subsites.

Typically access may be granted to contractors or consultants who need certain business data, to suppliers who want to monitor inventory levels to plan their own production schedules and to customers who want to check on the status of pending orders. A business with access rights can log on to the organisation's website and use a password to access the organisation's internal network. Once inside, they can access whatever the host of the extranet wants them to see.

Protection against unwanted intrusion on extranets is implemented via a hardware/software system known as a 'firewall' that examines incoming and outgoing data to prevent unauthorised transmission of, or access to, information.

Short Questions

1. What is a network? List three different sizes of networks.
2. Briefly describe how computers on a LAN communicate with each other on: (a) cable LAN and (b) wireless LAN.
3. List three benefits of a WLAN.
4. Distinguish between LAN, WLAN and WAN networks and suggest a suitable use for each type of network.
5. Compare and contrast two methods of connecting to the Internet.
6. List the three categories of broadband speed available.
7. Distinguish between the Internet and the Web.
8. What language is used to write a Web page? List an alternative way of producing Web pages.
9. What is meant by the term e-commerce?
10. Distinguish between a domain name and a URL.

11. Distinguish between 'search engines' and 'directory sites'.
12. List four guidelines you would give users of the Internet so that their searches are more productive.
13. Distinguish between an intranet and an extranet.

Chapter 12 — Information Systems

The quantity of data that is generated by a business can be quite significant. The data flow within a business must be organised to produce useful information that can be used to enhance the overall performance of the business. An information system is a method of arranging data and procedures to: capture, process, store and distribute quality information for decision-making purposes.

Levels of Decision Making

All levels of the business from operators to senior management use information to make informed decisions that affect the efficiency levels within the business. The types of decision made at the different levels of management are outlined in Figure 12–1.

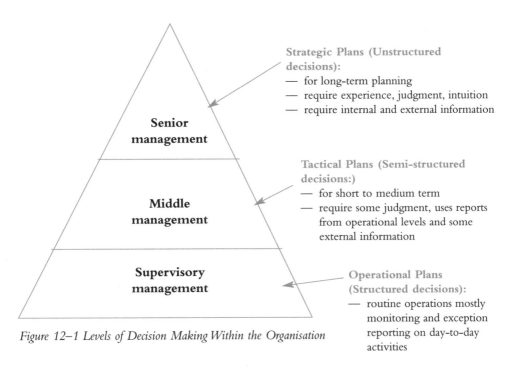

Strategic Plans (Unstructured decisions):
— for long-term planning
— require experience, judgment, intuition
— require internal and external information

Senior management

Tactical Plans (Semi-structured decisions:)
— for short to medium term
— require some judgment, uses reports from operational levels and some external information

Middle management

Supervisory management

Operational Plans (Structured decisions):
— routine operations mostly monitoring and exception reporting on day-to-day activities

Figure 12–1 Levels of Decision Making Within the Organisation

Senior management require information to make strategic plans for the long-term benefits of the business such as: decisions regarding large-scale investment, entering new markets and planning takeovers. At middle-management level, managers develop tactical plans for the medium term, such as staffing requirements, budgets and production requirements. These plans are then implemented and monitored by the supervisory or operational management level on a day-to-day basis.

There may be a variety of information systems operating within the business to facilitate different levels of decision making. The information system should provide up-to-date, accurate and relevant information, usually in the form of reports. Information systems can be divided into two categories:
1. Operational Support Systems
2. Management Support Systems.

Operational Support Systems

Operational Support Systems refer to a range of information systems that capture and process data of a routine nature relating to internal activities such as stocks, sales, personnel, production, marketing and finance. Examples of Operational Support Systems are *Office Automation Systems* and *Transaction Processing Systems (TPS)*.

Office Automation Systems

An office automation system computerises routine office tasks such as: managing correspondence, scheduling activities, accounting and payroll, using word processing, spreadsheets, electronic schedulers, databases and e-mail. LANs, WANs, intranets, extranets and the Internet are integral components of an office automation system.

Transaction Processing Systems (TPS)

A transaction processing system controls and organises data involved in the daily transactions of the business. A TPS typically consists of the following elements:
◆ data entry
◆ transaction processing
◆ file and database updating
◆ document and report generation
◆ enquiry processing.

An example of a TPS is the **EPOS** system (Electronic Point of Sale) used in most retail outlets. An EPOS system incorporates bar code pricing, stock controls and transaction sales data. Every product is bar coded and details such as price, product code, supplier and description are recorded on the in-store computer. When the product is scanned at the point of sale, and the sale is complete (ie, payment is made), an itemised receipt is produced for the customer and the stock levels are reduced by the product items and the sales total increases.

The reports available from the EPOS allow managers to make quicker and more informed decisions on the stock, sales and staff performances and help management to keep tighter controls over cash and stock.

In a retail-chain situation, all the branches are networked so that sales comparisons between branches can be made more easily. This also facilitates improved customer service, because sales assistants can view stocks in other branches to see if the item required is available.

Management Support Systems

Management Support Systems refers to systems that are designed to improve the quality of management decisions at a strategic rather than an operational level. Examples of Management Support Systems include *Management Information Systems (MIS)* and *Decision Support Systems (DSS)*.

Management Information Systems (MIS)

While operational support systems are concerned with capturing and recording data, middle and senior managers require more sophisticated reports to make tactical and strategic decisions. An MIS extrapolates and arranges the information from the operational support systems, to produce the reports necessary to make such decisions. Reports can be customised according to the type and frequency of information required, ie, periodically, by exception or on demand. For example, branch managers may receive a *summary report* such as the total amount of sales of product X per day, and an *exception report* showing products that have not reached the minimum sales level.

Decision Support Systems (DSS)

Decision support systems provide the tools necessary to analyse data so that non-routine decisions can be made. Such decisions may include planning resources, determining financial budgets, etc.

A DSS incorporates analytical modelling, allowing the manager to ask *sensitivity analysis* (or 'what if?') questions. For example, 'What happens to the profit margin if the cost price increases by 10%?' The DSS will use internal information and may incorporate external information to test a variety of hypothetical situations to achieve the optimum solution to a problem.

Airlines use a variety of decision support systems for analysing seating capacity to help management maximise seat utilisation, ticket pricing, etc.

Retail chains use a DSS called *Geographical Information Systems* to help analyse the demographics of a particular region, where to locate their outlets and how to optimise distribution routes.

Designing an Information System

When designing an information system, the following steps should be considered:

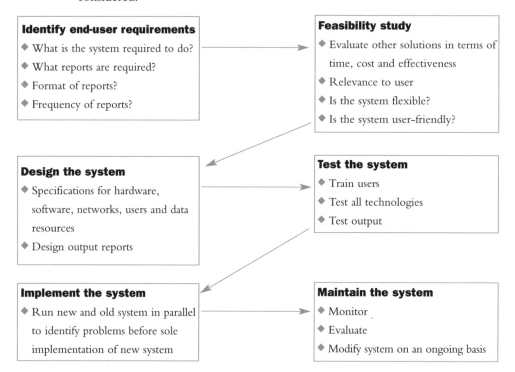

Identify end-user requirements
- What is the system required to do?
- What reports are required?
- Format of reports?
- Frequency of reports?

Feasibility study
- Evaluate other solutions in terms of time, cost and effectiveness
- Relevance to user
- Is the system flexible?
- Is the system user-friendly?

Design the system
- Specifications for hardware, software, networks, users and data resources
- Design output reports

Test the system
- Train users
- Test all technologies
- Test output

Implement the system
- Run new and old system in parallel to identify problems before sole implementation of new system

Maintain the system
- Monitor
- Evaluate
- Modify system on an ongoing basis

Potential Problems Developing an Information System

When designing an information system, the following list should be considered carefully to avoid problems such as:

1. **Information overload:** Ensure the system does not become bogged down with irrelevant and useless information, thus preventing 'real' information from being accessed.
2. **Technology v. People:** Employees may fear that changes in work practice using new technology may alter their status at work.
3. **Security:** Special consideration must be given to the protection of information, especially information concerning individuals (*Data Protection Act 1988 and Amendment Acts 1988–2003*). The system should be designed to limit access by setting controls via passwords and levels of access.

Whatever information system is implemented, the business must ensure that the information resulting from the system is appropriate to management requirements from supervisory to executive levels.

Accessing External Databases

As well as developing specific information systems, the business may subscribe to general information systems either on a private network or a public network such as the Internet.

Videotex is the term used to refer to an external central database that can be accessed by the user via a computer network or the television network. Two forms of Videotex are: Viewdata and Teletext.

1. **Viewdata:** Is a two-way information system, ie, the user can view and send information to the system, eg, extranets and the Internet.
2. **Teletext:** Is a one-way information system that is supplied through the television network, ie, the user can view the information on the system but cannot send information to the system. The information is general in nature, eg, timetables, stock market prices, weather, sports, news, shopping, TV guides etc. 'Aertel' is the teletext system supplied by RTE. Teletext is free to view and is financed by advertising. Aertel is also available on the Internet, allowing users faster access to the information database.

Short Questions

1. What is meant by the term 'information system'?
2. Briefly describe three types of decision made at the different levels of management.
3. Distinguish between an Office Automation System and a Transaction Processing System.
4. Briefly describe an EPOS system.
5. Distinguish between the type of information captured by an Operational Support System and by a Management Support System.
6. Give an example of an Operational Support System and a Management Support System.
7. List four points in which a Decision Support System assists management in making decisions.
8. What does the term 'videotex' refer to? List two forms of videotex.
9. Distinguish between 'viewdata' and 'teletext'.

Summary

Buying a computer can be very challenging, owing to the technical specifications that describe the computer's components and features. The type of computer you buy depends on its anticipated use — you should pay particular attention to processor speed, memory and hard-disk capacity.

It is also necessary to be familiar with peripheral devices such as printers, scanners and storage media. Common desktop printers are the inkjet and laser printer, of which there are many models. The types of scanner available are: sheet-feed scanners, flatbed scanners and versatile scanners; the type chosen depends on the type of material to be scanned and the volume of use. Storage devices range from magnetic media (ie, disks and tapes) to optical media (ie, CDs and DVDs) and to solid-state media such as the USB disk.

Computer application packages widely used in business are: word processing, spreadsheet, database and desktop publishing packages. Data stored on computer media must be protected from viruses and this is achieved by downloading software from secured websites, being suspicious of unknown e-mails with attachments and putting all files received through up-to-date anti-virus software.

Computer networks vary in size from a small local area network (LAN or WLAN, depending on technology), to a wide-area network (WAN), to a worldwide network known as the Internet. Services provided over the Internet include the Web, e-mail, newsgroups, chat and file transfer. The Web is an information-retrieval and interactive system with information available on almost any topic. Every website has a unique address known as a domain name. Within a website, the individual pages have addresses known as URLs — the full path to the file appended to the domain name. *E-commerce*, ie, buying goods and services over the Internet, is a growing industry. To find information on the Web a directory site such as *Yahoo* or a search engine such as *Google* can be used. A directory site provides a list of subject topics organised into major categories, whereas a search engine allows one to enter keywords of the topic being sought.

Web technology is also implemented internally within a business, eg, an *intranet* which is a 'private Web', generally implemented over a LAN and not accessible by the general public. An intranet is primarily used to publish internal information via a Web browser that is available to all employees on the network. An extension of an intranet is an *extranet*: this extends an organisation's intranet outside the organisation to a closed community such as business partners, suppliers and customers with special access permission to certain subsites.

Technology does more than just improve the normal routine functions of the office; it also impacts on information sources in the office and the transmission of correspondence, as well as enabling all levels of management to make informed decisions through well-designed information systems.

A variety of information systems usually operate within the business to facilitate decisionmaking at different levels of management. Information systems can be divided into two categories: Operational Support Systems and Management Support Systems.

Operational Support Systems capture and process data of a routine nature relating to internal activities such as stocks, sales, personnel, production, marketing and finance. Examples are Office Automation Systems and Transaction Processing Systems (TPS).

Management Support Systems are designed to improve the quality of management decisions at the strategic rather than the operational level. Examples are Management Information Systems (MIS) and Decision Support Systems (DSS).

As well as developing specific information systems, the business may subscribe to general information systems either on a private or public network. *Videotex* is the term used to refer to an external central database, of which there are two forms: **Viewdata** accessed through the computer network, and **Teletext** accessed through the television network, such as 'Aertel', supplied by RTE.

Assignments

1. Write a newspaper article entitled 'The Basics of Buying a Computer'. It should be easy to understand and yet comprehensive enough to cover all the basic issues. Your final report should be typeset using either a word-processing or a DTP program and should fit on a double-sided A4 page.

2. Your employer, a sole trader, has decided to upgrade the two computers in the business. He has asked you to research the computers in the middle range of the market and to supply three specifications within this category to include prices exclusive of VAT. His budget is €1,000 per computer. A printer is not required.

   Research the computers in this category using at least three different suppliers, as the same computer specification may cost more from different suppliers. To carry out the research, gather information from computer advertisements, computer magazines, brochures, computer stores, the Web, etc.

   Provide the employer with a report outlining your research methods and recommend one of the computers as being the best value for money, justifying your answer. At the end of the report, provide a comparison sheet (similar to the one below) outlining the specification of the three computers in the middle range from three different suppliers.

Comparison of Computers: Category_____	Company 1	Company 2	Company 3
Processor:			
Manufacturer			
Model (family name and number			
Features — clock speed — FSB — cache			
Memory:			
Type			
Size			
Monitor:			
Type			
Size			
Resolution			
Video memory			
Hard disk:			
Type			
Size			
Drives:			
CD-ROM speed			
DVD speed			
Other drives			
Sound:			
Card model			
Speakers			
Software Bundles:			
Price:			

3. Design a database to hold employee names, addresses, date of birth and gender. The relevant fields should be split up to enable the database to be searched and sorted by district, county, age and gender. Enter ten records.
4. Write a report that compares two ISPs that provide broadband in your local area on the following issues: monthly service charge, restrictions on downloads if applicable, Web space available, number of e-mail accounts and technical support service.

5. Search the World Wide Web for the following information:
   a) Iarnrod Eireann rail timetables
   b) stock exchange price for the Irish commercial banks
   c) night courses on computer basics in Dublin.

   Document the relevant findings in a report and provide the Web addresses of these sites for future reference. Outline how you conducted your search and the methodology used to refine your search strategy to deliver meaningful findings.

6. Select a specific topic from your syllabus 'Information and Administration' and use the Internet to research this topic further. Note the suggestions below:
   a) Using a search engine of your choice, write down your search criteria and print the search page that resulted from your search.
   b) Refine your search criteria, documenting the reasoning behind your new search criteria based on the results of your first search. Print the search page that resulted from your second search and comment on whether it is better or worse and the action to take.
   c) Keep performing a search until the required search page is found. Write down the search criteria used each time.
   d) Once a relevant site is found, save it to disk. Extract the relevant information and prepare a two-page report on your chosen topic.

Unit 4 — Postal, Electronic and Mobile Communication

Introduction

Information is the lifeblood of any business. All businesses communicate using a variety of means, such as the traditional postal system, or via electronic methods such as fax, e-mail and mobile phones. Unit 4 is divided into two chapters:

Chapter 13 — Post and Postal Services

Reviews the equipment that is typically used in the process of handling post, the general procedures for dealing with incoming and outgoing post in the office, and the wide range of services provided by An Post.
- ◆ Postal Equipment
- ◆ Dealing with Incoming Post
- ◆ Dealing with Outgoing Post
- ◆ Delivery Services Provided by An Post
- ◆ Other Postal Services Provided by An Post
- ◆ Marketing Services Provided by An Post
- ◆ Non Postal Services from An Post

Chapter 14 — Electronic and Mobile Communication

Reviews the electronic transmission of documents such as the fax and e-mail and other modes of communication used to stay in touch with the office, such as the pager and mobile phone.
- ◆ The Fax Machine and Features
- ◆ Compiling, Sending and Receiving Fax Messages
- ◆ Electronic Mail (E-mail)
- ◆ Creating, Sending, Receiving, Replying and Forwarding E-mail
- ◆ Managing Received E-mail
- ◆ Mobile Communication
- ◆ Mobile Network in Ireland

Chapter 13 — Post and Postal Services

To prevent delays in receiving or sending post, it is important to ensure that there is a proper procedure in place to deal with both incoming and outgoing post. In a large business, eg, a mail-order business, there may be a whole department dedicated to sorting, processing and distributing incoming and outgoing post. A medium-sized business may allocate post duties to a Post Clerk. In a small office, the receptionist or office assistant may take responsibility for dealing with the post.

Postal Equipment

The volume of post flowing through the business determines what type of equipment will be used in the post room. For example, a small business may not require a franking machine and may operate a manual weigh scales and a manual letter opener. A business with large volumes of post may operate up-to-the-minute electronic postal equipment. Typical equipment found in the post room includes the following:

Letter Openers

A paper knife is used to open sealed letters manually.

An automatic letter opener is used where there is a large volume of letters to open. Envelopes are fed automatically to the letter opener and a minute strip from the top of the envelope is cut by a blade. The width of the cut can be adjusted to open heavy envelopes. It is important to ensure that envelopes are faced correctly so that contents are not damaged.

Automatic letter opener

Date-stamping Machine

A date-stamping machine is used to stamp all incoming post with the date as evidence of receipt on a particular date. The day, date, month and year are adjusted by external controls. It is important to remember to change the date.

The Addressing Printer

The addressing printer is connected to a computer and accommodates different-sized envelopes and forms.

Date-stamping machine

The names and addresses are held on a computer file

Address-printing machine

and printed on the envelopes or forms as they are fed through the addressing machine.

Jogger Machine

A jogger machine aligns individual pages for stapling or for inserting into envelopes.

Folding and Inserting Machine

A folding and inserting machine is used to automatically fold and insert printed material into window envelopes (eg, invoices, statements). Some machines will also seal the envelopes.

Weighscales

A weighscales is used to weigh non-standard letters and parcels so that the correct postage value can be fixed on the post.

Modern postal scales can be programmed to calculate the correct postal charges and can be interfaced with a franking machine to print the appropriate frank value.

The Franking Machine

A franking machine places an impression of the postage value on envelopes or parcels which are accepted by the postal system as stamped post.

The envelopes are stacked on a feeder tray, and the required settings, ie, date, envelope width and frank value are set. As the envelope passes through the machine, the stamp value and date of postage are imprinted (franked) on the envelope. Some businesses place an advertising slogan on their 'frank'. Gummed postage stamps can be printed individually for large parcels or bulky envelopes that cannot be fed through the machine.

Franking machine

Modern franking machines can stamp up to 5,500 envelopes per hour and have a moistening device that seals the envelopes as they are passed through for franking.

The business can purchase or lease the franking machine from the manufacturer, but must obtain a licence and a franking card with franking units (similar to a telephone call card) from the Post Office. A meter displays the franking units remaining. Training should be provided in the use of the franking machine to avoid wasting franking units.

Postal Guides

Every office should have a copy of 'An Post's Guide to Mail Services' so that the correct value of postage is attached to the outgoing letter or parcel. Rates of postage vary according to the size and weight of the envelope or parcel and the customer's preference for standard or express delivery.

If the stamp or franking value is under the postal value, the addressee is charged with the difference in postage and a small fee. If the addressee refuses to pay the charge, the sender is obliged to pay.

An Post's Guide to Mail Services

Dealing with Incoming Post

The following procedure is generally implemented when dealing with incoming post to the office:

◆ Sign for registered post.
◆ Sort the post according to: general, private, confidential, personal and urgent.
◆ Open general post.
◆ Do **not** open:
  1. Post addressed to individuals as private, confidential or personal unless authorised to do so. These items should be handed unopened to the addressee.
  2. Post that is addressed to another business, eg, Allied Irish Finance, 12 Drury Street, Carlow, receives a letter addressed to Allied Irish Banks Ltd, 10 Main Street, Carlow. This letter should be returned unopened to the Post Office for redistribution.
◆ Date-stamp the post as it is opened.
◆ Check envelopes for enclosures. Secure enclosures with a paper clip or staple. Record missing enclosures as 'enc omitted' on documentation received.
◆ Record remittances (ie, monies received) in the remittance book.
◆ Distribute post to individual trays, pigeon-holes, or department post trays.

Remittance Book

A remittance book is maintained by an administrator/post clerk to record remittances received. The remittance book logs the date the post is received, who the remittance is from, the type and amount of remittance and is signed by the person opening the post.

Date	Addressee	Remittance Type	Amount	Signed
July 7	Star Ltd	Postal Order	€35.00	M Murphy
July 7	Cambridge	Cheque	€64.00	M Murphy
July 7	Calcus Ltd	Bank Draft	€13.00	M Murphy

Circulation List

The post may contain magazines which should be circulated to a number of employees. A *circulation list*, drawn up by an administrator/post clerk, is attached to the magazine for distribution. A circulation list is a list of all employees wishing to read the magazine. When the magazine is read, the list is initialled, dated and the magazine is passed to the next person on the list, usually within 24 hours. A circulation list is also used to circulate other internal information such as reports.

Name	Initial	Date
John Anslow Deirdre Browne Barry Carmody Margaret Doyle Louise Kiernan Brendan McArdle Aoife Ní Mhuirí		

Please read and circulate to next named person on the list within 24 hrs. Initial list and insert date when circulating.

A Circulation List

Dealing with Outgoing Post

Administration staff will usually have 'in/out trays' for receiving and dispatching post. The post will be collected from the out trays at specified times during the day. The following procedure is generally implemented when dealing with outgoing post:

Letters

- ◆ Ensure all letters are signed.
- ◆ Check all enclosures (eg, cheques, documentation) are attached.
- ◆ Check the address on the letter matches the address on the envelope.
- ◆ Fold letters and any attached enclosures neatly and place in an appropriate-sized envelope. Particular attention should be paid when inserting letters into window envelopes. Ensure address is visible and confidential information (eg, amount due on account) is not in view.
- ◆ Seal envelopes.
- ◆ Prepare post for franking, batching similar-sized envelopes together.
- ◆ Separate post requiring special attention (eg, post to be registered).
- ◆ Weigh heavy envelopes individually, and calculate the postage value. (Use *An Post's Guide to Mail Services*.)
- ◆ Frank post.
- ◆ Dispatch post to the Post Office.
- ◆ Register valuable post at the Post Office and obtain receipts.

> ### Example — Preparing Post for Dispatch
>
> A heavy envelope arrives at the post room from Purchasing, to be dispatched to the UK. Outline procedure for dispatch.
>
> 1. Check envelope is sealed and addressed properly.
> 2. Weigh the envelope and note weight (assume weight of 236 g).
> 3. Check postal guide for charges to UK for post weighing not more than 250 g. (Current charge is 96c for priority posting.)
> 4. Adjust franking machine to emit a stamp to the value of 96c.
> 5. Stick franking machine stamp to the envelope and dispatch.

Parcels and Packing

To ensure a safe delivery the following guidelines may be adopted when packing parcels for dispatch:

1. Pack the items tightly together to prevent movement. Foam or paper is often used.
2. Use protective wrapping around the parcel, ie, 'bubble wrap'.
3. Wrap the outer parcel with plain paper or place in a cardboard box.
4. Write the name and address of the recipient of the parcel clearly on the front of the parcel.
5. Write the sender's name and address clearly on the back of the parcel. Mark **'SENDER'S ADDRESS'** clearly to avoid confusion.
6. If using a bar-coded label, stick the bar-coded label on the left-hand side of the front of the parcel.

Delivery Services Provided by An Post

An Post is Ireland's national postal-service provider. While the primary task of An Post is to ensure the safe and efficient delivery of post, the Post Office also offers many other important services to the general public, which are discussed later.

An Post provides the following letter and parcel delivery services in conjunction with its subsidiary distribution companies: Air Business, JMC Trans Vans and Wheels Couriers. Many of the delivery services offer the customer a tracking service, whereby the customer is issued with a numbered receipt per item of post and can use the An Post website (www.anpost.ie) to track the progress of the delivery.

Letter Delivery Services – Nationwide

◆ **Standard Delivery Service:** Is the usual postal service used for letters and light packages. Delivery takes place within 24 hours and the minimum cost for a letter, weighing not more that 100 g, is 48c.

◆ **Swiftpost National Service:** Is an express postal service that guarantees next-day delivery to anywhere in the Republic of Ireland for items not weighing over 2 kg. The basic cost of Swiftpost national is €4.30 for post weighing less than 100 g.

Post marked with the Swiftpost label is easily identified and receives priority handling. The Swiftpost label is completed by the customer and handed to the Post Clerk for posting. The bar code on the label is scanned by the post office and the customer can track the item through the An Post internet tracking system. The receipt portion of the label is date-stamped and retained by

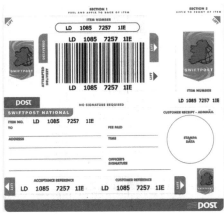

Swiftpost National label

the customer as proof of posting and for tracking purposes. There is a double-fee-back guarantee if the item is not delivered on time. Swiftpost labels can be obtained in advance from the Post Office.

Letter Delivery Services – Worldwide

◆ **Economy Service:** Is used where there is no urgency in delivery and therefore is cheaper than the priority service. The basic cost for a letter to Europe weighing less than 100 g is €1.10c.

◆ **Priority (Airmail) Service:** is a priority delivery service over the economy service, but there is no guaranteed day of delivery. All international priority post is sent by airmail. An Airmail label is placed on the item of post to help identify airmail

Airmail sticker

items from other post. Airmail labels can be obtained in advance from the Post Office. The basic cost for a letter to Europe, weighing less than 100 g, is €1.20.

◆ **Swiftpost Exprès:** Swiftpost Exprès is an international express service that operates within a specific zone. The countries in the zone are: Ireland, Britain, Denmark, Finland, France, Germany, Iceland, Netherlands, Norway, Portugal, Sweden, Switzerland and Spain. Swiftpost Exprès is faster than the Priority (Airmail) service and items sent are given guaranteed delivery times. Like the Swiftpost National Service, a label is placed on the item; post must not weigh over 2 kg; there is a double-fee-back guarantee if the item is not delivered on time; and a tracking system is used. The basic cost of Swiftpost Exprès is €7 for post weighing less than 100 g.

♦ **Swiftpost International:**
To send post urgently to countries outside the Swiftpost Exprès zone, a Swiftpost International mailing service is available for a flat fee of €4 in addition to the postage cost. However, Swiftpost International does not guarantee days of delivery and confirmation of delivery is not available.

Swiftpost International label

Parcel Delivery Service

The Express Mail Service (EMS) is An Post's courier service, which operates both nationally and internationally delivering letters and parcels. EMS operates three levels of service: Economy, Priority and EMS Courier. The maximum weight of parcels accepted by EMS is 30 kg. Most EMS services offer free insurance cover for loss or damage to the items, and further insurance can be taken out by customers for a fee. Customers can bring items for delivery to main post offices or to collection points assigned to major urban areas. International deliveries must have a completed dispatch label attached, with a detailed description of the contents for security purposes.

EMS label

The following table illustrates the EMS cost of sending a parcel weighing 5 kg within Ireland and to France.

EMS Parcel Delivery Service – Nationwide and Worldwide						
	National			**Worldwide**		
	Economy	**Priority***	**Courier**	**Economy**	**Priority**	**Courier**
Cost (€)	16.94	16.94	16.94	39.93	39.93	45.98
Delivery times guarantee	none	Next day	Pre-noon next day	None	3-4 days	Next day
Free insurance cover limit	€100	€150	€350	None	€150	€350
Internet tracking	Yes	Yes	Yes	No	Yes**	Yes
Proof of delivery	Yes	Yes	Yes	No	Yes	Yes

*   Priority also offers a Cash on Delivery (COD) service, within the Irish Republic, whereby the courier collects cheque payments and forwards the cheque to the sender for an additional fee.

**   Internet tracking is available only to the following: EU countries: Norway, Switzerland, Channel Islands, Canada and the USA.

Other Postal Services provided by An Post

Registered post

Post that contains valuable items or important documents should be registered at the Post Office. Registered post receives priority handling by An Post and the items are insured up to the declared value on the registered label (to a maximum of €320).

To register post, the sender completes a registration label, giving a description and value of the contents and stating both the recipient's and sender's names and addresses. The label consists of a **receipt** and an **identification** section with corresponding bar codes, so that the item can be traced through An Post's Internet tracking system. The completed identification section of the label is placed on the item for posting and the receipt is date-stamped by the Post Office clerk and given to the customer as proof of postage. A registration fee is charged; the amount depends on the value of the contents (see relevant Postal Guide).

Receiving Registered Post

When a registered letter/parcel is received, it is generally checked to ensure all contents are intact. A **Delivery Record Card** is signed as proof that the post was delivered successfully.

The postman removes the bar-code sticker from the identification label and places it on the Delivery Record Card as proof of delivery.

Advice of Delivery (Recorded Delivery)

The sender of the registered post may require proof from the Post Office that the post was delivered. Using the Delivery Record Card, the Post Office can issue an Advice of Delivery receipt which will have the recipient's signature. A small fee is charged to the sender for this service.

Redirection

This service redirects post to an address nominated by the customer for a period of time. The service is very convenient for people moving house or who spend periods of time working abroad. Booking forms for this service are available at the Post Office.

Mail Minder

An Post will retain post at the Post Office for up to 12 weeks while the customer is away from their usual address. Booking forms for this service are available at the Post Office, on which the customer enters the date when normal delivery is to recommence.

Poste Restante

Poste Restante or post 'to be called for' is a facility offered by An Post for those who do not have a known address, eg, people travelling. Post can be addressed to the recipient in the care of a specified Post Office. The post is held at the Post Office for three months.

Private post box

An Post operates a private post box facility for customers who do not have a regular address or who do not wish correspondents to know their address. The customer/business is allocated a private box number where post can be addressed and delivered. Private box numbers are common where employers have a job vacancy but do not wish to declare the location of the vacancy to the public. Respondents are given a box number to apply to and the employer collects the replies from the private post box.

Passport express

Passport application forms are available at the Post Office. The customer places the completed form in a special passport express envelope and returns it to the Post Office clerk with the appropriate fee, ie, the passport fee plus the cost of the service. All applications are sent by Swiftpost and the passport is delivered to the customer within 10 working days.

Sending Money Through An Post

It is not advisable to send cash through the post. An Post provides a range of services for transferring money nationally and internationally through the postal system and by electronic means. In all cases a receipt is given as proof of purchase.

1. **Postal Money Order**: Used to send money within Ireland, replacing the traditional postal order and money order. A Postal Money Order can be purchased for any amount up to a maximum of €650. A fee is charged depending on the value of the Order, ranging from 80c for an Order up to a value of €15 to €3.75 for an Order up to the maximum value of €650. The recipient can cash the Postal Money Order at any post office or can lodge it in their bank account. Proof of identity is required to cash the Postal Money Order.

2. **Sterling Draft**: Used to send money abroad. A sterling draft can be purchased to a maximum of £500 sterling. The sterling draft must be lodged in the recipient's bank account, so it is a safe means of sending money through the post.

3. **Eurogiro**: An international money-transfer system used to transfer money electronically in the currency of the receiving country up to a maximum of €1904.61. Eurogiro can be used in the following countries: Ireland, Belgium, Finland, Germany, Great Britain, Italy, Luxembourg, Spain and Switzerland. The money can be lodged directly into a bank account, collected at a nominated post office abroad, or sent by registered post to the recipient's address. It generally takes up to 4 working days for the funds to be transferred.

4. **Western Union Money Transfer**: A national and international money-transfer system available at selected post offices. Unlike Eurogiro, the transfer takes places within a matter of minutes and is used for urgent transactions. The recipient can collect the money in local currency at a designated post office and is not required to have a bank account; but proof of identity is required. The fee for the service varies depending on the amount of money that is transferred.

Marketing Services provided by An Post

An Post has a number of marketing subsidiary companies such as dm.works, PMI and Kompass. These companies offer services to businesses such as: compiling databases, preparing business listings, geographical customer targeting, business analysis and business surveying. Typical marketing services provided by these companies and distributed by An Post are:

Business Response Services

An Post provides businesses with opportunities to use the postal system to allow customers to reply to their business free of charge using **business reply** and **freepost** services. To avail of these two services, a business response licence is obtained from the Post Office and the business pays the postage charge plus a handling fee for every item that is received using these services.

Business reply service

The business reply service consists of special pre-printed envelopes or cards with the business licence number, name and address, followed by the words 'Business Reply' and the post district. No postage is paid by the recipient and the business pays only for the replies it receives.

Business reply envelope

Freepost

A business using the Freepost service **does not** have to enclose a pre-printed envelope or card. The customer replying to the business can use their own stationery and will address the envelope with the business Freepost address as agreed with the Post Office.

A Freepost address is used by a business that advertises in media such as newspapers, radio or TV where the inclusion of a pre-printed card or envelope is not possible.

Direct Marketing Services

Postaim

Postaim is a service that allows a business to distribute mailshots, product samples, leaflets, brochures or other promotional material through the normal postal system to a specific target market — for example, people on a mailing list with a specific interest. The material to be delivered is addressed by the business, and the postmen deliver the **addressed** items when they are delivering the normal post. The fee charged depends on the number and weight of the items to be distributed.

Publicity post

Publicity post is similar to Postaim, but it does not require names and addresses on the items to be delivered. It is therefore suitable for general promotions to a non-specific target market. The promotional material is delivered to every address in a postal district. The fee charged depends on the size of the district covered.

Non Postal Services provided by An Post

An Post operates many other services for the general public through the Post Office network. Such services include:

◆ social welfare payments
◆ deposit and savings accounts
◆ prize bonds
◆ bill pay (eg, telephone, gas, electricity)
◆ licences (TV and dog licences)
◆ insurance (via An Post's subsidiary insurance company, One Direct)
◆ banking (selected post offices offer cash lodgements and withdrawals and credit-card payments to AIB customers)
◆ retail services (such as: gift vouchers, National Lottery tickets, mobile phone top-ups, stationery, and developing of photographs via the Photoexpress service).

Short Questions

1. List four items of equipment used in the preparation of outgoing post.
2. List four features of a franking machine.
3. Outline a procedure for dealing with incoming post.
4. What mail should an administrator/post clerk not open?
5. Give an example of when the following items would be used:
   a) remittance book
   b) circulation list
   c) An Post's Guide to Mail Services.
6. Outline a procedure for dealing with outgoing post.
7. Outline the difference between the following national courier services offered by EMS:
   a) Economy
   b) Priority
   c) Courier.
8. Distinguish between the following international delivery services: economy, priority, Swiftpost Exprès and Swiftpost International.
9. Outline the procedure to follow when registering post.

10. Outline a procedure to follow for receiving registered post.
11. Distinguish between the following postal services:
    a) *Poste Restante*
    b) private post box
    c) COD.
12. Give an example of when it is more appropriate to send money through the post using:
    a) postal money order
    b) sterling draft
    c) Eurosure
    d) Western Union money transfer.
13. Which is the fastest way to send €250 to the UK through the post office?
14. Give an example of why a business might offer a Freepost address as distinct from a business reply service.
15. Distinguish between the following direct marketing facilities: Postaim and Publicity post.
16. List four non-postal services offered by An Post.

Chapter 14 — Electronic and Mobile Communication

Electronic and mobile communication devices enable one to stay in touch with the office while on the move. It refers to the sending, receiving or accessing of information through networks — for example, computer networks (ie, an intranet, extranet, or the Internet) or mobile phone networks).

Today, information can be transmitted directly from one electronic device to almost any other electronic device: for example, an e-mail or fax can be transmitted from a computer to a mobile phone or vice versa. This interconnection between devices has greatly facilitated employees on the move and has resulted in the so-called 'mobile office'.

Electronic document transmission is part of an overall electronic document-management system (EDM), ie, a large-scale computerised filing system where all information is captured, stored and distributed electronically (see Chapter 16).

The Fax Machine and Features

The Fax Machine

The word 'fax' is short for facsimile, which means an exact copy. A fax machine transmits an image of the page via the telephone line to another fax-capable device. A fax machine is generally assigned its own telephone line and number. Sharing the telephone line between the telephone and the fax is suitable only where the volume of incoming and outgoing faxes is low.

In a world that has gone largely digital, the fax machine still plays a major part in business communications and is widely used particularly to transmit signed documents. The traditional concept of a fax machine is a stand-alone or dedicated machine where documents are scanned and received by another stand-alone fax machine. However, with advances in technology and electronic communications this concept has become blurred, as a fax can now be sent and received from any fax-capable device such as:

◆ *Computer with a fax capability:* A modem device with a fax capability is connected to the computer and the telephone line. Using fax software, the fax message is typed or can be imported from a file on disk. The fax number is entered and the DIAL button is selected. A Message dialogue box displays the status of the fax, ie, giving messages such as 'dialling', 'sending', 'error', 'successful', etc. Received faxes are printed on a stand-alone fax machine or stored on the hard disk of a fax-capable computer. To fax a 'hard copy' — ie, a printed page — it must first be scanned into the computer.

◆ *Printer with a fax capability:* Multifunctional printers (MFP) are laser printers that incorporate a fax, scanner and copier. A fax can be sent directly from the computer, or a paper document can be scanned and then faxed via software to any fax-capable device. Incoming faxes are printed or stored in the printer's memory if the printer is busy.

◆ *Other technology:* A fax can also be sent via e-mail as an attachment using special software, or via several websites that offer the facility to send faxes. These technologies are generally used where one party has only one of the technologies, ie, either a fax or e-mail.

Features of a dedicated fax machine

Features	Functions
Automatic Document Feeder	Documents to be transmitted are stacked on the input tray and transmitted in sequence.
LCD (Liquid Crystal Display)	A panel which displays the fax number dialled and status of transmission, ie, 'dialling', 'sending', etc.
Fax/Tel. Auto Change	A function which automatically distinguishes between voice and fax calls when a telephone line is shared.
Automatic Redial	The number is automatically redialled if the receiving fax machine is engaged.
Speed Dialling	The machine can be programmed in alphabetical order by name to store frequently used numbers. To dial a fax number, the person's name is selected, which reduces the risk of misdialling a number.
Retrieval/Forwarding	Enables one to call from another fax machine to their own fax machine's memory to redirect faxes that have been sent — similarly to picking up voicemail messages. Useful if on a business trip.

Features	Functions
Store & Forward	Also known as **delayed transmission**. Documents can be scanned and stored in memory and a timer is preset for transmitting the fax at a later time. Useful to avail of off-peak telephone rates.
Confidential Reception	The fax is stored in the memory of the receiving machine. To print the fax an identification code is entered.
Substitute Reception	If there is no paper in the receiving machine to print the incoming fax, the fax is stored in the memory.
Broadcasting	Allows the same document to be sent to multiple destinations just by scanning it once and selecting the appropriate list of recipient fax numbers. A transmission report informs the sender which numbers received the fax and which did not.
Dual Access	Allows faxes to be sent and received simultaneously. The fax is scanned and stored in memory and sent automatically as soon as the machine is free.
Copier Facility	Modern fax machines incorporate a photocopying facility.
Automatic Log	A facility to log all incoming and outgoing faxes.
Fax On Demand	A facility used to give standard information to the public, eg, information on advertised products. The articles are stored in the memory of the fax machine. Individual articles are retrieved by dialling the fax number and entering the code associated with the particular article.
Fax Polling	A facility which provides a list of faxes available for retrieval at a single request. Each polling request results in the transmission of **all** documents in the polling list. Used by head offices to pass information to branches: a password is required.

Compiling, Sending and Receiving Fax Messages

Compiling Fax Messages

A business generally prepares its own fax coversheet using the templates available with software packages, ie, word processing. When designing a fax coversheet, the following information should be typed on the business letterhead: attention of; from; date; number of pages including this page.

SHARPMAN
Fax Message

Computer Books and Software
11 Northgate Street   Tel No: 0902 - 342675
Athlone   Fax: 0902 - 342677
Co. Westmeath   www.CBS.ie
       info@CBS.ie

Attention of: _____   Dept: _____

From: _____   Date: _____

Number of Pages including Coversheet:

Sending Fax Messages (via a dedicated fax machine)

1. Place the original(s) in the input tray.
2. Enter the fax number or use the 'speed dial' facility. If the message is to be transmitted at a later time (ie, after office hours) the 'store and forward' facility is used.
3. Press the 'start' button to dial the number.
4. When the receiving fax machine answers, the page is scanned through the transmitting fax machine. The mode and speed of communication depend on the capabilities of both machines and the quality of the telephone line.
5. At the end of the transmission, the fax machine prints a **transmission report**. This gives details of the date, time of the transmission, the receiving fax machine's number, the number of pages sent and whether the transmission was successful or not. The transmission report should be attached to the fax as proof that the fax was sent.

Receiving Fax Messages (via a dedicated fax machine)

1. Set the fax machine to ON.
2. Ensure sufficient paper is loaded to print incoming messages, unless the 'substitute reception' facility is available.
3. Check the fax to ensure that the number of pages received is correct, as indicated on the fax cover sheet.
4. Distribute the fax to the appropriate person(s).

Electronic Mail (E-mail)

E-mail allows messages to be sent from one computer to another over a **network**, or from a computer to a mobile phone, or vice versa. In this chapter, we concentrate on how to send and receive e-mail via the Internet.

E-mail messages are created, sent and received using e-mail software such as *MS Outlook*. When MS Outlook is loaded, the **Inbox** screen appears (Figure 14–1).

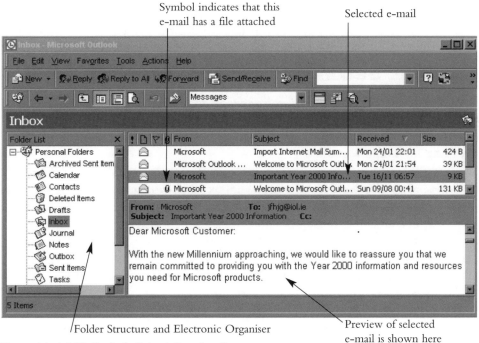

Figure 14–1 MS Outlook 'Inbox' Opening Screen

The **left side** of the Inbox window contains the folder structure to manage incoming/outgoing e-mail:

- ◆ **Inbox:** Incoming e-mail is stored in the Inbox
- ◆ **Outbox:** Queued e-mail (ie, e-mail not yet sent) is stored in the Outbox
- ◆ **Sent Items:** Sent e-mail is stored in the Sent Items folder
- ◆ **Drafts:** Unfinished e-mail (ie, e-mail not queued or sent) are saved to the Drafts folder
- ◆ **Deleted Items:** Deleted e-mail is placed in the Deleted Items folder but are not yet 'permanently' deleted

Other folders can be set up to manage e-mail. For example, regular e-mail received about a specific topic should be moved to a new folder created for this topic, thus making the 'Inbox' more manageable.

The **right side** of the Inbox window contains a list of messages received in the Inbox. Messages are arranged in date and time order of receipt, and display the sender, subject heading and size of e-mail. The paper-clip symbol beside a message indicates that this e-mail has a file attached (Figure 14–1).

To read a message select the message from the Inbox. The selected message is displayed in the lower half of the screen (Figure 14–1). To view the message in its own window, double-click its entry in the Inbox.

Creating, Sending, Receiving, Replying and Forwarding E-mail

Creating an E-mail Message

E-mail should be created off-line if you have a dial-up connection. When the option **New** is selected from the Inbox window (Figure 14–1) a new message window appears (Figure 14–2). The new message window is divided into a **header** and a **message** section.

Header section

In the header section, there are 'fields', ie, boxes labelled 'To:', 'Cc:' and 'Subject:'.

To: The recipient's e-mail address is entered here or it can be selected from the address book. To send the e-mail to more than one person, separate each e-mail address with a semi-colon or select 'multiply e-mail addresses' from the address book.

Cc: 'Cc' means carbon copy. The e-mail addresses of others who are to receive the e-mail for information purposes only are entered here. The person(s) listed in the 'To:' field, are responsible for replying to the e-mail. The 'Cc' field should be used only for internal communication. This is to protect the e-mail addresses of others, as all e-mail addresses are forwarded to each recipient.

Bcc: 'Bcc' means blind carbon copy. It does not appear in the header section by default and is selected from the View Menu. 'Bcc' should be used when sending e-mails to an external mailing list (ie, a subscription list or marketing list) to protect the identity of others on the list. In the 'To' field insert your own e-mail address; in the 'Bcc' field the e-mail addresses of those on the mailing list are inserted. When the recipients receive the e-mail, they will see your e-mail address in the 'To' field and their own in the 'Bcc' field; the identity of other recipients is hidden.

Subject: A heading to indicate the content of the message. Used by the recipient to prioritise the reading of e-mail.

Message section

The message section is where the e-mail message is typed. The message can be formatted using the appropriate buttons on the Format toolbar.

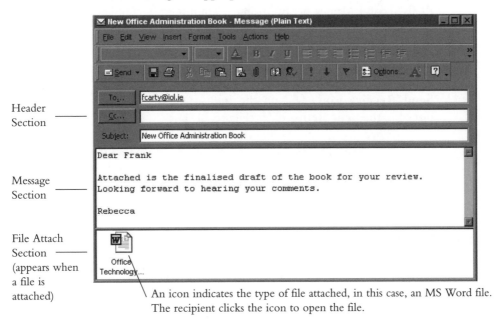

Header
Section

Message
Section

File Attach
Section
(appears when
a file is
attached)

An icon indicates the type of file attached, in this case, an MS Word file. The recipient clicks the icon to open the file.

Figure 14–2 MS Outlook E-mail Creation

File Attach section

Files (ie, word processing, spreadsheets, graphic files, etc) can be attached and distributed with an e-mail. To attach a file, the **File Attach** option from the **Insert** menu is used to select files from a disk. The file(s) selected will appear in the **Attach** section of the e-mail message with an icon indicating the type of file attached. For example, in Figure 14–2, the icon 📑 indicates it is an MS Word file. Other e-mail packages may just indicate the number of attachments without providing icons.

Format of an e-mail address

Every user has a unique e-mail address which typically takes the form of: *user_name@servername.country*

For example, the e-mail address of **nhegarty@iol.ie** is interpreted as: the *user name* is **nhegarty**, and his/her e-mail is stored on a *server* named **iol**, which is located in the *country* of Ireland (**ie**).

Typically, people use the initial of their first name and their full surname as their user name. However, the user name selected must be different from everybody else's on the same server. This is achieved by using the initial of their second name or by using a number, eg, nbhegarty@iol.ie or n2hegarty@iol.ie

Sending E-mail Messages

When the message is complete, it can be sent immediately by clicking the **Send/Receive** icon 📧 on the Inbox window. All 'sent' messages are placed in the **Sent Items** folder (Figure 14–1).

Where a 'dial-up' connection to the Internet is used, non-urgent messages are generally queued by clicking the **Send** icon on the New Message window (Figure 14–2). All queued messages are placed in the **Outbox** folder and are sent to the recipient's 'mailbox' for the price of one local telephone call when the **Send/Receive** icon on the Inbox window is clicked.

Receiving E-mail

E-mail addressed to a recipient is stored in a 'mailbox' on the ISP's server. To retrieve the e-mail, the recipient logs on to the e-mail system and selects the option to check for new mail. Any new messages are downloaded from the ISP's mailbox to the recipient's e-mail **Inbox**. The e-mail received is listed on the right side of the Inbox window along with previously delivered e-mail (Figure 14–1). The Inbox should be tidied up regularly by moving 'read' e-mail to specially created folders.

Replying to E-mail

In general there are two ways to reply to an e-mail:

1. *Reply by sending the message received with your reply:* When the **Reply** icon on the Inbox Window (Figure 14–1) is clicked, the screen displays the original message preceded by the '>' symbol with a space above it for typing the reply. This type of reply is not really suitable for ongoing correspondence as the e-mail message will become very long. This option has the following advantages:

   a) the recipient's e-mail address and the subject heading are completed automatically

   b) the sender can send a short reply as there is no need to remind the recipient of the content of the original e-mail

   The **Reply** icon sends the reply to all addresses listed in the 'To:' field; the **Reply to All** icon sends the reply to all addresses listed in both the 'To:' field and the 'Cc:' field.

2. *Reply by creating a new message:* The received message is not sent. A new message is created and the recipient's e-mail address and a subject heading is entered, along with the content of the reply.

Forwarding E-mail

E-mail can be forwarded directly to others by clicking the forward icon and entering the e-mail addresses of those who are to receive the message or by selecting e-mail addresses from the address book.

To forward e-mail internally within the business, a private e-mail system must be in place, ie, a network configured to manage e-mail.

Managing Received E-mail

When you use e-mail your correspondents expect a quick response, so read your e-mail regularly. E-mail should be managed properly; it is easy to let an overwhelming number of e-mails accumulate in your Inbox. Some tips to manage e-mail are:

◆ *Flag e-mails:* 'Flagging' e-mails is helpful in prioritising those that require follow-up. It is so called because a 'flag' symbol is placed on the e-mail. To set a 'Flag', right-click on the e-mail and select 'Follow-up' from the drop-down menu. In the 'Flag to Follow-up' dialogue box, the action required is selected with a date and time to act as a reminder.

◆ *Storing e-mail:* A folder structure should be set up for specific categories of e-mail.

For example, assume the business is constantly dealing with another business called 'Perfect Insurance Ltd' about specific topics such as: fire insurance, public liability insurance, etc. A folder for the business should be set up called 'Perfect Insurance', and within this folder sub-folders should be set up for the specific categories of correspondence, ie, fire insurance, public liability insurance, etc — just like organising files on a disk.

The e-mail sent should be stored with the reply so that a complete record of correspondence relating to a particular topic is stored together. This is achieved by moving the appropriate e-mail from the 'Inbox' and 'Sent Items' folder to the newly created folder. Storing e-mail in categorised folders makes the 'Inbox' and 'Sent Items' folder more manageable.

◆ *Delete e-mail:* Delete unwanted mail. Deleted mail is placed in the **Deleted Items** folder but is not yet permanently deleted, so this folder needs to be cleared on a regular basis.

◆ *Use other facilities:* Most e-mail packages provide other functionalities such as a task manager, calendar and filter options. The task manager can be used to schedule activities on a daily, weekly or future basis. It can be linked to the calendar to provide a reminder of specific dates to follow up on e-mails sent or received, or other activities. The filter option can be set up to automatically file e-mails (sent or received) to an appropriate folder based on the e-mail address.

Mobile Communication

Mobile communication has become an essential part of business communication. Examples of mobile communication include mobile phones and pagers. The pager, however, is facing strong competition from the mobile phone.

A mobile phone is a portable phone powered by a rechargeable battery, allowing calls to be made and received almost anywhere in the world. In addition to making and receiving calls, mobile phones offer extra facilities which include: sending text messages, photos and small video clips; accessing the Internet and e-mail; downloading games and music, depending on the generation of technology behind the mobile phone. The current generation of mobile phones use either 3G or 2.5G technology (also known as **GPRS** — General Packet Radio Service).

Features of the mobile phone

The features available on a fixed-line telephone are generally available with most mobile telephones, such as: call display, speed dialling, last-number redial, clear last digit, hold, call forwarding, call waiting and call barring. Additional features include:

Phone Book	Used to store phone numbers which can be accessed via the phone. The capacity of the phone book is dependent on the model of phone.
Ring Tones	A selection of ring tones — to distinguish the ring tone from other mobile phones. Ring tones may also be customised, ie, record your own message or song!
Vibration Alert	Lets the user know that an incoming call is being received via a vibration which is felt if the phone is close to your body. Useful if you don't want the phone to sound a ring tone.
Scratchpad	While on a call a telephone number can be entered in the scratchpad memory and saved to the Phone Book.
Organisers	Most mobile phones include a range of extra functions such as: a clock, stopwatch, calculator, calendar, diary, to-do list, alarm reminder, etc. These are useful features for employees on the move.
Voice Mail	If the phone is switched off or not answered, the caller is diverted to the mobile provider's answering service. Voice messages left are notified to the receiver when the phone is switched on and are retrieved by dialling the mobile provider.
SMS (Short Message Service)	Referred to as 'texting', text messages can be sent and received via mobile phones. Many businesses use SMS to provide a mobile information service to their customers, eg, information on the weather, lotto results, next DART), etc. The user enters the code for the service and dials a number.
MMS (Multimedia Message Service)	Referred to as 'picture texting' — a standard feature on camera phones. Messages can contain pictures, audio and longer text messages of over 160 characters. MMS is being used by businesses to provide an enhanced mobile information service, ie, pictures of products, previews of music releases, etc.
VMS (Video Message Service)	A short video can be recorded and sent to another compatible phone. In addition, VMS enables people to view each other as they speak on the phone. The

Dual Band/ Tri Band	service can be switched off when not required. There are three frequency bands allocated to use with mobile networks: 900 MHz, 1800 MHz and 1900 MHz. Dual band phones allow access to the 900 MHz and 1800 MHz bands used in Europe and Asia Pacific. Triband phones allow access to the 1900 MHz band which is used in North America and Canada.
Roaming	Allows international calls to be made from Ireland or while abroad. International calls **received** while abroad are charged as follows: a) the caller pays the charge to the mobile provider's network in Ireland b) the receiver pays the cost of the call from Ireland to the foreign country
Data and Fax Capability	A built-in data and fax capability. The mobile phone is connected to a PC or handheld computer (PDA) via a cable or an infrared link (built into the phone), allowing faxes and data files to be sent and received while on the move.
Internet Access & E-mail	Full Internet access and e-mail is provided via 3G phones and some GPRS (2.5G phones). 3G uses a broadband connection at up to 2MB per second and is the fastest technology to access the Internet. The cost of accessing the Internet via 3G and GPRS is based on the amount of data transferred, and not by the amount of time online as with earlier phones.
WAP (Wireless Application Protocol)	WAP is an older technology developed to access websites on pre-GPRS phones. The websites, generally known as WAP sites, are specifically designed basic sites with text and simple logos. However, WAP is not a fading technology and there are a huge range of WAP sites available through a mobile provider's network, giving the latest details on: sports, news and weather, entertainment guide, travel, traffic, finance, employment opportunities, etc. In addition, many '*m-commerce*' WAP sites are available such as banking, similar to banking over the phone.
Bluetooth	Bluetooth is a radio-based technology that enables devices such as: mobile phones, portable computers and PDAs to communicate with each other without

cables. The maximum range at present is 10 metres. Bluetooth is used to back up the mobile phone to a computer and is also the technology used with headsets, facilitating calls to be made or received without holding the phone or using cables.

Mobile Network in Ireland

The mobile network in Ireland is operated by four providers: O$_2$, Vodafone, Meteor and 3(Ireland) (a recent entry to the market). Mobile networks may also be referred to by their prefix number, eg, the O$_2$ network may be referred to simply as the 086 network. The prefixes for the other networks are 087, 085 and 083 respectively. However, as it is now possible to change networks and keep your old number, including the prefix, it is no longer possible to know which network a user is on from the prefix number.

This has implications for the charges paid when dialling a mobile phone. For example, dialling to the same network is cheaper than dialling from one network to another. So if a caller on the 086 network dials another 086 number which is on a different network, the caller will be charged more. However, the caller will hear a beep tone when dialling a different network using the same prefix number, the beep tone indicating a change of networks.

All mobile providers offer the following types of subscription connection to their networks:

◆ **Fixed contract:** A contract is entered into for a fixed term, generally one year. With a contract there is a range of payment options to choose from, depending on your usage of the phone. Each payment option has a different *monthly fee,* which will include a different set *of free call credit.* In addition, there is a greater selection of mobile phones to choose from and the cost of the mobile phone is subsidised by the network. However, if the phone is not used, or you switch to another network, the monthly subscription must be paid to the end of the contract.

◆ **Prepaid package:** The prepaid package is known by different names according to the network, ie, '*Ready-to-Go*' with Vodafone, '*Speakeasy*' with O2, etc.
With this option, there is no contract, monthly fee or phone bills. However, the choice of mobile phones and tarriff-rate options is limited. A prepaid phone is purchased which includes an amount of 'free call credit'. When the phone is running low on call credit, a message is sent to the phone. Call credits can be topped up via an ATM.

Guide to Connection Option

When deciding which type of connection to choose (ie, contract or prepaid) consider how many calls you would typically make (peak/off peak) per month. If the total cost is greater than the 'basic' monthly contract fee, a contract should be considered, as this has built-in free calls and the phone can be upgraded for a nominal fee at the end of the contract. The prepaid packages are suitable for low-volume or controlled usage.

If the decision is to go for a contract package, the first step is to compare the various *payment options* across networks (ie, the *monthly fee* and *free call credit*).

The next step is to compare the cost of the following services outside the free call credit, during peak and off-peak rates:

◆ call from a mobile network to a fixed-line phone
◆ call to SAME mobile network
◆ call to OTHER mobile network
◆ check voicemail
◆ send SMS (texting)
◆ send MMS (pictures)
◆ send VMS (video)
◆ access WAP sites
◆ access the Internet and e-mail.

Having done the analysis, choose the network provider that offers best value for your needs. Your needs could be just simply calls to all mobile networks, SMS and MMS, mostly during off-peak times.

Short Questions

1. Define electronic and mobile communication.
2. Define Electronic Document Transmission (EDM).
3. Outline recent developments in fax technology.
4. Describe the following features of a fax machine:
   a) broadcasting
   b) dual access
   c) confidential reception
   d) substitute reception.
5. Distinguish between the following features of a fax machine:
   a) store and forward
   b) fax retrieval
   c) fax on demand
   d) fax polling.
6. What information should be included on a fax cover sheet?

7. Define the term 'e-mail'.

8. Explain the format of an e-mail address.

9. What details should be included in the following fields of an e-mail message?
   a) To:
   b) Cc:
   c) Bcc:
   d) Subject:

10. Distinguish between the following features of e-mail:
    a) forward
    b) reply
    c) reply to all.

11. Describe how e-mails are received by a recipient.

12. List and briefly describe four ways to manage e-mail.

13. Describe the following features of a mobile phone:
    a) SMS
    b) MMS
    c) VMS
    d) Bluetooth.

14. Distinguish between the following features of a mobile phone:
    a) data and fax capability
    b) dualband and triband
    c) Internet access.

15. List four factors you would consider when deciding between a prepaid phone and a contract-based connection to a mobile network.

16. What is a WAP? List the services available via WAP.

Summary

In a small business, the administrator may be responsible for incoming mail, ensuring it is distributed to the appropriate persons. The office junior may be responsible for collecting outgoing mail from the different departments, packaging and franking, and ensuring it gets to the post office on time. Some postal items may need to be registered or a certificate of postage may be required. Staff dealing with the post should be familiar with the wide range of services available from An Post such as: registered post, airmail services, courier services, etc. Large businesses that rely heavily on the postal system, eg, a mail-order business, will have a separate mail department where all postal activities are carried out and elaborate equipment for sorting, addressing and packaging will be used.

Developments in mobile communication have facilitated the 'mobile office'. With electronic data transmission such as the fax, e-mail and services through a mobile phone, eg, faxmail, messaging services (ie, SMS, MMS, VMS), Internet and e-mail, it is now possible for employees to conduct their business as if they were sitting at their desk in the office.

Assignments

1. You have just been appointed Post Clerk for a new mail-order magazine company and are responsible for developing a procedure for handling the post. Write a report outlining, step by step, the procedure you intend to implement. Recommend the equipment you will need to accomplish the handling of incoming and outgoing post.

2. Your business needs a franking machine to deal with the increased volume of outgoing post. Examine three models of franking machine available and associated prices. Which would you recommend for the above mail-order magazine company and why?

3. Use the current Post Office guide to cost the following:
   a) parcel to France weighing 1 kg
   b) parcel to Zambia weighing 4 kg
   c) parcel to Roscommon weighing 2 kg 159 g.

   For each of the above, recommend one postal service and one courier service that will ensure that these parcels arrive by the fastest method.

4. Compare and contrast three types of fax machine available on the market today and write a report recommending one to the manager.

5. Mobile-phone operators in Ireland offer different packages which generally include: free-call value and different peak rates depending on the monthly subscription fee paid. Compare three operators on the assumption that your boss uses the phone approximately 500 minutes a month with approximately sixty per cent of these calls being made before 6 pm weekdays. Recommend the best option, justifying your answer.

6. Most businesses communicate to a large extent by e-mail. Prepare a presentation explaining how to send an e-mail with an attachment, how to reply to an e-mail and how best to organise incoming e-mail.

7. Learn how to use the e-mail system at your college. Briefly describe how you perform each of the following tasks:
   a) compose and send a message
   b) reply to a message you received
   c) delete a message you received
   d) forward a message you received to someone other than the person who sent the message
   e) send a carbon copy of the message
   f) send a message to a mailing list.

Unit 5 — Storing and Retrieving Information

Introduction

As organisations are constantly involved in business transactions, they generate a great deal of correspondence through various media: letters, memoranda, fax, telephone and e-mail. The business needs a system to store and protect all records (active and non-active) for future reference. Unit 5 is divided into two chapters:

Chapter 15 — Manual Filing System

Reviews the essential elements to consider when designing a filing system, the equipment necessary for filing and rules and procedures for a manual filing system.
- Devising a Manual Filing System
- Storage Arrangement of Files
- Categorising and Sorting Information
- Cross-referencing and Indexing
- Rules for Alphabetical Filing
- Filing Procedure

Chapter 16 — Electronic Document Management (EDM)

Reviews electronic filing systems where all files, including paper files, are stored either on microform or computer media such as disks, tapes, CD or DVD.
- Microform Filing System
- Electronic Document Management System

Chapter 15 — Manual Filing System

manual filing system is where files are stored in paper format in appropriately sized filing cabinets or folders. Filing is a methodical way of storing information so that it can be located when required.

An efficient filing system will ensure files:
a) are not lost or misplaced
b) are up to date and complete
c) are accurate (avoid duplication)
d) can be retrieved quickly
e) are secure and kept confidential.

Devising a Manual Filing System

When a manual filing system is being devised, the following factors are taken into account:
a) location of the files (centralised or decentralised)
b) equipment to be used
c) categories of information to be set up (eg, customers, suppliers, products)
d) methods of sorting within chosen categories (eg, alphabetical, numerical)
e) procedure for filing and retrieving documents
f) retention policy
g) security and access rights
h) assignment of responsibility to individuals to manage and control the system.

Location of Filing System

The location of the filing system will vary from one business to another depending on: volume of information, number of users, frequency of access and confidentiality of the information. Where information is used by several individuals, it is not advisable for each individual to have their own private copies of files. The duplication of information may lead to different versions of the same file as different amendments may be made to each copy.

An important question in designing a filing system for a business is, where should the files be located? The choices available are:

a) **centralised filing,** where all the files for the whole business are stored in one central location;
b) **decentralised filing,** where all the files for a department are stored centrally within that department;
c) **individual filing,** where individuals store their own files;
d) **a combination of the above**, For example, centralised filing could be implemented in respect of files which are not in constant use and those which are not specific to any one department. Decentralised filing could be used for files that are specific to a department, while files that are specific to an individual's work may be stored by that individual.

The decision as to where files are located is a management decision and each has advantages and disadvantages, as outlined in the following tables:

Centralised Filing	
Advantages	**Disadvantages**
1. The staff involved will be trained in the filing system. 2. Security of records is guaranteed because strict procedures will be devised regarding the retrieval of files. 3. Related matters from all departments will be filed together or appropriately cross-referenced, thus ensuring files are accurate. 4. Less equipment is required as centralisation ensures better utilisation of equipment, thus saving space and costs.	1. There may be a delay in obtaining files due to the location of the Filing Department and/or the file requested may be with another user. 2. The classification system chosen may not suit the needs of all departments, yet they have to conform to the standardised system.

Decentralised Filing	
Advantages	**Disadvantages**
1. Information relating to a particular department is stored within that department thus reducing delays in obtaining files. 2. The department can implement a classification system suitable for its needs.	1. Correct filing procedures may not be implemented. For example, a file may be removed without anyone indicating who has the file, a new file may be set up where one already exists or a file may be misfiled. 2. More filing equipment is required as full utilisation of equipment is not possible, thus increasing the space required and costs involved.

Equipment in a Manual Filing System

Filing equipment used in a manual system ranges from folders to cabinets.

Box file

◆ **Box file:** A box has a strong spring clip inside the box to hold the items inserted. It is used to hold *miscellaneous* items such as leaflets, catalogues or information which is not referenced frequently. The information is generally filed in **chronological order,** ie, date order, where the most recent item is placed on top of the pile.

◆ **Ring binder:** A ring binder is a folder with two or more rings used for filing *frequently referenced information*, such as price lists, lists of spare parts, etc. The document is punched with holes (generally two) so that it can be placed into the rings of the binder. Dividers which are pre-punched with holes are used to separate the information in the folder. The ring binder is opened by pulling the rings apart.

Lever arch binder

◆ **Lever arch binder:** This is similar to a ring binder except that there is a lever for opening and closing the rings. A lever arch binder is generally larger than a ring binder.

◆ **Concertina folder:** A folder that consists of a succession of pockets which open out; each pocket can be labelled by subject order or date order depending on its use. It is generally used for storing items which have yet to be processed.

◆ **Filing cabinets:** A wide range of different filing cabinets is available on the market. The models differ in size and in the way files are arranged in the filing cabinet.

Storage Arrangement of Files

The choice of storage arrangement depends on space available, suitability of access, cost and fitness for purpose.

There are four main storage arrangements:

1. **Vertical storage:** Files are stored **upright** one behind the other. This is the method used in a traditional filing cabinet. A vertical filing cabinet is fitted with frames which are positioned on either side of the drawer.

'Suspension folders', which are fitted with hooks, rest on the frames one behind the other. 'Name tags' are placed on the top of each suspension folder to indicate the name or number of the file. To subdivide the information which is held in a suspension folder, **manilla folders** are used. The drawers of the filing cabinet are also labelled for ease of reference.

Vertical filing cabinet

2. **Lateral storage:** Files are stored **side by side** like books on a shelf. It is a suitable arrangement for a large filing system. The filing equipment selected may be closed (ie, with doors or sliding shutters), open, or a carousel which is a rotary filing cabinet. Where the filing cabinet is used to store suspension folders, the filing cabinet is fitted with frames which are positioned to the front and back of the shelf. The suspension folders rest on the frames of the shelf side by side, maximising the use of space. 'Name tabs' are placed on the **side** of each suspension folder which indicate the name or number of the file.

Lateral filing system

3. **Horizontal storage:** Files are stored **flat**, one on top of the other. This method is suitable for small-volume temporary storage (ie, in/out trays) or to store large documents unfolded, such as plans and drawings.

4. **Combination of the above:** Filing cabinets can be purchased which accommodate all three types of storage arrangements, ie, vertical, lateral and horizontal. These filing cabinets are suitable for a small office which requires a versatile arrangement, ie, to store books, lever arch files, box files, large documents unfolded and suspension folders, etc.

Rotary filing system

Storage Arrangement — Advantages/Disadvantages		
	Advantages	**Disadvantages**
Vertical	1. All files in a drawer can be seen at a glance. 2. Files are stored at a height which is accessible. 3. Files are protected from dust by being enclosed in the cabinet. 4. Files can be made secure by locking the cabinet.	1. Utilises a large amount of floor space as extra space is required for opening the drawers. 2. Wasted storage space. There is a limit to the height of the cabinets for safety reasons. 3. Two drawers cannot be opened at the same time for safety reasons, (ie, weight would be unevenly distributed), therefore staff have to wait their turn to use the system.
Lateral	1. Less storage space is required for filing cabinets which are open or which have sliding shutters, as no space is required to open drawers. 2. Lateral filing cabinets can be built higher than vertical cabinets. 3. More files can be seen at the same time. 4. More than one person can access the files at the same time.	1. Difficult to read file titles, especially files placed at a height. 2. Difficult to access files stored higher up and lower down. 3. With an open shelf arrangement less protection is given to the files.
Horizontal	1. Simple equipment. 2. Cheap. 3. Can hold large documents flat. 4. Suitable for temporary storage or large documents.	1. Difficult and time-consuming to locate specific files. 2. Can become unmanageable. 3. Files are subject to wear and tear. 4. Can be difficult to replace file in correct position.

Categorising and Sorting Information

Information is held about several aspects of a business's life such as staff, stock, customers, suppliers, legal documents, financial position, etc. Therefore, when deciding how to organise information, we need to consider both the **categories** of information and how to **sort** the information within each category.

The organisation must decide on the broad categories under which to file its information. For example, customers could be one broad category, equipment could be another.

When the information has been categorised, the next decision is how to sort the information within **each** category. For example, using the customer category, are customers filed alphabetically by surname or is each customer allocated a number and filed in numerical order?

Files can be sorted in the following orders:

a) alphabetical
b) numerical
c) chronological
d) subject
e) geographical.

The method chosen depends on many factors, including:

◆ category of information (eg, customers, products)
◆ volume of information (implications for expansion)
◆ frequency of use (time factor in locating information, ie, direct versus indirect system)
◆ whether related information is to be filed together, ie, all details relating to a certain region (geographical) or all expenses for a business (subject) or all related books (Dewey system).

Alphabetical Order

The alphabetical order is a widely used method for filing correspondence. The files are sorted in alphabetical order of the category. For example, if the category is customers, the files will be sorted alphabetically by surname. Alphabetical filing systems are also known as **direct filing systems,** as there is no need to look up an index to find a file.

The filing cabinet will have labels on the drawer to indicate the contents, eg, Customers A–F, etc. Inside the drawers, **guide cards** are inserted to divide the alphabet, which makes locating a group of files easier. The customers' files whose surnames begin with the letter on the guide card are located behind the guide card.

Each file is labelled with the customer's name and filed alphabetically by surname. For example, in the diagram below, we have customers Leech, Doyle & Co. and Mr Harry Louth filed alphabetically after the guide card 'L'.

There may also be a file for **miscellaneous information** which is used for storing infrequent correspondence. For example, there could be other customers whose surname begins with 'L' but with whom the volume of correspondence is minor and infrequent. A separate file will not be opened for each of these customers; they are placed in a file called **miscellaneous 'L'**. If the correspondence increases for any of the miscellaneous 'L' customers, a new file is opened for that customer and the details transferred from the miscellaneous file to the new file.

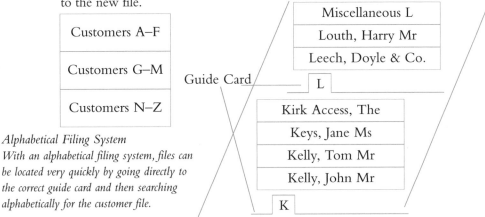

Alphabetical Filing System
With an alphabetical filing system, files can be located very quickly by going directly to the correct guide card and then searching alphabetically for the customer file.

Numerical Order

The files are allocated a number and a new file is simply given the next consecutive number. A **separate alphabetical index** will be kept to 'cross-reference' the file number.

Numerical filing is an **indirect system**, as you cannot go directly to the filing cabinet and locate the file. For example, if you do not know a customer's number, you would have to: (a) look up an alphabetical index of customers' surnames, (b) read the number associated with that customer and (c) go to the filing cabinet and search numerically to locate the file.

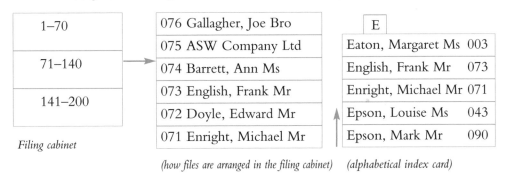

Numerical Filing System
To locate a file in a numerical system, an alphabetical index of customers' names is first referenced for the file number. The file is then located by going to the filing cabinet and searching numerically for the correct customer file.

Other Numerical Systems

There are other numerical systems used for more complex filing. These include:

Alphanumeric system

An alphanumeric system allocates a letter and a number to a document. For example, a document relating to a business called Office Supplies could be filed under OS/3. The letters 'OS' refer to the file called Office Supplies, and the number is the position of the document within the file. An alphabetical index of the files would be maintained.

Dewey decimal system

The Dewey decimal system is used for filing books in a library. It consists of three pairs of digits. The *first pair* refers to the subject, the middle pair refers to the topic within that subject, and the last pair refers to the particular book. For example, the following numbers could be allocated to **subjects**:

Business Studies 10

Accounting 20

Law 30

The **topics** within a subject are allocated the *second pair of digits* in sequence. For example, the subject Law 30 could be divided into:

Business Law 30.01

Company Law 30.02

Land Law 30.03

The **books** within each topic are allocated the *third pair of digits* in sequence. For example, using the topics Business Law and Company Law, you could have the following books:

30.01.01 *Business Law in Ireland*

30.01.02 *Business Law Simplified*

30.01.03 *A Guide to Business Law*

30.02.01 *Companies Act 1963*

Using this system, when a new book has to be added to the system it can be placed with the correct subject and topic, simply by giving it the next number within the subject and topic classification. For example, if the library purchased another business law book, it would get the number 30.01.04 and would be placed on the shelf beside the other business law books.

An alphabetic index is also maintained listing the books in alphabetical order of subject.

The Dewey decimal system could also be used in business. For example, in a college the following system could be used:

FULL-TIME COURSES	20		
Secretarial		20.01	
Certificate in Secretarial Studies			20.01.01
Diploma in Secretarial Studies			20.01.02
Business Studies		20.02	
PART-TIME COURSES	30		
Computers		30.01	
Spreadsheets			30.01.01
Database			30.01.02
Word Processing			30.01.03
EXAMINATION RESULTS	40		
Certificate in Business Studies		40.01	
Sept 2005			40.01.01
Sept 2004			40.01.02
Sept 2003			40.01.03

Terminal digit system

This is a numerical system which consists of three pairs of digits read from right to left. The last pair refers to a drawer, the middle pair refers to the position of the file within that drawer, and the first pair refers to a document within that file. For example, the number 20.02.04 refers to drawer 4, file number 2, document number 20 within that file. Every document will be numbered and placed in the correct position within the filing cabinet. An alphabetical index has to be maintained.

Other Classifications
Chronological order

Chronological means sorting by date order. Documents are filed according to the date, with the most recent date first. Chronological filing is not generally used as a core system, but it is the typical method of filing within files, ie, the most recent correspondence received will be placed on the top of the appropriate file.

It is used as a core classification method only where the date would have meaning; for example, in a school when files are archived (put away permanently) it is appropriate to file by academic year. You could have an 'examination results' file for 2004/05 and the results within that file sorted in alphabetical order by classes or subjects.

Subject order

There are certain categories of information where subject filing is appropriate. For example, in relation to insurances for a business, it may be more appropriate to have a file labelled insurance rather than filing under the individual insurance brokers' names. In this way, all information concerning insurance will be in the same place rather than split between the individual brokers.

The subject insurance may be subdivided into categories like fire insurance, public liability insurance, etc, where the volume of data in relation to each type of insurance justifies it. The subjects are filed in alphabetical order.

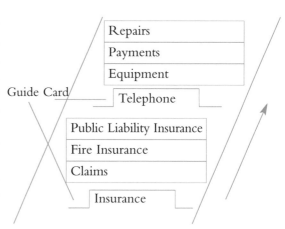

Subject Filing
The files are organised according to subject topic. Within each subject topic files are stored alphabetically.

Where subjects are subdivided into topics, the topics are also filed alphabetically within the subject.

Other examples where subject filing is appropriate are expenses, training, products, repairs, etc. Subject filing is used by students; their lever arch file is divided into sections such as office procedures, bookkeeping and communications.

Geographical order

Geographical classification is suitable for businesses with a high level of sales, mail order, imports, exports, etc. The organisation divides its business into regions. For example, a business with many sales outlets in Ireland would divide the filing system up into counties; the sales force in each county would then be filed in either alphabetical

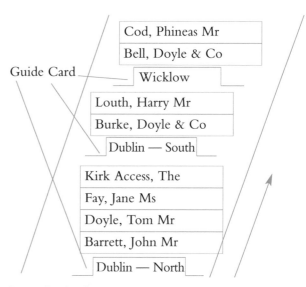

Geographical Filing
To locate a file in a geographical system, an alphabetical index of customers is first referenced for the geographical region. The file is then located by going alphabetically to the correct region and searching alphabetically for the correct customer file.

or numerical order. An index is required to link a person to a county. The index stores the names in alphabetical order and states under which county that person is filed.

It is therefore an indirect system like the numerical system.

Colour-coding system

Where the filing system is used to store different categories of information a colour-coding system may be used. The files are subdivided into their categories, and different-coloured 'name' tabs or folders are used for each category. This prevents someone placing a document in the correct 'name' file but in the wrong file.

For example, if the filing system contains customers, suppliers and employees, blue-coloured 'name' tabs may be used for customers, red for suppliers and yellow for employees. The files will be arranged in alphabetical order of category, customers followed by employees then suppliers. The files within each category will also be arranged in alphabetical order.

Colour-coding systems could also be used in a subject or geographical system; for example, in a geographical system counties could be colour-divided into north and south.

Comparison of Various Sorting Methods			
Sort Method	**Advantages**	**Disadvantages**	**Uses**
Alphabetical	• Easy to understand and operate • A direct system — no need to consult an index • Miscellaneous files can be set up	• The system is not easily expanded; considerable reshuffling of files may be necessary • Where surnames are the same, there is a danger of misfiling a document	• Generally where another system is not preferable • Suppliers, clients, personal records
Numerical	• System is easily expanded • No need to pre-allocate space in the filing cabinet • The file number can be used as a reference • The index provides useful information in its own right	• An indirect system — an index must be consulted • Files could be mis-filed if the number was read incorrectly	• Large filing systems • For business documentation, ie, orders, invoices, etc • By banks

Comparison of Various Sorting Methods			
Sort Method	**Advantages**	**Disadvantages**	**Uses**
Other numerical systems	• Each document can be given a unique number • Efficient in large filing systems • Unlimited expansion • High level of accuracy is possible • Dewey system is particularly suitable for libraries	• Intricate to learn and operate • Requires indexing	• Large filing systems, spread over different locations (terminal) • To file related topics together (Dewey) • Libraries (Dewey) • For more precision (alphanumerical)
Chronological	• The most recent correspondence is first in the file • Simple to accomplish	• For some applications, it can be difficult over time to locate specific documents, ie, you may forget the time period when a particular transaction occurred • Not a common core filing system	• Documents within files are stored in date order • For temporary storage before filing • Minutes of meetings • Bank statements • Newspaper archives
Subject	• Similar to the alphabetical system — direct • Related information is filed together	• The system is not easily expanded • Subject areas may overlap, therefore cross-referencing may be necessary	• To keep related topics together • Student folders • Educational institutions
Geographical	• A convenient way of subdividing customers or sales representatives • Colour coding can be used to speed up location of files	• An indirect system — an index must be consulted • A good knowledge of the geographical region is required	• Sales offices and mail-order companies • Businesses that deal in import and/or exports

Cross-referencing and Indexing

Cross-referencing

A cross-reference is used to relate one file to another. Examples of uses are:

1. **to locate information in an indirect filing system.** For example, in a numerical system when a file is requested and the file number is unknown, the alphabetical index is referenced to get the file number.

2. **where a file could be filed under two names.** For example, confusion sometimes arises as to where to locate a file. A file on VHI could be filed under VHI or Voluntary Health Insurance. There are rules for filing, but sometimes an organisation adapts the rules to suit its particular needs. To avoid confusion it may set up two files for that particular organisation; one file named VHI and the other named Voluntary Health Insurance. All the information would be stored in one file, say the Voluntary Health Insurance file and the other file, the VHI file, would be empty with a reference saying 'see Voluntary Health Insurance'.

A cross-reference card is set up and placed in the alternative location (in this case in the VHI file) so that staff are directed to the correct location.

Cross-reference card inserts in file

3. **to refer a person to a related file.** When a business changes its name, a cross-reference card is placed in the old file directing users to the new file. The old file is closed and the date noted. A card is also placed in the new file so that users can reference past data.

4. **where files are related or linked.** For example, where do we file documents relating to the maintenance of an item of equipment? Is it in the servicer's file or in the equipment file? The answer to this question may seem simple enough, but what if the servicer also services other equipment and the equipment is serviced by more than one person? Here we need separate files for each item of equipment and for each of the servicers. The servicer's file would contain correspondence and the equipment files would contain a service history. A cross-reference card is placed with each servicer's file, linking that person to all the equipment s/he services. A cross-reference card is also placed with each equipment file linking those files to the servicer's file.

This problem can also be overcome by putting a copy of the linked information in the appropriate files. For example, if Mr 'X' services the photocopier, then the details can be placed in both the Mr 'X' file and the photocopier file. Where the information is duplicated, a cross-reference is not necessary. However, this is not recommended, as the files become bulky. There is also the danger of the information being omitted from one file, leading to inaccurate records.

Indexing

An index is used with the numerical and geographical filing systems to locate files. The index is arranged in alphabetical order of file names and is referenced to find the number associated with the particular file.

An index will also contain some other information, which may be enough to eliminate the need for further reference. For instance, if a request is for a customer's phone number, the index may provide this information.

An index can be used to highlight or 'signal' particular items of information. This is achieved by using an alterable colour-coding method, where a coloured tag is placed onto the edge of a card or page. For example, a red tag may signal an overdue account. An index should be kept up to date: every time a file is added to the filing system an entry should be made in the index.

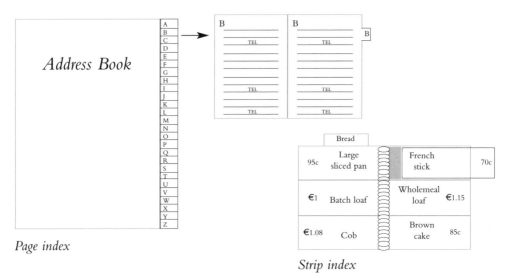

Page index

Strip index

Indexing equipment

Various types of indexing equipment are used to record information: page index, card index and strip index. The choice of indexing system will depend on:

◆ how much information needs to be recorded (strip versus card)

◆ space required for the system (visible card index versus vertical card index)

◆ maintenance of the system, ie, the removal or addition of information

◆ how frequently the information will be accessed (system needs to be close at hand).

Page Index: Is a book or loose-leaf binder which contains one or more pages for each letter of the alphabet. It is used to store small amounts of information which are accessed frequently, ie, price list, telephone numbers, etc.

Vertical Card Index: Cards, A6 or A7 in size are stored upright in a filing box. Alphabetical guide cards are used to separate. Coloured cards are available for classification purposes. With this system it is easy to add or remove cards as required, as the alphabetical order will not be affected.

Vertical card index

Visible Card Index: Cards overlap each other but the first line of each card is visible. The essential details are recorded on the first line to enable the card to be located.

Rotary Card Index: Cards overlap each other but are separated by alphabetical guide cards. The wheel is turned to get the required card section.

Strip Index: Consists of strips of cards which are inserted into plastic frames of a folder. The pages of the folder are arranged alphabetically. These systems are available in folder format or free-standing desk units. They are used for simple data which can be held on one or two lines, eg, telephone numbers, product prices, etc.

Rules for Alphabetical Filing

1. The surname is placed before the first name and if the surnames are the same, the first name decides the position. Titles are placed after the first name, eg:

Before Filing	After Filing
Prof John Keyes	Brady, Alice (Ms)
Ms Jane Keyes	Keyes, Jane (Ms)
Ms Alice Brady	Keyes, John (Prof)
Mrs Lucy Power	Power, Lucy (Mrs)

2. If no first name is given, the surname comes first. Nothing comes before something, eg:

Before Filing	After Filing
Mr John Smith	Smith
Fr J Smith	Smith, J (Fr)
Smith	Smith, John (Mr)

3. If the business name has a personal name, the surname is written first, followed by the first name and the remainder of the name, eg:

Before Filing	After Filing
Sharon Smith & Co	Black, Peter & Co
Peter Black & Co	Smith, Sharon & Co

4. If a business has several names, the first name is taken as the surname and filed accordingly, eg:

Before Filing	After Filing
Messrs Hegarty, Gallagher & Coghlan	Hegarty, Gallagher & Coghlan, Messrs

5. When 'The' is the first word of the name, it is placed at the end of the name, eg:

Before Filing	After Filing
The Open University	Open University, The

6. Prefixes such as De, La, etc are included as part of the name and filed accordingly. However, names beginning with Mac, Mc, M' are treated as if they were all spelt Mac and names beginning St and Saint are treated as if they were all fully spelt. However, the original spelling is kept, eg:

Before Filing	After Filing
Gerry Devries	De Vries, Ciaran
Jane De Vries	Devries, Gerry
Ciaran De Vries	De Vries, Jane
La Stampa Restaurant	La Stampa Restaurant
Thomas Laste	Laste, Thomas
Patricia M'Sparran	McCarthy, John
Gerald MacDonagh & Sons	MacDonagh, Gerald & Sons
Ciara MacSweeney	M'Sparran, Patricia
John McCarthy	MacSweeney, Ciara
St Brendan's College	Sain, Michael
Michael Sain	St Brendan's College
Saint Michael's Church	Saint Michael's Church
Ms Mary Sweeney	Sweeney, Mary (Ms)

7. The apostrophe is ignored. The word is treated as one, but the original spelling is kept, eg:

Before Filing	After Filing
Brian D'arcy	Darcy, Brendan
Brendan Darcy	D'arcy, Brian
ORM Sales Agents	O'Riordan's Pharmacy
O'Riordan's Pharmacy	Orlagh Park House
Orlagh Park House	ORM Sales Agents

8. Treat numbers as if they were spelt out in words but keep the original name, eg:

Before Filing	After Filing
400 Supercal Co.	500 ABC Ltd (filed under 'F')
500 ABC Ltd	400 Supercal Co. (filed under 'F')
60 Calls Ltd	700 Cab Call Ltd (filed under 'S')
700 Cab Call Ltd	60 Calls Ltd (filed under 'S')

9. Departments are filed by keyword of department, eg:

Before Filing	After Filing
Department of Foreign Affairs	Business Studies, Department
Department of Social Welfare	Foreign Affairs, Department of
Business Studies Department	Social Welfare, Department of

10. Treat **known** abbreviated names as being spelt out in full and file them under their full name (see cross-reference), eg:

Before Filing	After Filing
VHI	Educational Building Society
ESB	Electricity Supply Board
EBS	Voluntary Health Insurance

11. Leave **made-up** abbreviations in their abbreviated form, but file the same abbreviations in a group according to the word that follows the abbreviated name.

Before Filing	After Filing
ABC Computer Training Ltd	ABBA Taxis
ABC Services	Abbey Leisure
Abbey Leisure	ABC Computer Training Ltd
ABBA Taxis	ABC Services
Abco Interior Design	Abco Interior Design

Filing Procedure

To ensure an efficient filing system the following should be in place:
1. a clear cross-reference system
2. procedures for borrowing files
3. a 'follow-up' system
4. a policy relating to the retention of files
5. a policy relating to confidential files and security measures.

Filing should be carried out on a regular basis to avoid pile-ups and disorganisation. Whether you have dealt with the correspondence received, or intend to deal with it at a later date, it should be filed. A typical procedure for filing would be:
1. The documents are sorted into related batches; and the documents in each batch are sorted in chronological order.
2. The documents are inserted in the appropriate file on top of the previous correspondence. In this way, the most recent documents are placed first.
3. If no file exists for the document, a new file is opened. In a centralised filing system this will involve getting authorisation to open a new file to avoid duplication of files and misfiling.
4. Opening a file means getting the appropriate folder and writing up the 'name tag' with the correct classification, in the correct format. For

example, in an alphabetical system write 'Hegarty, Siobhan', not 'Siobhan Hegarty'. The folder is inserted in the correct position of the filing cabinet. In an indirect system, eg, numerical, the index will also be updated with the appropriate details of the new file.

5. Where a file cannot hold any more documents a continuation file is necessary. The original file is closed and labelled with a date. The continuation file is placed behind it.

How to Retrieve a File

When a file is borrowed, a record must be kept of the date the file was borrowed, the file name/number, the borrower's name and department. These details are recorded chronologically in a log book or on an '**outcard**' which is inserted in place of the file borrowed and remains in the filing system until the file is returned. When the file is returned, the date of return is recorded on the outcard and the outcard is removed from the system. The card can be used again when another file is borrowed.

Recording files borrowed in a logbook is suitable only for small systems, as the whole book may have to be searched to discover where the file is.

Outcard				
Date Taken	**File Identification**	**By**	**Dept**	**Date Returned**
7/6/05	File B009	JH	Marketing	

An outcard

In a large filing system a combination of a logbook and an outcard may be used. For example, to keep track of which files are out, the logbook will be checked; or when a file is requested, you know immediately who has the file by the details recorded on the outcard.

If more than one person needs to use a file, it may be passed from person to person without being returned to the filing department. However, in order to keep track of where the file is, a '**file-passing slip**' is filled in, detailing the file name, who passed the file, the new holder of the file and the date. The file-passing slip is returned to the filing clerk, so that the outcard can be updated.

Retention of Files

Documentation relating to the business may be used on a regular basis for a particular period of time and then may be referenced only on an occasional basis.

Retention periods vary for documentation. For example, some documents must be kept for ever, (ie, documents relating to the set-up of the business, financial accounts); other documents need to be kept only for a stated period, usually 6 years (ie, tax records, business transaction records); while other documents like correspondence, minutes of meetings, memoranda, etc are kept at the organisation's discretion.

The current filing system should not be clogged with information which is not accessed on a regular basis. The business should have a file-retention policy in relation to the classification of files. Files can be classified as:

- **Active files,** which are files in current use and generally span one year. These files are stored in the current filing system.
- **Semi-active files,** which are files no longer needed on a daily basis but which may be referenced on an irregular basis. These files are stored separately from the current filing system, ie, in a separate filing cabinet.
- **Non-active files,** which are files that are not referenced but must be kept until their retention period expires. These files are taken from the semi-active files and either stored elsewhere or converted into digital format and stored in an electronic document management system (EDM); the paper-based information can then be destroyed.
- **Dead files,** which are non-active files where the retention period has expired. Dead files are destroyed. Confidential information should be put through a '**shredder**' which reduces the information to strips of paper.

The output from the shredder can be used as packing material or recycled. If you are responsible for your own filing system, the decision to throw away documents should be taken with great care.

Follow-up System

A follow-up system (also known as a 'bring-forward' system or 'tickler' system) is a filing procedure implemented to enable documents to be filed until required by providing a reminder of the activity that needs to be attended to on a specific date, so that the appropriate file can then be retrieved.

A follow-up system can be implemented in many ways:

- A note is put into a diary indicating when the file is required again.
- A 'date file' is set up. This may take the form of a **concertina folder** with a pocket of the folder used for each day of the month and one pocket for the coming months. A note is placed in the appropriate pocket detailing the name of the file to be retrieved. Each day the appropriate pocket is checked — the notes act as a reminder to retrieve the appropriate file(s).

◆ When documents are sent to a centralised filing department, a pre-printed 'follow-up slip' is completed and attached to the document. The filing clerk detaches the 'follow-up slip' and places it in the appropriate pocket of the 'follow-up system' and the documents are filed away. The slips for each day are checked by the filing clerk. The files are then sent to the appropriate person with the 'follow-up slip' attached to the file. Details of the file sent are recorded on an outcard and/or logbook.

◆ If files are stored on a computer, the user can signal when the file is required again by placing an entry in a diary or more appropriately in an electronic diary.

Confidential Files

Strict procedures will be laid down for confidential files. These include: a list of authorised people who can access the files, which files cannot be copied or removed from the filing department. Files should be kept under lock and key. Valuable files should be stored in a fireproof cabinet, safe or at another location.

Short Questions

1. Distinguish between a centralised and a decentralised filing system.
2. Give two advantages and two disadvantages of centralised and decentralised filing.
3. What type of correspondence could be filed in the following:
   a) box file
   b) lever arch file
   c) concertina folder?
4. List and briefly describe the three main storage arrangements of files.
5. Give two advantages and two disadvantages of the three main storage arrangements of files.
6. List and briefly describe five main sorting methods that can be used in a filing system.
7. Distinguish between the following numerical filing methods:
   a) alphanumeric
   b) Dewey
   c) terminal digit.
8. Distinguish between a direct and an indirect filing system.
9. Place the following in alphabetical order:
   The Gainsborough Hotel
   Green & Patterson.
   Department of Education and Science
   St George's House

Saint Vincents
Sally Sainte
Patterson and Brown
Mr Tony MacDonnell
Ms Jane M'Donnell
5-Star Services.

10. List four factors you would consider when deciding on a method of sorting files.

11. List one advantage, one disadvantage and a typical use of the following sorting methods:
    a) alphabetical
    b) numerical
    c) geographical.

12. Give four examples of where it is appropriate to use a cross-reference.

13. When would a colour-coding system be used?

14. Outline the difference between, and one appropriate use of, the following indexing systems:
    a) card index
    b) visual card index
    c) strip index.

15. Distinguish between an outcard and a file-passing slip.

16. How are files generally classified under a retention policy?

17. Briefly describe what a follow-up system is and how it is used.

18. List four points for managing confidential files.

19. List four essential elements of an efficient filing system.

Chapter 16 — Electronic Document Management (EDM)

While the information age promised a paperless office, the reality is that it created a significant increase in the amount of paper needing to be sorted, filed and stored. One explanation for this is: the electronic *production* of documents was not matched with an equivalent system for the electronic *capture, storage* and *distribution* of these documents. For example, a word-processing file, while it is created electronically, is generally printed and distributed manually. Invariably, this electronically produced document must then be filed.

Paper-based filing has many problems, such as cost: the cost of paper, filing equipment and space. Other problems include filing mistakes, which can result in the business spending considerable time trying to locate misfiled documents.

Many businesses are considering a complete electronic document-management system (EDM) as a means to eliminate their paper storage and retrieval problems. With the advances in hardware and software EDM is now an affordable technology, which can be done in house or outsourced to an EDM agency.

An EDM System is in effect a large-scale, computerised filing system where all files, including paper files and microform (see below), are stored digitally, ie, on computer media such as hard disk, CD, DVD, etc) and distributed electronically via e-mail, an intranet, an extranet or the Internet, depending on the function of the information.

Before we get into a detailed discussion of an EDM system, we need to look at the other document-management systems used in the past and how this information can be integrated into an EDM system.

Microform Filing System

Microform Filing System

A microform filing system stores files in **film** format (like negatives of a photograph) and is used mainly to store archived paper files. It reduces the space required to store files, as many pages can be stored on a single film. The word 'microform' is the generic term used to describe the format of the film used, ie, a film strip or a microfiche (a 4″ × 6″ sheet of film about the size of a postcard).

In the recent past, microform was the storage media used by organisations with significant volumes of printed material, eg, the newspaper industry, libraries and the banks. Today, with the development of advanced digital technologies for scanning, storing and distributing information electronically, microform is not used to archive information by organisations that have never used it. However, some organisations that have extensively used microform are continuing with a hybrid approach, ie, a combination of microform and digitisation.

The hybrid approach being taken is: the archives are first transferred to microform and then the microform is scanned into digital format using a special scanner. Using this approach the microform is used for long-term storage, and the digital files allow direct access to the information. The rationale behind this hybrid approach is from a risk-management perspective. Microform is a known technology, has been around since the 1940s and is well supported, whereas with digital technology the fear is of being unable to access digital files in years to come, unless the files are continually migrated to current storage media.

Producing Microform

Microform can be produced in two ways:
1. *For paper documents*: A microform camera is used to photograph original documents. The camera is built into a unit that holds the documents, which are fed automatically to the camera like a photocopier.
2. *For computer documents*: A special printer, known as a **microform printer**, and software are used to print computer files directly onto film, thereby avoiding the steps of printing and photographing. The process of printing files directly to microform is known as COM (Computer Output Microform).

A microform duplicator is used to make copies of the microform (film or fiche). Microform is duplicated for distribution purposes.

Reading Microform

Microform cannot be read by the naked eye. A microform reader is used, which displays the image in an enlarged format on the screen. A search facility allows the required information to be brought into view.

Some readers have an in-built printer which allows the image to be viewed on-screen and printed on paper if required.

Microform reader/printer

Storing Microform

Microform should be stored in special sealed containers in a controlled environment, preferably in an air-conditioned room, and must be used only to make working copies. Extremes of temperature or humidity should be avoided, as well as direct exposure to sunlight. The equipment available includes:

Microfiche index box: Similar to a card index box but consists of plastic jackets to hold the microfiche. Each jacket has a tab for indexing.

Microfiche visible panel index: A ring binder consisting of panels in which to insert the microfiche. The top line of each microfiche is displayed, showing the details of the microfiche.

Microfilm jacket-strip index: A ring binder consisting of transparent jackets in which to insert a strip of film.

Various microfiche storage systems

Electronic Document Management System

EDM combines different technologies to scan, index and store paper-based documents in electronic format. Once information is in electronic format it can be: retrieved, searched, distributed electronically (ie, via e-mail, fax) and shared with others across a network.

EDM systems are available at different levels of complexity to cater for the level of computerised filing required in a business. This includes converting: paper-based information (ie, documents, books, catalogues, manuals, photographs, etc) and microform film to digital format, and converting analogue VHS tapes to DVD.

Before we get into a detailed discussion of the implementation and benefits of an EDM system, we need to look at the basics of how files should be organised on a computer to accomplish an efficient digital filing system.

Organising and Storing Files on a Computer

Consider a filing system for an auctioneering firm. A subset of the work involved in an auctioneering firm is the sale of houses. This part of the filing system could be organised as follows:

A folder-like structure is built using the operating system software, for example, Windows XP. A **folder** is an area for holding files, and folders may be divided into sub-folders.

In the example shown, the main folder, **sales,** is subdivided into sub-folders for the different areas where the auctioneering firm has houses for sale. These are: Dublin City, North Dublin, South Dublin and Other Areas (the software arranges the folders in alphabetical order).

An auctioneering firm may also categorise the houses within each area according to a price range. In the following example shown each area folder has further sub-folders to categorise the houses in price ranges of: Under €300k, €300k to €500k and Over €500k. Again, the software arranges the folders in alphabetical order.

Within each price range, the houses may be further categorised according to their condition. For example, excellent, good and repairs.

Using this filing system, the required file(s) can be located easily. For example, if information was requested on houses for sale in the Dublin City area which were under €300k and in excellent condition, the user of the system would go to the folder called 'Dublin City', select the sub-folder 'Under €300k' and in this folder select the sub-folder called 'Excellent'.

The 'Excellent' folder contains the relevant files for the information requested, ie, a list of houses in Dublin City under €300k and in excellent condition.

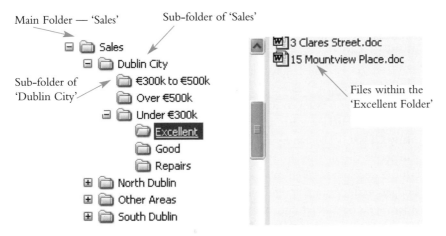

Main Folder — 'Sales'

Sub-folder of 'Sales'

Sub-folder of 'Dublin City'

Files within the 'Excellent Folder'

Layout of folders on a disk
The plus sign (+) beside each folder means that the folder is not opened. They are called expandable folders. If it was opened, you would see a breakdown similar to the 'Dublin City' folder.

Implementing an EDM System

To allow files to be shared among many users, a network of computers must be set up. Files which are shared by individuals are stored on the 'file server' and can be accessed by individuals sitting at their own computer.

To input paper-based information into the system, the information is generally batched, scanned and indexed.

1. *Batch Preparation:* Typically pages are sorted into batches of similar documents (ie, orders, invoices, etc) and then scanned.

2. *Scanning:* A scanner takes an image of the page (similar to a photocopier) and inputs it into the computer. Document scanning falls into two requirements:

   a) where a 'digital **permanent** image' is required: such as vendor invoices, signed contracts, handwritten text, legal documents, etc. Such documents must be saved with the entire look and content of the original.

   b) where a 'digital **editable** image' is required: (such as typed documents of general information), where the need is to be able to edit the content of the documents. This is achieved by opening the scanned document with *Optical Character Recognition (OCR)* software, which converts the scanned image into text that can be edited.

3. *Indexing:* Indexing is the most critical and time-consuming step in the capture process. To assist with the retrieval of files, keywords are defined for each document. The keywords would include common things such as the customer's name and file reference, as well as words that would be appropriate for searches in the future.

4. *Storing:* Where the files are stored depends on whether the files are active or should be archived. If the files are active, they are generally stored on the 'file server' to be available to network users. If the files should be archived, a decision has to be made as to whether these files should be stored on-line or off-line.

If the decision is taken to store archived files on-line they are generally stored on optical media, ie, CD/DVD. A jukebox (capable of holding many CDs/DVDs) can be added to the network so that the network users can access the files on-line.

If the decision is taken to store archived files off-line, then depending on budget and personal preferences, the files can be archived onto tape, microfiche or indeed optical recordable media. However, the CD/DVDs would not be available on the network, ie, they would be stored off-line in an appropriate holder. Most EDM systems archive onto optical media — CDs/DVDs.

Benefits of an EDM System

1. Saves storage space and eliminates the need for filing cabinets.
2. The cost associated with storing paper documents, printing and publishing internal information (ie, safety manuals, company policies manuals) is eliminated, as this information can now be published on the intranet for employees to view.
3. Files exist on the file server and can be viewed simultaneously by authorised users across a network.
4. No duplicate files exist, which means that all files are current. For example, there is no danger of recording a person's change of address in one department and not in another department.
5. Electronic files can be linked with existing applications. For example, in a customer database, a 'field' could contain a link to all correspondence relating to a particular customer.
6. No time is wasted searching or waiting for files. The search facility allows network users to find specific information in multiple electronic documents.
7. Software tools can be used to emphasise or clarify information in a documen: for example, information can be highlighted, notes can be added using electronic 'sticky notes' and vocal comments can be recorded with a document.
8. It is easy to transfer non-active files to off-line storage.
9. Strict control procedures can be implemented using software. Certain users can be locked out of the system by means of passwords and access rights can be set up to control what individuals can do within the system, ie, which files they can view, update, etc. Documents can be password-protected,

thus facilitating the safe e-mailing of documents without the fear of an unauthorised person viewing the document.

10. Retention and deletion procedures can be enforced, by the system administrator in charge of the file server.

Short Questions

1. Describe a microform filing system and give one example of its use.
2. Distinguish between a microfiche and microfilm.
3. Briefly describe two ways of outputting documents to microform.
4. How is microform read and stored?
5. What is an EDM system?
6. List the component features of implementing an EDM system.
7. Briefly describe two requirements of document scanning in an EDM system.
8. Compare and contrast the choices available for storing files on-line and off-line in an EDM system.
9. State five benefits of an EDM system.

Summary

Every business must maintain an efficient filing system, be it a manual system or an EDM system. In a manual system files are categorised according to the information to be filed, eg, customers, suppliers. Files are sorted either alphabetically, numerically, chronologically, etc within a category. Manual systems suffer many disadvantages such as the cost of storage space, misfiled documents and time involved in locating documents.

Electronic document management (EDM) is becoming essential and increasingly popular in medium-sized businesses owing to the volumes of information generated today. EDM combines different technologies to scan, index and store paper-based documents and microform in electronic format to facilitate the distribution of documents across a network. With the advances in digital technology, microform has been repositioned to a backstage role, owing to the capacity and active retrieval capabilities of optical media.

Regardless of the filing system, all files must be carefully maintained and procedures must be in place to prevent unauthorised access to files.

Assignments

1. Assume you have been employed as office manager of an existing business. The business wants to improve the operation of its centralised manual filing system and you have been asked to:
   a) write a report detailing a procedure to follow in relation to:
      (i) borrowing files
      (ii) retention of files
      (iii) confidential files and security arrangements;
   b) write guidelines (which should fit on a double-sided A4 sheet of paper) to be followed by all staff in relation to the filing of documents alphabetically. Examples should be given where necessary.

2. Place the examples below in alphabetical order — then combine the three examples and place them in alphabetical order.

Example 1	Example 2	Example 3
Fred B. Walsh	Dr Tom Healy	Dr J.P. O'Sullivan
Walsh Family Foods Ltd	John Healy and Associates Ltd	Department of Education
The Highway Lounge	Ms Marie Collins	The Business Studies Department
Gerry McGovern	Collins Conor	O'Meara (Auctioneer) Ltd
Hugh McGovern	Arthur Gibney and Partners	Pro William O'Meara
Tom MacGovern	The Kerry Company Ltd	Finlay's Lounge
Oasis Design Ltd	William Farrell Ltd	Fr F. Carthy
O B Marine Ltd	Saint Clare's Nursery	The Two Sisters
Frank O'Brien	St Theresa's Swimming Pool	2's Company (Artists)
Star Society	Colm De Buitlear	David Twohig
The Three Bears Ltd	John Deasy	1-Hour Repairs
1st Cleaning Services	One Hour Photo	One-to-One Swap Shop

3. You have been asked to devise a computerised folder structure for storing exam results at a college-based on the information given below, and to indicate where the files should be stored.

   The main folders should be organised by *course category* (ie, Business and Computing) with sub-folders for the *course names*. Within each *course name* folder there will be further sub-folders for *exam years*. The *exam results* files are stored in the appropriate *exam year* folder. You should use appropriate abbreviated course names and file names.

Course Names: Business Studies, Multimedia Computing, Computer Programming, Marketing, Secretarial, Business Administration, Computer Applications, Banking and

Auctioneering

Exam Years: 2002–3, 2003–4, 2004–5

File Names: Class A (Business Studies for year 2003–4)

Class B (Business Studies for year 2003–4)

Class A (Multimedia Computing for years 2002–3 and 2003–4)

4. You have been employed as the office manager of an existing business. However, your manager is very reluctant to change from the manual filing system. While there is a computer network in place, staff print off e-mail, and file them.

You have spoken to your manager on numerous occasions about the benefits of transferring over to an EDM system, but he is not convinced.

Research appropriate EDM systems available for a medium-sized business with capability of expansion. Use the Golden Pages or other relevant sources, ie, the Internet, for businesses that sell EDM systems. Write a report detailing the benefits of an EDM system. Construct a table comparing the EDM systems available from three different sources.

Appendix — Blank Documents for Business Transactions

Materials Requisition Form

Materials Requisition   No: _____
From: _____

To: _____

Qty	Details

Signature   Date

Purchase Requisition Form

Purchase Requisition		Ref. No: _____

Department: _____

Supplier's Name: _____

Supplier's Address: _____

Qty	Details	Cat. No.	Unit Price €

Signature	Date

Order Form

Order No: _____

VAT No: 284 3455 89

Tel. No:_____

Fax No: _____   Date: _____

Quotation No: _____

Please supply the following:

Qty	Description	Cat. No.	Unit Price €	Total Price €

Terms of Sale

Delivery Note

Delivery Note No: _____

VAT No: 284 3455 89

Tel. No: _____

Fax No: _____   Date: _____

Quotation No: _____

Qty	Description	Cat. No.

Delivery:

Received by:

Goods Received Note

Goods Received Note No:

Supplier: _____

Date Received: _____

Delivery/Advice Note No: _____

Order No.	Description	Qty Received

Received by:	Date:		Entered in stock by:	Date:

Inspected by: Date:

Shortages:

Damage Recorded:

Invoice

Invoice No: _____

VAT No:_____

Date: _____

Tel. No: _____

Fax No: _____

Delivery Note No: _____

Order No: _____

Qty	Description	Cat. No.	Unit Price €	Total Cost €

Credit Note

Credit Note No: _____

VAT No:_____

Date: _____

Tel. No: _____

Fax No: _____

Delivery Note No: _____

Order No: _____

Qty	Description	Cat. No.	Unit Price €	Total Cost €

Debit Note

Debit Note No: _____

VAT No: _____

Date: _____

Tel. No: _____
Fax No: _____
Delivery Note No: _____
Order No: _____

Ref.	Description	Cat. No.	Unit Price €	Total Cost €

Statement

Statement

VAT No:_____

Date: _____

Tel. No: _____.

Fax No: _____

Date	Ref. No.	Details	Debits €	Credits €	Balance €